FRAGILE PEACE

Dr. Borko B. Djordjevic, M.D., Ph.D., F.I.C.S.

The views and opinions expressed in this book are solely those of the author and do not reect the views or opinions of Quipper Prints. Quipper Prints is not to be held responsible for and expressly disclaims responsibility of the content herein.

Fragile Peace

Published by Quipper Prints
875 North Michigan Avenue,
John Hancock Center,
31st Floor,Chicago, IL 60611
www.quipperprints.com

Copyright © 2024 by Dr. Borko B. Djordjevic, M.D., Ph.D., F.I.C.S.

All rights reserved. Neither this book, nor any parts within it may be sold or reproduced in any form or by any electronic or mechanical means, including information storage and retrieval systems, without permission in writing from the author. be only exception is by a reviewer, who may quote short excerpts in a review.

ISBN (paperback): 978-1-77839-101-9
eISBN: 978-1-77839-102-6

T. S. Eliot (1888–1965)

"War is not a life: it is a situation,
One which may neither be ignored nor accepted."

A Note on War Poetry, Stanza 5

*These writings are dedicated
to all victims of Yugoslavia's disintegration*

Contents

PART ONE

THE LAST MISSION 2
JIMMY CARTER REMEMBERS THE 8
SERBS 8
THE SMELL OF WAR 18
I WAS TREATING CHILDREN 23
BEATEN BY NATO'S STICK 28
KARADŽIĆ SUMMONING CARTER 31
RIGOROUS CHECKS 41
A SECRET TRIP TO GEORGIA 44
A CARPENTER AND A GUSLAR [11] 53
CLINTON ON THE LINE 66
FRAGILE PEACE 74
CARTER'S NONACCEPTANCE 83
HOLBROOKE'S JIGGERY-POKERY 88
THE BULLDOZER DIPLOMAT 94
A DANGEROUS SERB 106
DOUBLE-DEALING IN THE ARMY 113
SLOBA'S BIRD 119
BATTLING FOR BILLIONS 126
A SCHEME TO TRICK THE NATION 137
THE FRIGHTENED SERB 144
SECRET CORRESPONDENCE 155
RAY CARTER PROTECTING RADOVAN 161
SURRENDER YOURSELVES, SERBS! 168
ON PAIN OF DEATH 175

MOMCILO KRAJISNIK'S AMERICAN DEFENSE	183
RADOVAN'S WITNESS?	187

PART TWO

SON OF A PARTISAN 1941 VETERAN	194
GRANDPA'S BOY	210
PLASTIC SURGEON	222
AMERICAN FIRST LADIES	230
ROSALYNN CARTER'S FRIEND	239
MARSHAL TITO – CARTER'S SPY	245
Reagan's Man	250
Save Yugoslavia!	258
COMMUNIST-WAY TRANSITION	273
KPMG and Sloba	280
Selfish Rulers	286
Saddam Hussein's Man	292
MY PRIVATE WAR	300
A PLOT: LIBEL AND BADMOUTHING	309
A PROFITEER ON HIS SERBIAN IDENTITY	320
	320
MY SON FOR AMERICAN PRESIDENT	324
BARACK OBAMA'S NEIGHBOR	333
DOCUMENTS	336
BORKO DJORDJEVIC, MD: CAREER OVERVIEW	361
	361
PHOTOS & PRESS CLIPPINGS	367

PART ONE

THE LAST MISSION

When I Visited Jimmy Carter in Georgia, in late September of 2015, he looked very good at first glance, but felt rather bad intimately. He kept refusing to go to hospital for chemotherapy treatment of the cancer diagnosed earlier that summer.

– The result of such treatment is highly uncertain – Jimmy told me in confidence.

His wife Rosalynn, their children and the rest of the family were shaken when they became aware that the former American President was taken ill with pancreatic cancer that also threatened liver. This was my first impression upon entering Jimmy Carter's home at Plains, Georgia.

We greeted each other warmly and had a brief talk about the days of 1994 when we, together, brought the first peacetime to the Serbs, Muslims and Croats in Bosnia, one that lasted for nearly four months. That truce was the forerunner of Dayton Accords, the settlement reached at the Ohio military base in November, 1995.

– I did my best for the Serbs which was possible at the time! I brought peace – Jimmy Carter said to me.

In his latest book, *A Full Life*, published in early summer of 2015, the former U.S. President Carter openly admitted that his recollections of the Serbs at Pale[1] and Belgrade were favourable. Moreover, there was a hint of the cease-fire agreement accomplished in Bosnia in December, 1994, being one of the arguments in his nomination for the Nobel Peace Prize.

Namely, two decades had passed since the first cease ire agreement in Bosnia-Herzegovina (abbr. BH) had been reached at Pale and Sarajevo by the Croats, Bosniaks and Serbs. On December 20, 1994, the former U.S. President Jimmy Carter visited Sarajevo and Pale and managed to accomplish an agreement whereby the three warring sides pledged to desist from hostilities. Many referred to it as a „fragile peace". The creator of that historic arrangement, Jimmy Carter, still lectures on the event.

Despite his serious illness, Carter lives a normal life which includes presentations of his new book and lecturing on international relations and crises-stricken regions around the globe.

Jimmy Carter is a strong man psychologically, for he draws his spiritual strength from Baptist faith and the strong belief that he should be giving his goodness as long as he lives. As he is a sincere friend of mine and a man who put his special trust in me, I offered help on the part of my colleague Shimon Slavin, M.D., an internist from Tel Aviv famous for successful cancer treatment. Doctor Shimon has specialized in alternative therapies by stem cells. This recent method has proved very efficient in cancer treatment, and less difficult for patients than chemotherapy. Carter, who had stepped into the ninth decade of his life, answered:

– Dear Borko, thank you. I'm gonna consider your suggestion and give my answer directly to Dr. Slavin Shimon in Israel!

– We hope to save you, Mr. President, for the benefit of the world and the Serbian people – I said to my friend Carter at farewell.

When I left his home at Plains, Ga., I believed that Carter and I would undertake yet another good and fruitful mission. Namely, Jimmy is the sole American president who has had an honest attitude to Radovan Karadzic and other 'dangerous Serbs', as they are held by the international community and the White House. What I wanted to do at the time was to arrange with him a new meeting with Radovan Karadzic, who was then awaiting the sentence by The Hague Tribunal, in the fall of 2015, so that they could undertake a fresh peace-making effort in Bosnia-Hercegovina. Although both men are seriously ill, I have not lost the hope. I believe that Carter and Karadzic can still save the peace in Bosnia.

Two decades have passed since the sanguinary war in Bosnia, and peace is still lacking there. Why is that so? Probably because the rulers of the world and the Muslims do not need peace in BH. At the 20th anniversary of Dayton Peace Accords, the situation in BH implied that –as an eminent military commentator put it – "one should not underestimate some secret hopes on the part of certain military and political circles in Sarajevo that the Republic of Srpska has to be liberated by an army-led blitzkrieg".

Today, Bosnia-Herzegovina is a Western protectorate in the most pugnacious sense. The state of BH does not have sovereignty, for it was 'given birth' to as a 'child' of the Clinton Administration and, as such, has been maintained in life by force. Sticking together, the Muslims and the Americans wish to rule across the former Yugoslavia resorting to a policy of violence. Moreover, the West on the whole prefers to keep the Balkans verging on warfare.

The Serb side, the first one which offered its hand in reconciliation during the war conflicts of 1990's, is currently in a repeated situation of waiting to see what is going to befall the Serbian people in BH. That is why the official Belgrade has continued to cooperate with Washington D.C., for America has come to absolutely dominate the globe economically, technologically and politically. However, in the process of building Serbian-American relations, one should choose full truth as the point of departure, not the fairy-tales about Western/American democracy preached in Serbia for years now through non-government groups, pro-West organizations and lobbies.

- *We, the Serbs, are not a genocidal nation!*

That is the sentence I have to utter loud enough in order to make my American friends dissuaded from belief in what has been written down in the Srebrenica Resolution adopted by the U.S. Congress in July of 2015, and then also by the European Parliament. The Resolution renders that the Serbs committed genocide over the Muslims in Srebrenica in the summer of 1995. Arguing for my claim that opposes the American stance, I am presenting the story about the Serbs and not others being the first to offer peace to Muslims in Bosnia toward the end of 1994. The Muslims rejected the Serbian hand of reconciliation.

Out of hatred and in revenge for the peace offer, what they did do on that very day, December 19, 1994, was – behead 70 Serbs in a Serbian village in Bosnia.

At the moment when Jimmy Carter was signing the Comprehensive Peace Agreement with Radovan Karadzic at Pale, several hundred Muslims and Croats from Banja Luka attacked the Serb civilians in Glamoc and Bosansko Grahovo. Commander Naser Oric bestially massacred the Serbs by the Drina river. It was only later, on July 6, 1995 that the crime against the Muslims in Srebrenica took place. The United States is a ruthless swayer. The country exploits 45 percent of the world's raw materials. Over the past 40 years, it has been carrying out a large-scale dollar-based deception – ever since the 'gold standard' was abandoned and frantic printing of the money began, linking all prices, especially that of oil, to this currency. Today, the U.S.A. is a country indebted for between three and four thousand billion dollars while ruling the globe. That the Americans have accustomed themselves to toppling regimes across the planet in the name of democracy has been exemplified in the dismemberment of Yugoslavia, but also in the cases of Libya and Syria. The analysts Noam Chomsky and John Perkins have publicly exposed the American pattern in foreign politics applied in the destruction of other countries, thus building the status of the Unites States as the dominating number one leader of the world. For that purpose, the U.S. has been instrumentalizing the NATO which protects capital and investments, and the European Union. These facts must be observed and reckoned with instead of being suppressed for the sake of Serbian cooperation with the Americans.

My book *Fragile Peace, or Jimmy Carter and the Dangerous Serbs* – as the subtitle reads – is a recollection of the truce that we, the Serbs, led by Radovan Karadzic and together with the former U.S. President Jimmy Carter, created toward the end of 1994. That first peacetime in Bosnia lasted for four months. It was brought to an end through a political intervention by the Americans, Croats and Muslims. The book has no ambition to disentangle the highly intricate issue of war and peace in BH or the overall Serbian-American relations. Unfortunately, however, it offers some hints of why the Americans labeled the Serbs as a genocidal nation.

These political memoirs of mine are also an abridged story of my life in Serbia and America, one showing how the American dream of a Belgrade physician came true and more than that: the conduct of the Serbs and the Americans over the last quarter of a century.

Author

On Christmas, 2016[2]

---

[1] **Pale** is a town and one of the six municipalities in the City of Istočno Sarajevo (Eastern Sarajevo) within the Post-Dayton Republic of Srpska entity. From 1992 to 1998, it was the seat of Srpska's administration. – *Translator's note.*

[2] January 7, since the Serbian Orthodox Church observes the Old Style/Julian calendar. –*Translator's note.*

JIMMY CARTER REMEMBERS THE SERBS

As soon as I realized, in the year 2015, that real peace was lacking in Bosnia because some people from the U.S.A. and E.U., as well as some Bosnia's Muslims, have tried to dismantle the Dayton Accords and trigger off new wrangling and new war conflicts, it occurred to me that I might ask the former U.S. President and Nobelist Jimmy Carter to revisit Sarajevo and Pale in order to establish lasting peace there. At the time (in the year 2015)when former President Radovan Karadzic and General Ratko Mladic were on trial at The Hague Tribunal for the alleged war crimes committed during the war in Bosnia-Herzegovina in the 1990's, the Serbian people became object of renewed satanization. The fresh target of the political firebrands was the Republic of Srpska as the Serbian entity/state within the federal Bosnia-Herzegovina.

It was then that Great Britain submitted her seventh draft of the Srebrenica Resolution to the member-countries of the UN for adoption; however, Russia blocked London's political action by deploying veto. Yet the resolution re-emerged outside of the United Nations, in some other parts of the world. Having adopted the Srebrenica Resolution, E.U., the U.S.A. and France have stigmatized us, the Serbs, as a genocidal nation. Our people will have to pay a much too high price for that, because this resolution and the condemnation it articulates will serve as a political alibi to the European Union and the United States for the destruction of the Republic of Srpska. Next, they would drive a wedge between Aleksandar Vucic and Milorad Dodik, the current PM of Serbia and President of Srpska respectively, and sever the links of Banja Luka with Belgrade. This would lead to the obliteration of the Serbs west of the Drina river and to Bosnia-Herzegovina becoming a country of the Muslims and the Croats.

Although worrying for my people in Bosnia, I was patiently waiting for further developments in order to prevent any act out of panic.

Addressing an Easter card to the Carter Center, I wrote to my friend Jimmy Carter to remind him of the trust he had put in me and of his deed for which I shall be grateful for ever.

"Dear Mr. President!

It's been two decades since our joint efforts to bring peace to Bosnia alongside the presidents R. Karadzic, A. Izetbegovic and F. Tudjman. We managed to calm the warriors and provide a peaceful sleep to people. Thanks to you, Serbian nation was saved and lives in its own country. I hope you have written about your peacekeeping mission in Bosnia 1994 in your memoirs.

My wish is to visit you and to thank you in person for the salvation of the people in Bosnia. Many more happy Easters and Christmases!

Sincerely yours, Borko dr Djordjevic"

I sent a similar card to President Radovan Karadzic, in custody of the ICTY[3] at the Scheveningen detention center, whom I intended to visit during his trial at The Hague. It was just in those days that the Trilateral Commission, that secret swayer of the world, warned the public that a new escalation of misunderstandings, conflicts and even collapse of Bosnia-Herzegovina emerged as a threat. The assessment was confirmed by an event at Srebrenica: Serbia's Prime Minister Aleksandar Vucic was stoned, that is, he faced an assassination attempt there.

Peace in Bosnia-Herzegovina has not been established firmly. There are inter-ethnic tensions and threats coming from major powers which endanger the security of the people living there. It became clear to me that BH needed the former U.S. President Jimmy Carter in the role of a peacemaker. By his respectability and experience, Carter was capable of alleviating the political tension and bringing lasting peace.

To Borko: Thank you for your nice note. I describe our effort in my next book "A Full Life" that will be published in July.

Jimmy Carter

Dear Mr. President,

Happy Easter to you and Rosalynn !

It's been two decades since our joint efforts to bring peace to Bosnia alongside the presidents R.Karadzic, A.Izetbegovic and F.Tudjman.

We managed to calm the warriors and provide a peaceful sleep to people.

Thanks to you, Serbian nation was saved and lives in its own country.

I hope you have written about your peacekeeping mission in Bosnia 1994. in your memoirs.

My wish is to visit you and to thank you in person for the salvation of the people in Bosnia.

Many more happy Easters and Christmases !

Sincerely yours,

Borko dr Djordjevic

THE CARTER CENTER

Borko B. Djordjevic
Sava Ilica 5
85347 Igalo
Montenegro

Fearing a repetition of the history of ethnic conflicts in Bosnia, I got the idea that Jimmy Carter, as the sole American President who displayed an honest attitude to the Serbs, and Radovan Karadzic, as an honest leader of the Serbs, could – together – undertake a new mission of peacemaking. That the two men at least could agree about, sign and release a Peace Appeal for Bosnia in an effort to prevent years of war from happening again or to prevent BH from turning into another 'Ukraine'. The following step would be (provided that Karadzic is acquitted of all charges before The Hague Tribunal) to sign – with Carter at Pale once again – a new agreement, a kind of 'Charter of Peace among the Peoples of Bosnia'.

I was aware of the fact that, on principle, the two respectable men who exercised politically sound reasoning would accept this idea of mine; that both Jimmy Carter and Radovan Karadzic suffered from serious illnesses was something that worried me. Carter had liver cancer diagnosed in August of 2015; early in September, Karadzic complained to the Tribunal of elevated blood sugar level, high blood pressure and intense pains. The situation required my support in the first place, so I left for the United States and the Netherlands to visit them.

I am a Serb, a physician/surgeon and a missioner. That is how I describe myself today. In my biography, personal, professional and social aspects of life are entangled to the extent that they can hardly be discerned or described separately. As a professional physician and plastic surgeon, I have met a great many famous people and joined in the elite circles of both America and the former Yugoslavia. My stance was one of a man who does not just pose any problems while abstaining from the search for their causes; my choice was to be a man who in life's challenges only pursues solutions. I did not wish to waste time on the past; while trying to get an insight into the roots of my nation's unfortunate destiny, I set out to ind solutions to the problem. The attitude invigorated my personality and spread positive energy around me. That is why people easily accepted me, trusted me and shared with me their expectations of the resolved issues leading us through life toward a better future.

THE WHITE HOUSE
WASHINGTON
July 5, 1995

Thank you for passing on the letter from Bosnian-Serb President Karadzic.

It is always beneficial to maintain open channels of communication when seeking to resolve situations as complex as those confronting us in Bosnia. In this case, unfortunately, Karadzic seems to be seeking an end to the international isolation of the Bosnian-Serbs without offering any new elements in his negotiating posture. In particular, he continues to seek a solution that would destroy Bosnia-Herzegovina's territorial integrity by recognizing the sovereignty of his self-styled "Serbian Republic."

Nevertheless, like you, I intend to look carefully at any proposal that might lead to a successful and honorable negotiated solution to this conflict, and I appreciate your passing along Karadzic's message.

Sincerely,

Bill Clinton

Bill Clinton's Letter

Since I had practically been convinced that Jimmy Carter and Radovan Karadzic thought and behaved in a like manner, I turned to them in order to suggest a new peace mission as outlined above.

JIMMY CARTER

October 24, 2002

To Dr. Borko Djordjevic

It is a great honor to be awarded the Nobel Peace Prize, and I am touched by your warm congratulations. Rosalynn and I appreciate your support for The Carter Center's work to promote peace, health, and human rights around the world. In a very real sense, you share this tribute with us.

Sincerely,

Jimmy Carter

Dr. Borko Djordjevic
American Academy of Plastic Surgery
1091 North Palm Canyon Drive
Palm Springs, California 92262

Jimmy Carter responded with a handwritten message:

"To Borko: Thank you for your nice note, & best wishes. I describe our efforts in my next book 'A Full Life' that will be published in July. Yours, Jimmy Carter"

In his memoirs, Carter openly stated that his recollections of the Serbs from Pale and Belgrade were favourable, giving a hint of the cease-fire agreement from December, 1994, was one of the elements supporting his nomination for the Nobel Peace Prize which he received in the third attempt, in 2002. The earlier American Presidents-Prize laureates included Theodore Roosevelt (Republican, 26th president of the U.S.A., for the peace settlement established between Russia and Japan and as the founder of the League of Nations) and Woodrow
Wilson (Democrat, 28th president, for his role in the Paris Peace Conference at Versaille). As the Nobel Committee in Oslo put it in their press release, President Carter was awarded "for his decades of untiring effort to ind peaceful solutions to international conflicts, to advance democracy and human rights, and to promote economic and social development".

Now I can say that my contribution to the Nobel Prize was considerable – owing to the peace efforts in Bosnia, for which Jimmy Carter and his spouse Rosalynn Carter thanked me in 2003.

Jimmy Carter won the Nobel Prize among the record-beating number of nominees – as many as 117. Other candidates included the U.S. President George Bush and the British Prime Minister Tony Blaire. However, although deservingly awarded, the Committee's decision roused some controversies after Gunnar Berge, Chairman of the Committee, had left the public wondering whether the honor was paid to Jimmy Carter personally or it was a 'a kick in the leg' to President George Bush.

The Americans who – because of the 'silent rage from the White House' – do not like Jimmy Carter still claim that he went to Pale and visited Radovan Karadzic in December, 1994 as a 'Nobel Peace Prize hunter' and as "a friend of the Serb aggressors". The fact which is kept suppressed thereby is that Carter's mission provided a basis for the formulation of the Dayton Peace Accords, and that the mission enjoyed the support and coordination by the then-President Bill Clinton in person, and later by the former U.S. President Gerald Ford, too. During the last week of January, 1995, I had a two-hours' meeting with Gerald Ford, the former Republican President of America, at Palm Springs, California. I gave him the details of the situation in the Republic of Srpska. Since Mr. Ford was a Republican, I felt a need to address the Republican Party on the same subject. Ford supported Carter's peace plans and promised to do as much as possible personally, and on the part of his party. But political games minimized and hushed Jimmy Carter's peace efforts in Bosnia.

Borko Djordjević and Gerald Ford (1999)

How did that happen? In the years 1994 and 1995, Carter still had his men and women in the American Administration. However, when he revealed his sympathies and understanding for the 'dangerous

Serbs' such as Radovan Karadzic and Ratko Mladic, these people were removed from Washington, D.C., and some were even murdered. That is why I wondered about the response of the Americans when I tried to arrange a new peace encounter between Jimmy Carter and Radovan Karadzic for the year 2016 – at The Hague or Pale – so that they could save Bosnia-Herzegovina. For a long time, Radovan Karadzic failed to answer my messages. He was in a very delicate situation: awaiting the final conviction by The Hague Tribunal. All alone, he had to right for his life and for the image of the Republic of Srpska, in the midst of what he called "the anti-Serb kangaroo court". And I relied on him, for Karadzic himself knew best of all that the Serbs are not a genocidal nation. I sent him a message about a political request being under way –following the adoption of the Srebrenica Resolution in the U.S. Congress, the E.U. and France – that the Republic of Srpska should be abolished, while the Serbs should pay war damage compensation to the Muslims and the Croats. This – I believe – should motivate Karadzic to work with Jimmy Carter and me on a renewed peace offer to Bosnia-Herzegovina.

[3] **ICTY** – International Criminal Tribunal for the former Yugoslavia was established in 1993 by the UN Security Council. – *Translator's note.*

THE SMELL OF WAR

MODERN YUGOSLAVIA, the one (re)created after World War II[4], existed as a federation of six republics and two provinces for 45 years. In Slovenia, Croatia, Bosnia-Herzegovina, Serbia, Montenegro, Macedonia, as well as in the Autonomous Provinces of Kosmet[5] and Vojvodina, people of ten different nationalities lived. The Serbs made the largest part of the total population – 36 per cent. They lived not only in Serbia, but also in the Province of Vojvodina, Montenegro and Bosnia-Herzegovina (BH). They were a substantial minority in Croatia and in the Province of Kosovo-Metohija. In terms of numbers, Croats (20 %) and Muslims (nearly 10 %) were second and third nation respectively in the Socialist Federal Republic of Yugoslavia (S.F.R.Y.).

Almost three per cent of the country's citizenry classified themselves as Yugoslavs by nationality. Half-Slovenian and half-Croat (some claim that he was a Jew of Polish origin), Josip Broz Tito, the lifelong president of that country, carefully structured the Federal Government and the Communist Party of Yugoslavia, i.e. the executive and political powers, in order to ensure that none of the ethnic groups could dominate the political scene.

Kurt Waldheim, President of Austlia om 1986, former UN Secretar-General, proven member of Wehrmacht's units that commied atrocities during WW II

Subsequent to 1945, Tito turned the inhabitants of the southernmost Republic of Macedonia into the Macedonian nation; in 1960's, he officially labeled the Muslims as a constitutive nationality of Yugoslavia. On the part of Broz, it was an attempt to establish balance among ethnic groups and thus confront Serbian domination. In daily life and routines, most Muslims did not differ significantly from their Serbian and Croat neighbors. They spoke the same language, ate the same food, and prevailingly maintained secular life habits. The rather small Muslim population in BH lived scattered all around the republic. The only areas with concentrated Muslim inhabitants were in the northwestern most part of the republic, around Bihac, plus several small pockets in Eastern Bosnia.

During World War II, the Serbs, Croats and Muslims waged a brutal civil war in which Croats and a number of Muslims allied with Germany and the Axis Powers, while most Serbs associated with Western and Eastern Allies. Since both the 'First Yugoslavia', as a kingdom, and the 'Second Yugoslavia', as a Communist-ruled country, spread on the crossroads of Western Christianity, Eastern Orthodoxy and Islam, some political analysts concluded that the three religions/civilizations could not coexist voluntarily for long. And that falling apart was their inevitable destiny, owing to the pernicious influences of Catholicism, Orthodoxy and Islam, that is, of the West and the East.

The argument that the three civilizations differed too much mutually and therefore could not function united regardless of their long history of living together in peace was the argument most frequently exploited by the leaders of nationalist parties which prevailed on Yugoslavia's political scene in late 1980's and early 1990's; it served them to justify the war for the independence of their entities. That is why this 'Third World War', waged in the Balkans from 1992 to 1995, and extended into 1999, took the course of a historical scenario designed in advance.

The Yugoslavia built by Tito over four decades was undone within five years. The Yugoslav National Army (YNA) fell apart and Yugoslav economy collapsed. The citizens became beggars who dashed around in pursuit of a job and a chance to earn their living.

In the beginning, the nationalists in Slovenia and Croatia – under the influence of Germany and Austria – demanded independence, which was by the Serbian nationalists taken as evidence of Fascist revival in the S.F.R.Y. and of the German ambition to establish 'the Fourth Reich'. Traditional support coming from Russia to the Serbs and from Turkey to Bosnia's Muslims roused additional fears in other communities and spread the smell of war across the Balkans.

In spite of the 'announced' bloodshed in Yugoslavia, the international community failed to interfere with the conflict prior to its mature stage. The American Secretary of State James Baker had visited Belgrade in 1991, a few days before Slovenia and Croatia declared independence, and expressed his hope that Yugoslavia could survive voluntarily united, giving no support to either unilateral declarations of independence or any use of force aimed at preventing these. Twelve foreign ministers of the European Community (EC) agreed not to recognize the one-sided declarations of independence.

In reality, the international community had no plan to resolve what had meanwhile become inevitable. As the summer was advancing into fall, and as the pictures of the war between the

Serb-dominated YNA and Croatia became breaking news in the world's evening newscasts, the concern of the global community kept growing. In September of 1991, the European Community appointed Lord Peter Carrington of the U.K. the mediator in the conflict; in response to his views articulated in the Carrington Plan, Germany launched pressures aimed at international recognition of the two breakaway republics.

In December of 1991, the United Nations appointed former U.S. Secretary of State (under Jimmy Carter) Cyrus Vance Special Envoy for Croatia in the peace negotiations. The Vance Plan, announced at the end of December, envisaged deployment of UN force in Croatia's three Serb-held pockets in order to protect the local people therein. In return, the Yugoslav National Army was supposed to retreat, the Serb paramilitary had to be disbanded and cease-fire established. Croatian President Tudjman agreed with the plan, for Germany had convinced him that Croatia was going to acquire international recognition. Milosevic agreed, too: he had already taken control of the YNA and the offer was his best chance to 'freeze' the frontline demarcations and establish new *de facto* borders.

Through the U.N. Resolution No. 743 of February, 1992, the disposition of the United Nations PROtection FORce (UNPROFOR) was approved. Following a referendum in Bosnia-Herzegovina (BH) which was boycotted by Bosnia's Serbs, and expecting international assistance in case of warfare, Alija Izetbegovic won his struggle for the independence of BH in March of 1992. The leading politicans of Bosnian Serbs proclaimed their own state – the *Srpska Republika* ('Serbian Republic', later renamed as the Republic of Srpska). In mid-1992, following the independence of Slovenia and Croatia respectively, the reduced Federal Republic of Yugoslavia was formed (F.R.Y.).

---

[4] The heterogeneous country known as **Yugoslavia** was first created in the aftermath of World War I (the Great War), on December 1, 1918 as the Kingdom of Serbs, Croats and Slovenes under the Serbian Karadjordjevic Dynasty; it was later (1929) renamed as the Kingdom of Yugoslavia ('Yugoslavia' meaning 'Land of Southern Slavs'). During World War II, when Germany and Italy overran the country (1941), a fascist puppet state, Independent State of Croatia, was established; its territory consisted of most of modern-day Croatia

and Bosnia-Herzegovina, plus some parts of Serbia and Slovenia. The Author here describes the situation in the country refounded in 1945, the official name of which was the Federal People's Republic of Yugoslavia first, then changed (1963) into the Socialist Federal Republic of Yugoslavia – S.F.R.Y. – *Translator's note.*

[5] Kosmet is an abbreviated name of Kosovo-Metohija, which has been the official name of that province according to Serbia's (formerly Yugoslavia's, too) constitution; since recently, the local/ethnic Albanian and international communities have been referring to it as 'Kosovo' only, thus eliminating the historical implications of the full name. Namely, the Metohija part mostly consisted of the (Serbian Orthodox) Church property, *metoh* meaning 'appendage of a monastery'. – *Translator's note.*

I WAS TREATING CHILDREN

THE WAR WAS RAGING ON. I alternately stayed at Igalo (Montenegro), Pale (Bosnia) and Belgrade (Serbia). In the coastal town of Igalo, I owned and ran the Mediterranean Surgery Center for Plastic and Reconstructive Surgery. In Montenegro, BH and Serbia, people described me as a man who celebrated Yugoslavia in his heart while carrying an American passport in his pocket. I had to endure the malicious and satirical label attached to me as a person, for I had 'other fish to fry' which were pressing on my mind.

As a doctor, I was tackling the horrible consequences of the war, saving the innocent and young victims of the bloodshed. Owing to the efforts of the Norwegian Government, French President François Mitterrand, and also the Norwegian missioner Thorvald Stoltenberg and his daughter Camilla, a prominent humanitarian, it was in cooperation with Bato Djurovic, Director of the Institute6 at the time, that a department for the treatment and recuperation of the children injured in the war was established in Igalo. One of the WHO physicians working at IOM – International Organization for Migration, Dr. Harald Siem, authorized me to work at that department. Children used to be injured by bullets which crushed their bones or damaged the vital organs, and frequently had extremely bad burns and cuts. For a year I worked with my colleagues on providing care, treating and operating on these children. At Igalo and Pale, I treated children that had dangerous burns from lame bombs and injuries inflicted by the ammo ired by the Muslims, Croats, and Serbs as well. Whenever I saw those innocent victims of the mad conflict on the territory of what had been no-longer existing Yugoslavia, I could not help racking my brain and trying to think up a way to help the horrors come to an end – once and for all.

INTERNATIONAL ORGANIZATION FOR MIGRATION (IOM)
ORGANISATION INTERNATIONALE POUR LES MIGRATIONS (OIM)
ORGANIZACIÓN INTERNACIONAL PARA LAS MIGRACIONES (OIM)

Telephone: 717 91 11
Cable Address: Promigrant Geneva
Telex: 415 722
Telefax: 798 61 50

17, route des Morillons
P.O. Box 71
CH - 1211 GENEVA 19
SWITZERLAND

TO: DR B. DJORDJEVIC MISC 9093

FAX NO: 47 22 60 12 22

10 DEC. 1993

COPY: IOM BELGRADE GEBG 472

DATE: 10 DECEMBER 1993

DEAR DR DJORDJEVIC,

I ENJOYED VERY MUCH YOUR VISIT THE OTHER DAY. I HAVE BEEN IN CONTACT WITH NORWEGIAN AUTHORITIES WHO CONFIRMED THAT IGALO WAS VERY MUCH ON THEIR MIND, AND SUGGESTED MORE DETAILED TALKS WHEN I VISIT THE MINISTRY OF FOREIGN AFFAIRS IN OSLO THIS COMING 17 DECEMBER.

IT IS UNDERSTOOD THAT YOU, WITH SOME ASSISTANCE TO SHIP IN SUPPLIES, HEATING OIL, MEDICINE AND FOOD, COULD RECEIVE FOR TREATMENT A LARGE NUMBER (HUNDREDS) OF THE PATIENTS THAT ARE REFERRED TO IN THE IOM SPECIAL MEDICAL PROGRAMME. IT IS HOWEVER UNCLEAR HOW IOM CAN ASSIST WITH SUPPLIES. IT IS HOPED THAT THE NORWEGIAN AUTHORITIES COULD BE HELPFUL WITH THIS ASPECT.

THE IOM OFFICE IN BELGRADE WILL BE BRIEFED AND WILL STAND READY TO ASSIST IF AND WHEN OUR COOPERATION COMES INTO PLAY.

REGARDS

DR HARALD SIEM

COORD IN DRAFT: NORTON

Letter by Dr. Harald Siem

Their fate moved me so much that I was unable to sleep. I wondered: Is it possible that the warriors attack, injure and kill – children? Why? Because of the sick politics of the Balkan leaders. I treated the children of the Muslims, the Croats and the Serbs alike, without any biases. At the Igalo Institute, treatment of children and encounters of their families led to a kind of small-size inter-ethnic cooperation in BH. America recognized my humanitarian activities and awarded me the 2010 Ellis Island Medal of Honor, and a star on Palm Canyon Drive for humanitarism at Palm Springs, Ca.

Everything else I participated in was a matter of natural course of events.

International peace efforts for Bosnia started in February, 1992, with the so-called Cutilheiro Plan proposed at a conference in Lisbon by the Portuguese diplomat José Cutilheiro as an attempt to prevent BH from sliding into war. The plan envisaged a partition of Bosnia-Herzegovina and formation of ethnic territorial units within Bosnia. During the debate on the plan, two leaders of nationalist/ethnic parties stepped onto the international political scene for the first time: they were Radovan Karadzic of the Serbian Democratic Party (abbr. SDS in Serbian, for *Srpska demokratska stranka*) and Mate Boban of the Croatian Defence Council (abbr. HVO in Croat, for *Hrvatsko vijeće obrane*). Unwilling to accept such a division, while representing the Bosnian authorities, Alija Izetbegović rejected the plan.

Soon after Izetbegović's refusal to accept the said plan, the war broke out in April 1992. Fighting was going on following the pattern of that in Croatia: Supported by the Yugoslav National Army, local Serbs would take control of a territory. In the summer of 1992, the world was shocked by the footage and news reports about the massacres committed in Bosnia and concentration camps reminiscent of those from World War II. This led to a conference regarding the conflict in BH, summoned in London by the British Government and the United Nations, in August 1992. Radovan Karadzic appeared at the conference in the capacity of the Bosnian-Serb leader. The conference resolutely condemned Milošević and Karadžić, and established the ICFY –International Conference on the Former Yugoslavia.

With Cyrus Vance, who represented the U.N., and Lord David Owen who represented the European Community, as co-chairmen, the International Conference on the Former Yugoslavia departed from the principles agreed to in London while seeking solutions for the war in BH; early in 1993, the Vance-Owen Peace Plan (VOPP) was adopted to become subject of international debates due to the envisaged division of Bosnia into 10 provinces/cantons. The map launched by the VOPP offered to the Serbs mere 43 percent of the Bosnian territory at the moment when they held control over 70 percent. Sarajevo was seen as a demilitarized zone unrelated to any one of the ethnic groups in particular.

The plan additionally supported a broad protection of human rights. The American Administration never backed up the VOPP in full; instead of sending in troops, the newly-elected President Bill Clinton introduced the 'lift and strike' policy, that is, air-raids against the heavily 'entrenched' Bosnian-Serb lines. The Europeans and the UNPROFOR[7] did not approve of this American doctrine, for their own troops were thus threatened as well.

By a referendum held in 1993, the Bosnian Serbs rejected the VOPP with great majority because they would have had to cede large areas back. Even Slobodan Milosevic, who wanted lifting of the UN sanctions against Serbia, failed to talk Radovan Karadzic into acceptance of Vance-Owen Peace Plan. In consequence, he closed the borders between Bosnia and Serbia for everything but food and medical drugs.

In early summer of 1993, a new and comprehensive Owen-Stoltenberg Partition Plan was launched under the auspices of the ICFY (Thorvald Stoltenberg representing the U.N.); it led to recriminations between the three involved sides while the fighting on three fronts went on. Each of the armies in Bosnia-Herzegovina was trying to take hold of as large territory as possible before drawing of final maps. If this plan had been put into practice, the Serbs would have been given 53 percent of the BH territory, the Croats could have taken 17 per cent, and the Bosnian Government would have taken the rest of 30%. A Serb delegate put in this remark during the talks: "The Turks [derogatory reference to Muslims] are going to be like walnuts in a Serbo-Croat nutcracker".

In the beginning, Izetbegovic indicated acceptance, yet changed his mind and rejected the plan in September, 1993.

It was earlier in 1993 that my interest in the state of affairs in Serbia had begun, when I tried to get a closer insight into the official policies of Belgrade and Pale re the war crisis. In order to obtain an expert opinion, I asked Janusz Bugajski of the Center for European Policy

Analaysis in Washington, D.C. to assess my chance of taking President Dobrica Cosic[8] to the U.S. for secret consultations.

Bugajski sent me an answer on March 24, 1993: A lady, official of the National Security Council in the States had told me no one in the White House was willing to meet the 'grey-haired man', for they were angered by the Serb actions in Eastern Bosnia; Belgrade had to make a great change in its policy; the new administration prioritized the Russian issue and some other issues during the transition in the White House. Yet the lady wanted to know more about the initiative, and Bugajski asked me to let him know of the trip to Washington, for he wanted to meet 'the guy'.

---

[6] **Dr. Simo Milosevic Institute** at Igalo, Montenegro, is an internationally renowned medical institute/spa for physical medicine, rehabilitation and rheumatology; founded in 1949, it started Physiotherapy College in 1976; since 2004, it has had the status of the Faculty of Applied Physiology and, accordingly, member-faculty of the University of Montenegro. –*Translator's note.*

[7] The United Nations Protection Force, **UNPROFOR**, was established in February of 1992 for the war in Croatia, to extend to Bosnia-Herzegovina with somewhat different tasks that changed and/or multiplied in the years to come. In March of 1995, the Force was restructured into three coordinated peace operations. – *Translator's note.*

[8] **Dobrica Cosic** (1921-2014) was the first president (June 15, 1992-June 1, 1993) of the Federal Republic of Yugoslavia (1992-2003) which consisted of Serbia and Montenegro, two of six republics in the former Socialist Federal Republic of Yugoslavia. A member of the partisan forces in WWII and an outstanding figure as politician and novelist, he became a dissident in 1960's and earned the attribute of the "Father of the Serbian nation", for his opinion about the Serbs being imperilled in the multinational country. – *Translator's note.*

BEATEN BY NATO'S STICK

THREE WEEKS LATER, on April 13, 1993, Janusz Bugajski, an associate of the director of the Center for Strategic and International Studies (CSIS) wrote to me again about the expectations the U.S. had from the Serbian leaders in the areas of politics and the military. These included as follows:

Politically, the Serbs had to unambiguously recognize the independence, sovereignty and territorial integrity of BH; to openly back up the principles of Vance-Owen Peace Plan (with or without changes under negotiations); to demonstrate the willingness to meet with Izetbegovic and Tudjman, to distance themselves from Milosevic's option for war; to declare opposition to an armed conflict as an instrument in pursuing political goals. In terms of military-related issues, the Serbian leaders had to condemn breach of truce or refusal to let humanitarian aid reach Eastern Bosnia; to condemn military threats against UN/NATO operations in Bosnia in Bosnia; to send strong signals about Belgrade supporting demilitarization of Sarajevo; to exert pressure on the Serb forces re the bombing of Sarajevo; to help establishment of a UN or NATO mission in the city; and, to demonstrate good will and let the UN observers patrol along the Bosnian-Serbian and Bosnian-Montenegrin borders, overlooking possible breaches of the truce.

By the beginning of 1994, the armed conflict in Bosnia had lasted for more than 18 months. Over the period, four comprehensive peace plans had been launched, yet none of them resulted in peace. Of all the factors in this regrettable outcome, the absence of any strong American participation in the peacemaking process is perhaps the most important.

Following the February raid at Sarajevo's city market of Markale, NATO – led by France and the U.S.A. – presented an ultimatum to the leaders of the Bosnian Serbs demanding the withdrawal of heavy artillery from around Sarajevo (20-kilometer-wide 'total exclusion zone') or submitting these weapons to the U.N. control. The Serbs were warned that otherwise they would expose themselves to NATO'S air raids. Before March, 1994, the American Government brokered cease-fire to end the Croat-Muslim conflict, which further led to the creation of the Muslim-Croat Federation as an entity within the present-day Bosnia-Herzegovina.

Soon thereafter, NATO ordered limited air-strikes (the first such operation in the 47-year history of the Alliance) against the Serb-held lines. The raids were launched in response to the attack against the town of Gorazde, one of the 'safe areas' according to the Joint Action Plan, by Gen. Ratko Mladic. In revenge for the NATO bombings, Mladic undertook an attack against the town of Tuzla, another 'safe area', and took 150 U.N. personnel hostages, thus violating the international standards of humanitarian access and protection. Mladic's moves hightened Milosevic's rage, for Serbia's president had expected the sanctions on the F.R. of Yugoslavia to be lifted.

The foolhardy actions by Gen. Ratko Mladic drove the Russians out of BH and the gap between Milosevic and Karadzic grew additionally.

In April, subsequent to the attack on Gorazde and the first round of NATO air-strikes, an appeal on the part of Boris Yeltsin, President of the Russian Federation, at an international summit led to the establishment of the Contact Group. The members of the Group were representatives of France, Germany, Russia, Great Britain and the U.S.A. Over the next few months, they worked out some details for a peacemaking program, based on the European Community Action Plan. The plan of the Contact Group, made public in July of 1994, envisaged that 51% of the territory should come under Bosnian-Croat Federation, and 49% under the Bosnian Serbs' control. The plan reckoned with 'carrot and stick' policy, reward and punishment that would be applied on either party in conflict. Provided the BH Government refused the plan of the Contact Group, the sanctions on Yugoslavia would be slackened; provided the Bosnian Serbs rejected the plan, the weapons embargo on BH would be lifted. When the plan was released, the Contact Group issued a statement which emphasized that the acceptance of the plan was the essential first step to open the negotiations.

The statement was interpreted by the Bosnian Serb and Muslim authorities respectively as the request for their acceptance of the territorial partitioning of BH followed by negotiation on constitutional formulas. Next, the word 'acceptance' turned into a stumbling block to the opening of Serb-Muslim negotiations which lasted to the end of the year.

Slobodan Milošević, who still wanted the sanctions against the F.R. of Yugoslavia to be lifted, accepted the proposed plan; the rejection on the part of the Parliament of the Republic of Srpska enraged him greatly. Annoyed, he imposed economic blockade on the Bosnian Serbs in early August 1994. In November, the Bosnian Government launched offensives on three fronts: in central Bosnia, in the vicinity of Sarajevo and in Bihac enclave. The Serb leaders found themselves isolated diplomatically, even by Slobodan Milosevic. The Contact Group refused to talk to Radovan Karadzic, the sole person who seemed powerful enough to stop the war.

The latest of the comprehensive peace plans was delayed. The negotiations on a long-term cessation of hostilities, conducted by the U.N. Representative Yasushi Akashi and the UNPROFOR Commander Lt. Gen. Michael Rose looked like going nowhere. Boutros Boutros-Ghali, U.N. Secretary General, tried to meet with Radovan Karadzic in order to negotiate a cease-fire, yet this was rejected. Even the talks on some minor cease-fires proved to be hopeless. The world lost faith in the possibility of stopping, or at least slowing, the war by anyone from the international community.

In such a tense and uncertain situation, Dr. Radovan Karadzic asked me in despair:

– Bring Henry Kissinger or Jimmy Carter here to Pale so that we can make a peace settlement and put an end to the war.

KARADŽIĆ SUMMONING CARTER

I was contacted by Slavko Lazarevic, a man enjoying full trust by Radovan Karadzic. He was in charge of economic affairs (business and money) of the Republic of Srpska. In June, 1994, he took me to Pale in order to discuss the possibility of my help in their big business deals with Americans.

– Help Radovan Karadžić! – Slavko Lazarević said to me quizzically. It was then that I was present at a session of the Parliament of the Republic of Srpska; other outstanding figures there were Dr. Radovan Karadžić, Vice-Presidents Dr. Biljana Plavšić and Dr. Nikola Koljević, Speaker of the Parliament Momčilo Krajišnik and other officials. There I learned that Ambassador Milan Milutinovic (Yugoslavia's foreign minister from 1995) had been trying to persuade Radovan Karadzic of the necessity that the Republic of Srpska gets international credibility through American recognition of it as a partner, unofficially at least.

Karadzic and I discussed this matter and agreed that the advice by Milan Milutinovic, my schoolmate, was good and worth following. At that point, Karadzic lushed with excitement over an idea he had just hit upon. He said:

– I want you to bring Henry Kissinger or Jimmy Carter to me, here in Pale, so that we can ensure peace and lift the embargo imposed on the Republic of Srpska and Yugoslavia.

I was not taken by surprise. Karadzic had been cornered and understood that it was the Americans only who could pull him out of the Bosnian darkness and his quarrel with Milosevic. I knew that Milosevic's attempt to engage Carter had failed and believed that my capability was greater than that of Milosevic's team, that is, that I could reach Jimmy Carter in person.

At Pale, with Radovan Karadžić and Momčilo Krajišnik

– I accept. You know me as a man of my word. Give me a certificate that I am your representative in the United States, and an authorization for the talks to the Americans! – I answered.

Karadzic was seeking a way to re-enter negotiations and offer some concessions without being forced to make the politically suicidal decision to accept the Contact Group plan.

As soon as Karadzic signed my first appointment as a representative of the Republic of Srpska in the United States, I asked my friend Thomas F. Hanley, attorney working at „Whitman Breed Abbott & Morgan LLC" of Los Angeles as real estate lawyer, to mediate my contact with Jimmy Carter.

Hanley is a tall man with bushy eyebrows and thick hair, my friend and a business partner in the purchases of some houses in the States, whom I had last met in Santa Barbara, in early summer 1993. On that occasion we did not talk politics. Tom represented numerous foreign investors in their American business transactions, but that could hardly make him prepared to work with us, that is, the Serbs.

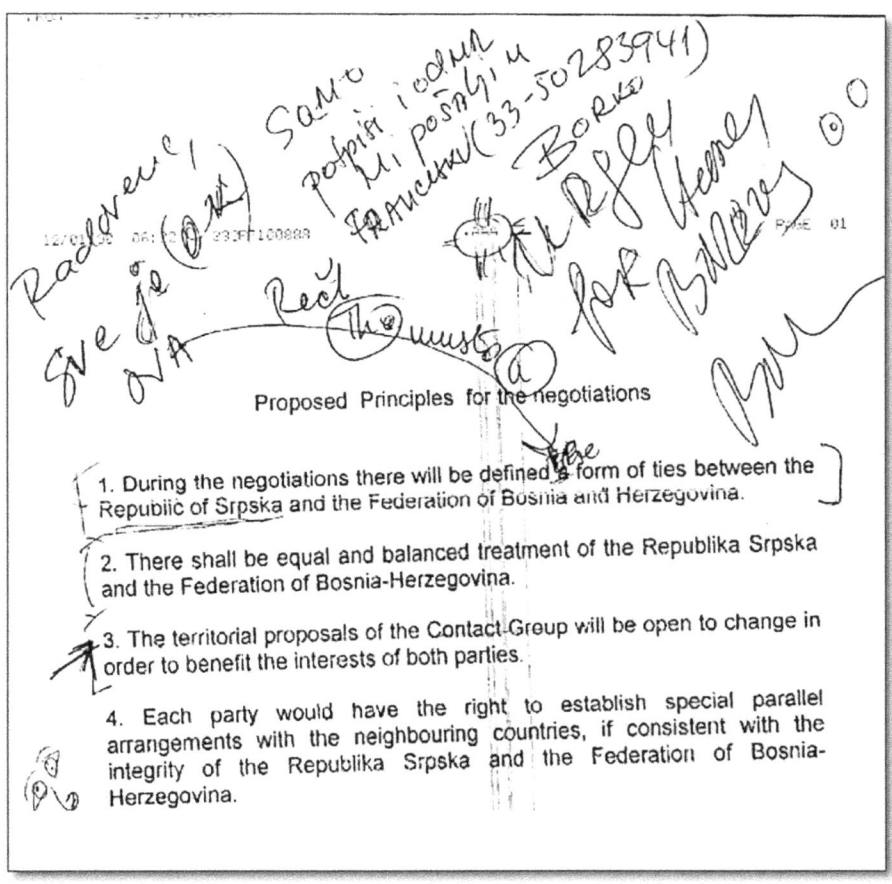

A draft paper for the Pale negotiations (Dec. 1994) re the establishment of the Republic of Srpska, when Dr. Borko Djordjević insisted that it should be an entity within the federal Bosnia-Herzegovina.

Relying on Tom Hanley in the effort to involve Jimmy Carter in the peace-making affairs in Bosnia was not a political thing. It was a commonsense thing. I explained to Tom Hanley that politics in BH and Yugoslavia had not proved productive. The Bosnian arena needed someone capable of bringing peace and helping the misunderstandings being solved, for they had resulted in a horrible civil war. Politicians had failed to stop the clash, and I persuaded myself and my friend Tom Hanley that the influence of someone outside of the system – someone like Jimmy Carter and his Carter Center – could possibly bring peace to both the Serbs and the Muslims.

Bill Clinton and Borko Djordjević

The Carter Center was founded in 1982 by former President Jimmy Carter and his wife Rosalynn Carter and registered as a non-pro it, non-partisan organization which addresses the issues of democracy and development, global health and urban revitalization in the U.S.A. and abroad. The Center was built by private donations from individuals, foundations and corporations (29 million dollars) that keep supporting its annual operation budget of 20 million. It works in partnership with Emory University, which provides a solid basis for research and scholarships and all of the Center's activities. It has some 250 employees, most of whom work from Atlanta, Ga., plus 80 volunteers and about a hundred of students and graduates, prevailingly from Emory. The Center's field representatives have been stationed in Guyana, Liberia, Ethiopia, Nicaragua and other countries.

What I found most appealing was the fact that most of the Carter Center's programs are run by professors of Emory University who relied on the leadership of President Carter and the former First Lady Rosalynn Carter. Important elements of the profile lay in Carter's inclination to consulting other world leaders and finding partners among organizations and communities both in the Unites States and abroad in the effort to enhance changes and implement programs aimed at solutions in conflicts, in the field of human rights, administration systems in Africa, Latin-American and Caribbean studies, as well as worldwide advance of democracy. For instance, in 1993, the Carter Center hosted a meeting with the Sudan People's Liberation Army United to explore possibilities for reconciliation with the SPLA, another southern Sudanese faction.

BORKO B. DJORDJEVIC, M.D., Inc.
Plastic and Reconstructive Surgery

Cosmetic Surgery Center
Yugoslavia 85347 Igalo
Save Ilica 1
Phone: (3882) 59-395
Fax: (3882) 53-805

Vladimira Popovica
Suite B39
11070 Beograd
Yugoslavia
Phone: 38-11-222-3956
Fax: 38-11-222-4011

```
TO : MR MILAN PANIC
FAX: 38-11-662-917
```

Aug.19, 1992

Dear Mr Panic,

      I've received the copy of the fax that You sent to my mother in law. We are making preliminary arangement for President Carter to meet You in Geneva preferably without publicity.

      As I told You when I met You, I've been here for the last two years trying to identify major problems in which I can help with some of my Friends from Washington and Europe. I think the problems are right here and some of the steps that have been sugested to me, is one process of privatisation which I have worked out with KPMG - Washington office, and made some inroads here, but as You know, it is very hard to work outside the Goverment chanels. If Yugoslavia would sign the KPMG agreement, I can activate very powerful PR machine that They have, including some serious possibility of canceling the embargo. We can talk about it.

      I am sending You in the separate envelope the contract that KPMG signed pre embargo and the Letter of Intent that Mr Maljkovic, Deputy Prime Minister signed prior to that. Mr Milosevic is aware of this. I do not see any reason why this program can not be implement in whole Yugoslavia and give You a powerful argument against the foreign press. There are many more programs that I started Here and in which I was using American business - man and politicians who spoke in our favour, but as I said, I need official chanels.

      As soon as Betty notifies me about President Jimmy Carter, I would let You know.

Sincerely,
Dr Borko Djordjevic, M.D.

Letter to Milan Panić

At my Mediterranean Surgery Center for Plastic and Reconstructive Surgery I had faced many tragedies and sufferings of people afflicted by the Bosnian war. They sought salvation at the clinic, and I reacted –naturally enough – with overwhelming emotions which motivated me as a humanist to do something which could contribute to the cessation of the sanguinary civil war in Bosnia. It had earlier occurred to me that Jimmy Carter would be the right person to appeal on: his adroitness and experience could help stop the fighting in Bosnia-Herzegovina. On August 19, 1992, I had written about it in a letter to Milan Panic[2], Yugoslavia's Prime Minister, but with no response.

The idea of Carter as a mediator was revived by Karadzic himself; he told me that *he was aware of the necessity to ind way to the Americans*. Like a stage manager who stays behind the scene, in this case I undertook – on November 28, 1994 – to inform the U.S. President Bill Clinton and the Secretary of State Warren Christopher about the issue, asking them to give it a little bit closer attention. Yes, I was a Serb, but I was also an American who wanted to know if my country would allow me to co-work with Dr. Radovan Karadzic as my fellow-Serb and the missioner Jimmy Carter as my fellow-American. I knew the usual result of such letters when lateral political backup was missing.

РЕПУБЛИКА СРПСКА 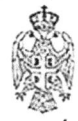 REPUBLIC OF SRPSKA
ПРЕДСЕДНИК РЕПУБЛИКЕ PRESIDENT OF THE REPUBLIC
САРАЈЕВО SARAJEVO

From: Dr Radovan Karadzic

To: H.E. Jimmy Carter

Dear Exellency,

It is a great pleasure for me to send a message to you. Mr. Slavko Lazarevic´ and Mr. Borko B. Djordjevic´, M.D., are entitled to pass the message, in a form of a non-paper, to your exellency. Your possible visit to Pale could mean a great break-through in the peace-process.

We would try to create a new public statement which could enable President Clinton to change the attitude towards the crisis in former Yugoslavia, if he is seeking such an opportunity.

This is of the greatest importance that President Clinton recently stated that in Bosnia there is a civil war, and not a war of an agression, since we, Bosnian Serbs, didn't come from Serbia.

We are shure that the U.S. may bring about peace in Bosnia. We are looking forward to meeting such an important American, which may be a turn-over in the crisis. The Serbs are ready to improve their own relationship with the U.S. particulary since we always have been friends of America, hopeful that America would help us to instole the democracy after the communist dictatorship.

Looking forward to meeting your exellency in my country, I wish you all the best.

Sincerely yours,

Радован Караџић
(Radovan Karadzic´)

P.S. Passport number of mr Slavko La[zarevic´]
is: S 021566

R. Karadžić's letter to H.E. Jimmy Carter

A positive political signal came through Tom Hanley who had worked in the same firm as the lawyer Warren Christopher before the latter became a statesman. Their secretaries were rather close, too: a seemingly trivial fact in a big deal, yet one should know that even minor opportunities to win over as many people as possible for such a mission are not to be wasted.

Together with Tom Hanley I contacted the Carter Center and reached Ambassador Harry G. Barnes Jr. who faxed a letter to us. I informed Radovan Karadzic thereof, asking him to contact me urgently "re the fax by Mr. Harry Barnes".

Like every loyal American, my associate Thomas F. Hanley kept the State Department informed on the ongoing activities, including those of mine; the latter were the subject of his letter sent from Los Angeles on November 28, 1994.

Therein, he referred to my and Karadzic's idea, and the latter's wish to have the U.S.A. organize the peace settlement for Bosnia-Herzegovina with the help of his emissaries, including Dr. Djordjevic, and himself (Hanley). A prompt consideration of the proposal was asked for.

A week later, on December 5, 1994, Tom Hanley addressed an almost identical letter to Jimmy Carter in the capacity of the Carter Center Chairman. Again, he mentioned me, Dr. Djordjevic, himself and Slavko Lazarevic as participants in peace negotiations, as well as a letter I was going to hand in to him personally which was summoning President Carter to come to Pale for such negotiations. Thomas Hanley named himself as a contact for this matter. Thereafter, Hanley's related correspondence also included President Bill Clinton and his staff (James Steinberg, Carlene Ackerman, Mark Steinberg).

Then I gave Tom Hanley Karadzic's hand-written letter which he (Tom) – on behalf of his 'client' forwarded to the White House, State Department, Carter Center in Atlanta and Jimmy Carter in Plains. The letter appealed on them to come to Bosnia and help a peace settlement to be accomplished. On December 6, 1994, Hanley wrote to the former U.S. President about an approved enclosure of a copy of Dr. Karadzic's letter for Carter, the original of which, together with a war-terminating proposal, was going to be handed in to him by Mr. Slavko Lazarevic and Dr. Borko Djordjevic.

The White House and the State Department did not respond. The Carter Center did. Harry G. Barnes Jr., Director of the Center's Conflict Resolution and Human Rights Programs wrote to Thomas F. Hanley on December 7, 1994 about President Carter being ready to receive Dr. Karadzic's emissaries in his home at Plains on December 13 or 14.

In a telephone conversation, Barnes repeated that "the former U.S. President takes great interest in the peace in Bosnia", but it was necessary that Radovan Karadzic called Jimmy Carter and confirmed his proposal.

Upon my request, Hanley sent Barnes a few details of our itinerary: departure from Belgrade on Dec. 12, via Zurich, to Atlanta and Los Angeles; trip back from L.A. would start on Dec. 26, via Zurich and Geneva, to Belgrade. Such a plan was implied by the political protocol on our cooperation. Moreover, the need emerged for a check on who Thomas Hanley and Borko Djordjevic were, and whether we were legitimate official representatives of the Bosnian-Serb leader.

---

[2] **Milan Panic** (b. 1929) is a Serbian-born American businessman with a lengthy career in pharmaceutical industry. In July 1992, he assumed the post of the Prime Minister of the Federal Republic of Yugoslavia at the request of Yugoslavia's President Dobrica Cosic and the President of Serbia Slobodan Milosevic. In the 1992 general elections in Serbia, Panic ran for presidency but only came in second to Milosevic. Peace in Bosnia was on the agenda of his presidential race platform. His office of PM lasted from July 14, 1992 to February 9, 1993. – Translator's note.

RIGOROUS CHECKS

Di Mari Ricker, a lawyer and former staff writer for the *Boston Globe* and the *Los Angeles Times*, told me in confidence that Harry Barnes, a director at the Carter Center, had been investigating the way in which Thomas Hanley turned out to be *the* person conveying Radovan Karadzic's message to Jimmy Carter.

Here is what Ambassador Barnes later told Di Mari Ricker for an article published in the ABA *Journal* of January 1996:

"Hanley's letter came [to the Carter Center] out of the blue." For, "in the preceding week or two we had received other inquiries regarding possible Carter involvement" in the peace efforts for Bosnia, through some people who were much closer to Belgrade and had clearer connections with Yugoslavia. The letter was thus a true surprise. "We did some checking with the State Department to determine whether Djordjevic's contacts were such that Karadzic inquiry – through him [and Tom Hanley] – was plausible. We came upon sort of a chain of plausibilities, so we went forward with it". The Carter Center carefully monitored the situation in Bosnia, so the appeal on the part of Radovan Karadzic appeared to be extremely serious.

The very idea of involving the former U.S. President Jimmy Carter as a peacemaker in the war conflict had come from the Serbian leader Slobodan Milosevic before the Contact Group was formed in June 1994. Milosevic sent his emissaries to the States with the assignment to find Jimmy Carter whom he knew as a man who had respect for Yugoslavia owing to his friendship with Josip Broz Tito.

Two Milosevic's emissaries visited the Carter Center in the belief that – with Jimmy Carter – they could find a novel and impartial approach to peace-making in the region. They intended to meet Carter in person and talk him into a consent to encounter and have a dialogue with Slobodan Milosevic. They reckoned with Carter – after the assumed agreement with Milosevic – as a missioner and catalyst to peace.

As Milosevic's envoys had no concrete proposal as to the way in which a visit by the former American President could help peace efforts in Bosnia-Herzegovina, Jimmy Carter refused to receive them. And it was not by mere chance that the American ex-President decided to help Radovan Karadzic.

When I told Karadzic that Carter's team suggested a personal phone call to Jimmy Carter whereby he would repeat his proposal, Radovan responded with a counter-question:

– What makes you think that the former President of the United States would come to see me at Pale? Milosevic has deceived all those Americans. Why should Jimmy Carter trust us, the Serbs?

– Because you're gonna prove that you are a good Serb. That you're struggling for peace, for democracy and for capitalism – I answered.

He instantly understood what I meant. For, Karadzic had learned from the American Serbs who had previously visited him that he had to strive for peace, democracy and capitalism. At that moment, Karadzic needed a distinguished man with whom he could make some concessions by accepting the Contact Group plan, yet somewhat altered in order to save his reputation as a man of honour. Since the Carter Center had been renowned for peace-making activities, it was Jimmy Carter whom Karadzic needed. Radovan Karadzic directly invited Carter to visit him at Pale and offered to send a couple of representatives to see him in Georgia; the goal was to work out a proposal which Karadzic had in mind. The former U.S. President instantly informed President Bill Clinton about his contacts with the Bosnian-Serb leader, and President approved of Carter's cooperation with Karadzic.

Namely, Bill Clinton and Jimmy Carter, as well as the American Administration, assessed that Karadzic could replace Slobodan Milosevic as a new leader of all Serbs, both in Serbia and the F.R. of Yugoslavia. In 1994, Clinton and his administration were fed up with the dirty and volatile politics of Slobodan Milosevic and the renewed communist ideology and politics exercised by his spouse Mirjana Markovic.

Moreover, the Americans assessed that Ratko Mladic as commander of the Bosnian Serb army and the leading figures of the Serbian Orthodox Church held Karadzic in higher esteem than Milosevic, reckoning with their support to Karadzic as the new leader of the Serbian nation.

As a witness, I can say that Carter accepted Radovan Karadzic because he understood that this Bosnian Serb was prepared for an honest cooperation with the Americans. So the once number one American informed President Bill Clinton about the contact.

Carter's representative Harry Barnes consulted Ambassador Charles Thomas, U.S. delegate to the Contact Group, who explained a couple of points: the military position of the Bosnian Serbs was not as strong as to imply occupation of nearly 70 percent of Bosnia; General Ratko Mladic, the Serbian military leader, was loyal to Karadzic rather than Milosevic; the Contact Group had made an attempt to clarify to the Bosnian Serbs that they could accept the Group's plan as a *basis for negotiations* and not as their superimposed final result.

Having consulted Bill Clinton, Carter gave his consent to the visit of us the Serbian representatives at his home in Plaines. The members of Radovan Karadzic's delegation were Tom Hanley, Slavko Lazarevic and myself.

A SECRET TRIP TO GEORGIA

IN ORDER TO PREPARE OURSELVES for the talks to Jimmy Carter as thoroughly as possible, Hanley and I had to read some 500 pages of documents referring to the situation in Bosnia. Another issue I faced was how to ensure a passport and the American visa for Slavko Lazarevic, Karadzic's confidant, and his aide Milan Reljic – avoiding the disclosure of the fact by Serbian leader's spies or by Slobodan Milosevic himself. For, our envisaged mission with Jimmy Carter was kept hidden from Milosevic so that he would not be able to sabotage it in order to humiliate Radovan Karadzic. My personal fear was that Milosevic, if he found out about my role in bringing Jimmy Carter to Pale, could order my exclusion from the circles around him. Our journey to Georgia and visit to Carter had to be a deep secret. So I persuaded Lazarevic to submit a visa application to the U.S. Embassy in Belgrade, to which I –on my part – sent a letter asking them to facilitate my friend's private visit to me in Palm Springs, California.

Dr. Borko Djordjević, Slavko Lazarevic and Tom Hanley at the Atlanta airport, heading to the Carter Center

Borko Djordjević at the Frankfurt airport

It was through Senator Dianne Feinstein that I urged the U.S. Embassy in Belgrade to promptly issue entrance visas to Lazarevic and Reljic. On November 14, 1994, Senator Feinstein wrote to Consul Robert Sorensen, using diplomatic phrasing, in order to convince him of the necessity for the two visitor visas to be issued:

I am writing to you on behalf of my constituant, Dr. Borko Djordjevic, a respected Southern California surgeon. He has asked for my assistance in obtaining visitor visas for his friends, Milan Reljic and Slavko Lazarevic, citizens of Serbia.
Dr. Djordjevic informs me that because of procedural constraints the visa applications submitted to your post by his friends will not be reviewed until December. I understand that their trip is scheduled for later this month. For this reason, I ask you to process their applications as soon as possible.

DIANNE FEINSTEIN
CALIFORNIA

COMMITTEE ON APPROPRIATIONS
COMMITTEE ON THE JUDICIARY
COMMITTEE ON RULES AND ADMINISTRATION

United States Senate
WASHINGTON, DC 20510-0504

November 14, 1994

Mr. Robert S. Sorensen
Consul
U.S. Embassy
Belgrade, Serbia-Montenegro
C/O Department of State
Washington, D.C. 20521-5070

Dear Mr. Sorensen:

I am writing to you on behalf of my constituent, Dr. Borko Djordjevic, a respected Southern California surgeon. He has asked for my assistance in obtaining visitor visas for his friends, Milan Reljic and Slavko Lazarevic, citizens of Serbia.

Dr. Djordjevic informs me that because of procedural constraints, the visa applications submitted to your post by his friends will not be reviewed until December. I understand that their trip is scheduled for later this month. For this reason, I ask you to process their applications as soon as possible.

While I am aware of the statutory restrictions placed upon applicants for non-immigrant visas, I believe that this request deserves the strongest consideration. Dr. Djordjevic has stated that he intends to send his friends back to their home country at the end of their appointed stay.

Please grant Mr. Reljic and Mr. Lazarevic every available courtesy that is consistent with applicable law. If you require any additional information, do not hesitate to contact David Swerdlick in my San Francisco office.

Thank you for your efforts in this matter of mutual concern.

Sincerely yours,

Dianne Feinstein
United States Senator

DF:ds6

Dianne Feinstein's letter

While I am aware of the statutory restrictions placed upon applicants for non-immigrant visas, I believe that this request deserves the strongest consideration. Dr. Djordjevic has stated that he intends to send his friends back to their home country at the end of their appointed stay.

Please grant Mr. Reljic and Mr. Lazarevic every available courtesy that is consistent with applicable law. If you require any additional information, do not hesitate to contact David Swerdlick in my San Francisco office.

Thank you for your efforts in this matter of mutual concern.
Sincerely yours,
Dianne Feinstein, United States Senator

In addition to the visas, Lazarevic and Reljic obtained the permits to carry their handguns. Fortunately enough, Slobodan Milosevic did not find out about the visas for the two Serbs and never discovered our plan. That is how I found myself inside international high politics, although becoming a gynaecologist and not a peacemaker had been the dream of my life.

We arrived in Plains, Ga., on December 14, 1994. We met first with the Carter Center officials at Country Corner, a local restaurant. It was a breakfast session with Joyce Neu and Ambassador Harry Barnes. They insisted that we, as a delegation representing Radovan Karadzic, should demonstrate, in a vivid manner which could persuade Carter, Karadzic's willingness and ability to conduct some particular measures. In return, Carter would pay a visit to the Republic of Srpska and Radovan Karadzic at Pale. Specifically, Carter – as had been said by his team –requested Karadzic's acceptance of the following six preconditions for his involvement in a peace mission:

– permit free movement of the regular U.N. relief convoys throughout Bosnia;
– remove any of the existing restrictions on the free movement of the UNPROFOR representatives;
– release all Muslim prisoners of war age 19 or below;
– honor a cease ire around Sarajevo;
– open the airport in Sarajevo; and
– guarantee human rights now and in the future.
During the discussion on these measures, the phone at the

counter rang insistently, and the waitress said:
- "Must be for y'all. They're talking foreign languages."
It was Radovan. He wanted to know our whereabouts and when we were going to see Carter. I conveyed to him Jimmy Carter's proposal and conditions of his visit to Pale.
- Tell Mr. Carter that I accept all of his measures, they will be honored within 48 hours!

After the confirmation, we boarded a van for Carter's home. He waited for us in his yard and waved. His attitude was extremely genial. Mr. Carter stood in front of an unpretentious house of some 150 square meters and surrounded with a high iron fence. We could see cottonfields in bloom stretching behind. Before we entered the house of our host, Carter's guards (security agents) searched us, despite our status of announced guests.

Carter ushered us into a small and modest living room that exuded homely atmosphere. He offered us to take seats on the chairs he had crafted personally or on the sofa. My friend Tom Hanley and I described the situation in Bosnia in detail. We presented a map of Bosnia-Herzegovina where 72% of the territory was controlled by the Serbs, 26% by the Muslims and the Croats jointly, while the rebel Fikret Abdic[10] held some two percent.

We emphasized Karadzic's view: in his cooperation with Carter he saw a channel which should take the Serbs toward a new cessation of hostilities that would further lead to the resumption of peace negotiations.

- The split between Karadzic and Milosevic is irreconcilable due to their differing visions about the future – I pointed out. – Karadzic wants democracy, and Milosevic wants a communist Serbia. Isolated by Milosevic and the Contact Group, Karadzic claims to be the sole person in charge of the developments in Bosnia and to need this way, your way, to re-enter the talks. He, Mr. Carter, takes you as a political figure through whom he can make concessions he didn't want to make before in order to reach peace – I underlined.

Then Carter put in a call to Karadzic, for he wanted a confirmation by the Bosnian-Serb leader that he would comply to certain conditions.

He talked to Karadzic in person first, then to Ratko Mladic. Telephone extensions were scattered all around the house, so we could witness their conversation: Carter was at his kitchen table, I was in Mrs. Rosalynn Carter's bedroom, while Hanley was sitting at Carter's desk in the home office, surrounded by presidential books. Radovan Karadzic was assuring Carter of his acceptance of all the conditions put forward and repeated that all of the proposed measures were to be carried out within 48 hours.

– Do come to Pale as soon as possible, we'll be waiting for you, Mr. Carter! – Karadzic said in the end.

Within a short while, Carter called the UNPROFOR in Sarajevo to make sure Karadzic had lifted road blockades. The CNN reported meanwhile that "the Bosnian-Serb leader had opened the traffic corridor". Jimmy Carter reached for the wall phone in his kitchen to inform President Bill Clinton that the implementation of the six measures by the Bosnian Serbs was successfully under way.

– I'm going to Bosnia-Herzegovina to make peace there. I'm going with Dr. Borko Djordjevic to see Radovan Karadzic!

– You can't go on behalf of the United States, you can only go as a private citizen – Clinton responded.

– I know, I'm going there as a representative of the Carter Center. This is an opportunity to stop ire and bloodshed in Bosnia!

– All right – Clinton agreed.

I understood that the U.S. President Bill Clinton, in spite of a certain skepticism as to the likelihood of success, was satisfied by the effort Jim Carter was investing and therefore approved of his journey to Pale. Carter said that the timing of his trip depended on the progress made in fulfilling the said six conditions, but he was ready to leave very soon. Some people from the Carter Center asked me if it was safe in Bosnia-Herzegovina, if Sarajevo was free, if one could get to Pale without risk. I would answer:

– Go freely! Radovan Karadzic personally guarantees for your lives!Just a few hours later, the Carter Center issued a press release about the pending peace mission of Jimmy Carter, due to start in three days' time, on December 17, 1994. In the meanwhile, Hanley, Lazarevic and I flew to Frankfurt. A U.S. military aircraft was to transport us on to Zagreb, but the White House withdrew the light suddenly, so we travelled by car. The trip to Pale via

Zagreb and Belgrade was rather exhausting, for customs officers questioned Hanley's credentials at every border crossing. The trouble culminated in Belgrade where he was detained by Interpol agents who suspected him of being an international smuggler.

Having crossed into Bosnia, we were exposed to gun ire, yet survived. As our visit to Jimmy Carter and his consent to come to Bosnia for a meeting with Karadzic had proved fruitful, we let his staff take full initiative in further activities; the Carter Center staff were kept extremely busy. On the one hand they were exposed to both praise and criticism of the public, while on the other they had to follow the advice from the U.S. administration regarding their work.

Carter's closest associates Dr. Joyce Neu and Ambassador Harry Barnes maintained steady contacts with the American State Department and the United Nations. In Washington, D.C., Barnes discussed the upcoming mission with Assistant U.S. Secretary of State for European and Canadian affairs Richard Holbrooke and with Charles Thomas from the Contact Group. He also met with the representatives of the Central Intelligence Agency and the National Security Council. The State Department briefed Jimmy Carter on the situation in Yugoslavia and Bosnia-Herzegovina, as well as on the measures put forward to Karadzic as preconditions for Carter's visit to Pale.

Bill Clinton sent his own representatives to brief Jimmy Carter on the American position on the stalled negotiations over the previous Contact Group plan. They advised Carter that he could help the peace process move forward by convincing the parties involved to agree to a cease-fire and doing what he could in order to bring them back to negotiating table so that territorial 'barter' is discussed.

The other points of Clinton's confidential messages to the missioner Jimmy Carter concerned the importance of preserving Bosnia-Herzegovina as one (though in firm and unconvincing) country/state, the relations along the line Milosevic-Karadzic-Mladic and the situation at the town of Bihac, as well as the extent to which Karadzic was fulfilling the conditions imposed.

In essence, Karadzic, who – as was admitted by the State Department – necessarily had to be included in any peace agreement, was looking for a 'bridge' he could use to leave the 'island' whereon he had found himself isolated. Hence, one of the primary goals of Carter's initiative was to bring the parties to a negotiating table while 'constructing' the 'bridge' for Radovan Karadzic and the Bosnian Serbs.

---

[10] **Fikret Abdic** (b. 1939) is a Bosnian businessman and politician. In 1980's, he turned the *Agrokomerc* agricultural company based in the municipality of Velika Kladusa into one of Yugoslavia's biggest conglomerates. Himself a Sunni Muslim, in 1990's he opposed the official Bosnian government and proclaimed the Autonomous Province of Western Bosnia (1993-5) which covered the town of Velika Kladusa and the villages in its vicinity. – *Translator's note.*

A CARPENTER AND A GUSLAR [11]

Accompanied by Joyce Neu and Harry Burnes, Jimmy and Rosalynn Carter set out on a trip to the Republic of Srpska on December 17, 1994. They flew an official U.S. aircraft. Through Christiane Amanpour and the CNN, the former U.S. President made it public that he was to travel to Bosnia-Herzegovina on a peace-mission; the news evoked stirring in the U.S. Congress. On December 17, 1994 *Los Angeles Times* published the article "Carter, Driven to Do Good, Looks to Bosnia Quagmire" written by Jack Nelson. Here is an excerpt therefrom:

There he goes again. First it was North Korea. Then it was Haiti. Now he's talking about trying to help negotiate a solution in Bosnia.
[...]
By now, almost everyone knows that Carter is different. He was different as an obscure state legislator. He was different as governor of Georgia and different as President.
The mystery is what drives him. At an age and stage in life when others opt for a dignified deceleration. [...] In little more than a decade, the 70-year-old former President transformed himself into one of the world's busiest and--arguably--one of its most successful dogooders.
[...]
Now he hopes to visit Bosnia-Herzegovina at the invitation of Bosnian Serb leader Radovan Karadzic to try to mediate an end to the most intractable of all of today's bloody regional disputes. Although no plan had been announced as of Friday night, Karadzic's intermediaries--including Dr. Borko B. Djordjevic, a Santa Barbara plastic surgeon--expected to accompany Carter to the Bosnian capital of Sarajevo as early as today.
To his critics, the explanation for all this is relatively simple: He is driven by a desire to rehabilitate his image and his place in history after a failed presidency. In that vein, many believe that he is shamelessly seeking the Nobel Peace Prize.

At this point, two opinions seem worth quoting: To Stephen E. Ambrose, biographer of Dwight Eisenhower, Carter was the *"greatest living ex-president"*. David McCullough, author of biographies on Harry Truman and Theodore Roosevelt, described Carter as an *"extremely interesting and ethical man whose standing historically is going to increase as time goes on".*

On that same day, December 17, 1994, the *Los Angeles Times* also published my statement that I had a phone talk with Mr. Karadzic the day before, and that he had been told that all six articles of the plan had been implemented, including the release of the Muslim detainees; Karadzic felt that he had never been given a fair opportunity, but he trusted Jimmy Carter's unbiased approach, due to fact that the Serbs and the Americans had a history of traditionally good diplomatic relations. The newspaper also conveyed skeptical attitude on the part of Mr. William Perry, U.S. Defense Minister.

The information about Jimmy Carter's visit to Dr. Radovan Karadzic, Bosnian-Serb leader, enraged Slobodan Milosevic who swore at his (in)competent adviser, Ambassador Milan Milutinovic.

– They've grabbed Carter right under your very nose!

At Pale: Radovan Karadzic and Jimmy Carter during dinner

Upon their arrival in Frankfurt, the Carter team had a meeting with the American representatives in the Contact Group. There followed a stop-over at Zagreb, on December 18. There, the Carter delegation met the Croatian President Franjo Tudjman and informed him on the mission and the degree of its coordination with Bill Clinton and the Contact Group. Expectedly enough, Tudjman blamed the Serbs and the Muslims for the war, threatening to postpone the re-opening of economic ties with the Serbs in Croatia (i.e. those of the Srpska Krajina). He told Carter that he was going to demand withdrawal of the UNPROFOR from the Croatian territory if the Serbs refused to 'reintegrate' in the country by the end of March, 1995.

Leaving the Banski Dvori government palace [in Zagreb], Jimmy Carter set out to have a lunch meeting with U.N. Representative Yasushi Akashi in the residence of Peter Galbraith, U.S. Ambassador to Croatia. Akashi expressed his pleasure over this fresh initiative to break the delay in the Bosnian negotiations. After the lunch, Carter went to the Zagreb's Embassy of Bosnia for a brief talk to the Bosnian P.M. Haris Silajdzic. Silajdzic stressed the importance of the Bosnian-Serbs' acceptance of new conditions, yet pounced on Carter's use of the formulation "on the basis of Contact Group plan" labelling the phrasing as unacceptable, for his view was that the Serbs had to accept the plan unconditionally. Then he added an emotional appeal to Carter to get the Serbs stop the attacks on Bihac which enjoyed the status of a 'safe area' yet had been put under siege.

The Author at Pale, with Jimmy Carter, Radovan Karadzic and Ratko Mladic

The town of Bihac was a 'springboard' for one of the three directions of the planned Bosnian-government's offensive. The Serbs of Bosnia and the Serbs of Croatia had allied with the rebel Muslim leader Fikret Abdic of Velika Kladusa, managing to resist the offensive by mid-December and reinforce the siege of the area. Silajdzic claimed that the Bosnian Serbs were taking advantage of Carter's mission in order to divert the world's attention from their military operation at Bihac and the ethnic cleansing under way. Therefore, any cease-fire – he insisted –had to be conditioned by stopping the fighting there.

With all of those information and interpretations in mind, Carter left for Sarajevo. Aboard the UNPROFOR plane, everybody had to wear a lak vest and a helmet, although the light route kept the plane above the Bosnian government-controlled territories.

Landing over, Carter met several UNPROFOR officers and staff. One of them, the American Tony Branbury, was attached to the delegation as an adviser during the forthcoming talks. From the UNPROFOR headquarters, Carter and his team went to an evening meeting with Alija Izetbegovic and Vice-President Ejup Ganic. The city was still under siege, and Gen. Ratko Mladic was shelling Sarajevo from Mt. Romanija. One could see torn sacks covering the windows instead of curtains, while houses were full of damages made by shells and bullets, or even bombed down. The streets were deserted. The former President and First Lady were driven in a black Chevrolet.

With Jimmy Carter, Rosalynn Carter and Biljana Plavsic at Pale

Djordjevic with Jimmy Carter and Radovan Karadzic

Jimmy Carter was assuring Izetbegovic that he came to Bosnia in support of the Contact Group plan. Izetbegovic expressed readiness of the Bosnian government to back up a limited three-month cease-fire, yet added that the talks on a comprehensive settlement could only commence after the Bosnian Serbs accepted the plan of the Contact Group. He admitted that there was some room for mutually acceptable alterations in that plan which could include shifting of the land demarcations. Yet he could approve of these only after the Bosnian Serbs accepted the plan.

*

At that time, toward the end of 1994, the Islamic countries and, first and foremost, Saudi Arabia, provided the Party of Democratic Action, locally abbreviated as SDA (*Stranka demokratske akcije*), and Alija Izetbegovic with 50 million dollars per month. The support lowed in through the Chemical Bank owned by the family of James Baker III, former U.S. Secretary of State. The money enabled the Muslims to finance the warfare and buy off some territories in BH. In return, they let the mujahedins from Iran and members of Al-Qaeda fight against the Serbs. Those were the 'buds' of Al-Qaeda and Osama bin Laden on the European continent.

*

On December 17, the *New York Times* published a report by Roger Cohen titled "Seeking Carter Visit, Bosnia Serbs Ease Up". In a polemical tone, the article presents the political situation in Bosnia-Herzegovina at the time of Carter's arrival in the war zone, realistically depicting the balance of forces between the Serbs and the Muslims, and their leaders. Here follows an excerpt from Cohen's article:

Consulting Jimmy Carter

Intent on luring former President Jimmy Carter to Bosnia, the Bosnian Serbs declared the Sarajevo airport open today after a break of almost one month and eased their hold on United Nations convoys.

A convoy carrying 106 tons of food was allowed into the encircled northwestern Muslim enclave of Bihac, and the United Nations said that it would resume lights into Sarajevo on Saturday. The airport, the chief conduit for food aid into the capital, has been closed since Nov. 21 because of threats from new Serbian surface-to-air missiles.

Freedom of movement for the United Nations and the opening of the Sarajevo airport were among the six steps promised to Mr. Carter this week by the Bosnian Serbs' political leader, Radovan Karadzic. Dr. Karadzic's compliance with the promises is viewed by Mr. Carter as an essential condition for a visit.

But the forced expulsion this week of 15 Muslim civilians from the Serb-controlled own of Bijeljina, in northeastern Bosnia, suggested that perhaps the most signi icant of the six Serbian promises made this week --respect for human rights -- was still far from being honored.

If Dr. Karadzic keeps the pledge to "guarantee human rights now and in the future," that would represent a turnabout. He has often made such pledges to United Nations officials, only to continue with "ethnic cleansing" of Muslims and to blame local commanders. [...]

Western officials here said it was still unclear if Mr. Carter would come this weekend to Sarajevo and to the Bosnian Serbs' headquarters in Pale, just southeast of the capital. The former President was briefed in Atlanta today by State Department and C.I.A. officials on a war that has de ied countless attempts at mediation.

He faces a cool reception from the Bosnian Government. "If Mr. Carter is coming in order to put forward a new peace plan for Bosnia, then I think his visit would not be productive," President Alija Izetbegovic said.

In essence, some American officials say Mr. Carter's presence in Pale might allow Dr. Karadzic to save face and begin peace talks on the basis of an international plan he has previously rejected.

That is the chief goal of the United States, Russia, France, Britain and Germany -- the five countries that devised the plan, which offers 51 percent of Bosnia to a Muslim-Croat federation and 49 percent to the Serbs.[...]

РЕПУБЛИКА СРПСКА  REPUBLIC OF SRPSKA
ПРЕДСЕДНИК РЕПУБЛИКЕ   PRESIDENT OF THE REPUBLIC
САРАЈЕВО   SARAJEVO

TO WHOM IT MAY CONCERN

This is to certify that Mr Borko Djordjevic, MD Ph.D. Passport No: 035192453, USA, a special representative of The Republic of Srpska (Bosnian Serbs) is fully authorized to negotiate the matters of peace agreement, and madiate in creation of the maps between us and others concerned parties, which will be subject to our final aproval.

He is also authorized to represent The Republic of Srpska in mediation in variety other matters, such as economic and financial activities.

Pale, 28.12.94.

Dr Radovan Karadzic
President, The Republic of Srpska

Radovan Karadzic's letter

A western official said that the visit might prove useful provided Carter could offer Karadzic an outlet from the deadlock and a way to start the talks on the basis of the said plan.

The Carters spent their first night in Sarajevo in the apartment of Michael Rose, Canadian general, who was on leave. Barnes and Neu were staying at the Holiday Inn Hotel. By the next morning, Carter prepared a draft for his talks with Karadzic. Meanwhile, a Western official who was the first to go to Pale was preparing Karadzic for the talks from noon to 5 p.m.

After breakfast, Carter's delegation got on the armored vehicles and, up the winding mountain roads, arrived in the headquarters of Bosnian Serbs at Pale. During the ride, bearded soldiers of the Republic of Srpska would here and there emerge from the forest; their look was fearful.

Mrs. Rosalynn Carter felt uneasy. Her husband uttered just a soldierly comment:

– This is a hilly area, hard for fighting. The Serbs hold a better position...!

Karadzic greeted the guests warmly. In Pale, Carter was welcomed in the congress hall of the Parliament of the Republic of Srpska. Five hundred people attended the occasion. As the guests were hungry, lunch was a priority, and the whole political leadership was there, as well as many clergymen. Toasts were drunk and good mood prevailed, for both parties were pleased by the fact that the eyes of America were diverted from Belgrade onto Pale.

Karadzic addressed Jimmy Carter with 'Your Excellency, Mr. President', and Carter responded with 'Mr. President'. Karadzic's spouse, Mrs. Ljiljana Zelen, had by herself knitted a white winter cardigan, made of wool of the sheep from the free Serbian mountains, which she handed in to Carter ceremonially. Carter was moved by the Serbian gentility.

– I do not represent the United States of America. I am here as a private citizen, but whatever we agree upon will be conveyed to President Bill Clinton – Jimmy Carter said.

In that way, he detached himself from the official America, yet also backed away from the exaggarated Serbs' expectations or possible promises to them. With a smile, he accepted a little glass of *loza*, the local grape brandy. Karadzic presented his guest, the former U.S. President and a carpenter from Georgia, with his inely carved *gusle*.

The official talks of the two delegations, American and Serbian, took several hours. At one point, they were discontinued, for Carter asked for a private talk with Karadzic, which lasted for more than an hour.

Harry Barnes passed to Carter my report on the points Karadzic had agreed upon. Two presidents, one former and one currently in office, sat at Carter's laptop computer and started to negotiate. Carter presented his draft cease-fire agreement which Karadzic – with a couple of minor alterations – accepted, suggesting also a text of the statement they would jointly go public with. Karadzic's proposal included the idea of the division of Sarajevo into two parts and lifting of the U.N. embargo, for – as he claimed – if the Serbs did not get some bene its from relaxed economic embargo, he could not confirm the just-reached agreement with Carter. Carter explained that the issue of embargo was an international one which he, as a private citizen, could not control for it was outside of his purview; therefore, such a clause would make no sense in a document he would sign.

On the other hand, Vice-President of Srpska Biljana Plavsic kept insisting on the lifting of sanctions. Carter responded angrily and said that the talks could not be continued that way and that he was ready to leave. At that moment, Harry Barnes entered the room in order to clarify some contentious articles regarding the U.N. sanctions. Ambassador Barnes advised Carter to suggest a pause, which was accepted by Karadzic. Barnes immediately told me about the dispute between Biljana Plavsic and Carter, asking me to warn Karadzic: as Carter, in the capacity of a private citizen, could not resolve the issue posed through the new demand, the whole peace mission could be discontinued. Tom Hanley openly said the same:

– Carter is a private person now. He can't put an end to the U.N. embargo. If you insist that the embargo end now, you're telling me that you don't want peace!

Again, I brought Carter and Karadzic together and suggested to Carter that in his meeting with Milosevic, scheduled for the next day in Belgrade, he should tell Serbia's leader that Radovan was ready to negotiate on the basis of the Contact Group plan, for that might suffice to get Milosevic lift the sanctions the F.R. of Yugoslavia had imposed on the Republic of Srpska. Radovan agreed at first, but then gave up the demand re Milosevic's lifting the embargo.

This concession on the part of Karadzic manifested his trust in the former American President, so Jimmy Carter accepted to stay for a late dinner and resume the talks. A peace settlement was designed which made it possible to start the cease-fire on December 27. The cease-fire was to be implemented through the interposition of the U.N. forces along the line of confrontation after military activities end and exchange of detainees takes place.

---

[11] **Guslar** means '*gusle* player', that is, interpreter of Serbian epic poetry who sings/recites accompanying himself on the one-string instrument. The tradition is related to the Serbs of Serbia, Montenegro, Bosnia-Herzegovina and Macedonia. The most popular of the cycles of such long poems deal with historic personages and events (such as Prince Marko Kraljevic or the Battle of Kosovo). This part of the national literary heritage survived owing to Vuk Stefanovic Karadzic (great language reformer and educator, 1787-1864) who collected them from famous *guslars* of his time as informants. It was through Jacob Grimm, Goethe and the historian Leopold von Ranke that Serbian folk poetry reached renown and admiration Europewide. The practice of playing the gusle has been maintained to the present day, but on rare occasions. – *Translator's note.*

CLINTON ON THE LINE

DURING THE INITIAL TRUCE, the parties were to start negotiations of a four-month cessation of hostilities with an intention to conclude such an agreement by January 15, 1995. During those four months, the parties were to negotiate a comprehensive peace treaty.

Carter had a satellite phone and – straight from Pale – regularly informed President Bill Clinton on the current stage of the talks and the obstacles emerging at those moments. Thus, the former U.S. President Jimmy Carter called Washington, D.C. and obtained approval of the proposed agreement by the State Department and Bill Clinton's Of ice.

The talks on territorial demarcation of peoples and the partition of Bosnia-Herzegovina operated with two division plans – A and B. Plan A envisaged the Republic of Srpska spreading on 51% of the country's territory, while Muslims and Croats would take hold of 49%. Karadzic was determined in his insistence on such a share. General Zdravko Tolimir, whose family house and property lay on the Serbiam-Muslim demarcation line, and myself took this map from Karadzic's table to that of Jimmy Carter.

Karadzic had redesigned the Contact Group plan with us, his associates, and proposed that the Serb-held territory had to have some cities and industry, too, and not only villages, meadows and mountains. I have managed to safeguard this original map of BH on which Carter and Karadzic had been working. Plan B envisioned cease-fire, cessation of war operations and establishment of peace. That part followed the plan of the Contact Group. I was authorized by Karadzic to work with the representatives of the Contact Group as assistant to Minister of Foreign Affairs Dr. Aleksa Buha. Through Charles Thomas, the Americans expressed their support to Plan A, and this was confirmed by the representatives of the Contact Group. It was that night, following a nine-hour round of the talks, that Radovan Karadzic and Jimmy Carter signed the *Agreement on Complete Cessation of Hostilities* [full text provided in the supplemented "Documents" in this book].

Mapping the partition of Bosnia

During the talks at Pale, Clinton was repeatedly called via satellite phone. Calls were also made to Izetbegovic and the UNPROFOR. This led to creation of the document about the cease-fire which came into force that day. Carter was not too concerned about his own security. What he did fear was the high degree of mutual distrust between the parties in conflict. That is why he insisted that substantial force of Blue Helmets should instantly be deployed along the demarcation lines, lest the agreement should not be broken.

For Radovan Karadzic, this was a huge success. In just one CNN program, Carter's and his initiative was discussed for more than an hour. Even the Milosevic-controlled media in Belgrade, that censored whatever Bosnian-Serb leaders said, were forced to convey some of Karadzic's views. In the meanwhile – according to some media – Zoran Djindjic, leader of Serbia's Democratic Party, departed for Moscow in order to convey Karadzic's views to the Russian leadership and ask them to side with the Bosnian Serbs and enter the negotiations.

The essential idea of Djindjic's appeal on the Russians resembled mine on Jimmy Carter: direct negotiations with the backup from Moscow yet without American mediation. The message did reach Moscow: for, Russia seemed to be the loudest opponent to Jimmy Carter's trip to Pale, as their assessment was that the mission was an attempt to undermine the Contact Group plan, and, moreover, to diminish Russia's impact on the events in Bosnia-Herzegovina. Moscow firmly played with Milosevic, while Radovan Karadzic wanted – through Djindjic – to dissuade the Russians from such an attitude to the situation in Bosnia.

– Each war must end one way or another, and if today is the day of the beginning of this war's end, we welcome it – Radovan Karadzic said. – We are ready to negotiate a stable political solution so that we can step out of politics and into the field of economy, democracy, social development and stabilization of the Balkans.

With Radovan and Ljiljana Karadzic, Ratko Mladic and Biljana Plavsic

Ratko Mladic commented:
– This is a big step toward peace, but I think it could even be bigger if all the parties involved in this conflict signed it.

What Mladic had in mind was the side of Bosnian Croats and Croatia, the neighbor-country which, as the Bosnian Serb leaders claimed, had its own troops deployed in Bosnia.

– Life here is going to suffer a considerable change owing to this agreement – said, noticeably satis ied, Yasushi Akashi, U.N. Secretary-General's Personal Representative for the war in former Yugoslavia.

Delighted with the welcome at Pale, Mrs. Rosalynn Carter tried to persuade Jimmy to stay overnight with Radovan Karadzic. Carter refused to do so, and his delegation went back to Sarajevo that night. At the UNPROFOR headquarters in Sarajevo, he received a report on the shelling of Bihac that same day. Carter was deeply upset, for he took the event as violation of the spirit of his talks with Karadzic. He immediately called Karadzic:

– Mr. Karadzic, in the name of peace, please stop the fighting at Bihac. I suggest the cease-fire implementation date is postponed to December 27.

THE WHITE HOUSE

WASHINGTON

July 5, 1995

Thank you for passing on the letter from Bosnian-Serb President Karadzic.

It is always beneficial to maintain open channels of communication when seeking to resolve situations as complex as those confronting us in Bosnia. In this case, unfortunately, Karadzic seems to be seeking an end to the international isolation of the Bosnian-Serbs without offering any new elements in his negotiating posture. In particular, he continues to seek a solution that would destroy Bosnia-Herzegovina's territorial integrity by recognizing the sovereignty of his self-styled "Serbian Republic."

Nevertheless, like you, I intend to look carefully at any proposal that might lead to a successful and honorable negotiated solution to this conflict, and I appreciate your passing along Karadzic's message.

Sincerely,

Bill Clinton

Letter by Bill Clinton

Karadzic denied his responsibility for the fighting at Bihac, but they agreed that he should investigate the situation there and inform Carter on the findings that evening.

As Alija Izetbegovic was not available for a meeting that night, on December 19, 1994, a notice came from the BH Presidency that Vice-President Ejup Ganic was to pay visit to Carter at the UNPROFOR headquarters. During the meeting with Ganic, Carter made an account of his previous encounter with Karadzic earlier that day and the steps he had taken upon the news on resumed battling around Bihac. Next morning, Carter required one more visit to Pale so that he could personally discuss the cease-fire agreement and the situation at Bihac with Karadzic. At first, Karadzic denied Carter's demand for another meeting face-to-face; he said that there was one way only to his consent to immediate cease-fire which would include Bihac: the Fifth Corps of the Bosnian Army had to be disbanded and the Bihac pocket demilitarized. The condition was rejected.

Carter responded to Karadzic's condition by a threat that he was going to pronounce his mission as a failure and lay the blame on the Bosnian Serbs. Fearing defeat, Karadzic eventually agreed to have another meeting later that morning, on December 20.

Before leaving for Pale for the second time, Carter met with Alija Izetbegovic and members of his cabinet. The two leaders signed the slightly altered cease-fire agreement. Following the exhausting talk to the former U.S. President, Izetbegovic made the following statement:

– As far as I understand it, Mr. Carter has not come here to revise the Contact Group plan. Carter has come to mediate in order to make the Serb side accept the plan.

The second meeting with Karadzic and the members of Srpska's cabinet began around noon. It was held in a less comfortable and less formal room than the previous one. The duration of the meeting was limited due to the circumstances at the airport: Carter was to fly to Belgrade, but lights could not leave after sunset. Carter firmly insisted on ixing the cease-fire date which implied cessation of the fighting at Bihac; otherwise, he would go public with a statement on the Serbs' unwillingness to establish truce at that town. Karadzic put forward a counterclaim: Bihac was attacked by the forces of Fikret Abdic and not the Serb army.

Vice-President Biljana Plavsic accused Carter of humiliating the Serbs by this dispute on the shelling of Bihac, for, as a peacemaker, he was supposed to tackle the major problems of war and peace.

– You have offended me by your opinion that peace in any part of Bosnia is unimportant. My visit is important for you, because it shows that the Bosnian Serbs are ready to make peace. The continuation of the attack on Bihac would make the message impossible. I will tell the media that you have broken the promises given to me, and that you are not willing to make peace – Jimmy Carter, angered, warned.

A short break helped the passions calm down. Carter and Karadzic composed a draft for a supplemental agreement which called for the cease-fire coming into effect as of December 23. The Annex also called for negotiations on a four-month cessation of hostilities beginning on December 23 with the intent to conclude a corresponding agreement by January 1, 1995.

Radovan Karadzic then raised another issue asking Carter to help about withdrawal of the Bosnian-government troops from Mt. Igman, a strategic point above Sarajevo. Mount Igman had been supposed to turn into a demilitarized zone, but the government's forces occupied it in order to control the major road for the entry of humanitarian convoys into the city. The new request was incorporated in the supplemental agreement, too.

Prior to his departure from Pale, Jimmy Carter said: – We hope and pray for peace. Your readiness to respect human rights makes us very happy.

Karadzic's TV broadcaster also ascribed to Carter a statement about his impression that the American public failed to understand the Bosnian Serbs properly.

When the Carter delegation left the meeting at Pale and set out downhill toward the Sarajevo airport, Jimmy Carter called Alija Izetbegovic and obtained his consent to the supplemental agreement, including the shifted dates of cease-fire and withdrawal of soldiery from Mt. Igman.

To sum up, Jimmy Carter's peace mission resulted in two extremely signi icant agreements being signed by Radovan Karadzic and Alija Izetbegovic, with his own signature in the capacity of peacemaker and crown witness to the arrangement accomplished between Bosnian Serbs and Muslims. The two documents bore the following titles: the *Comprehensive Peace Agreement* and the *Agreement on Complete Cessation of Hostilities.* Karadzic received congratulations from both the U.N. and the Contact Group.

Before leaving Bosnia, the former U.S. President and current conciliator Jimmy Carter read a statement prepared for the media; it summed up the main points of the agreements, emphasizing that what was still missing was a formula for restarting peace talks.

While the airplane with Jimmy Carter was taking off on its light to Belgrade, the sun was setting above Sarajevo.

FRAGILE PEACE

Upon the end of their mission in December 1994, the Carter delegation left Sarajevo in a somewhat somber mood. As soon as during the light to Belgrade, they began to contemplate their achievement. Carter had arrived in Pale with two basic goals in his mind: first, to persuade the warring sides to sign a cease-fire, and, second, to re-establish contacts between chief negotiators. The former U.S. President accomplished both – partially. Jimmy Carter and the members of his team were hoping that their visit could embetter the conditions for some of the war's victims, as well as motivate the protagonists to recommence sensible peace talks.

The change of course left the American allies in the Bosnian government very angry. Through the Carter mission, the United States opened a channel toward the Serbs in the hope that the nearly three-years' war could be brought to an end. The Bosnian PM Haris Silajdzic confirmed receipt of the letter by Warren Christopher, U.S. Secretary of State, which said that the American officials would maintain the contact with the Serbs despite their repeated rejections of the international peace plan. Christopher's letter marked a change of U.S. tactics, re lecting an effort to build informal relations with the Bosnian Serbs, the grounds for which had just been laid by Jimmy Carter's visit.

Each of the members of the Carter delegation feared whether the effort invested would bring a change. Moreover, Carter was exposed to attacks as soon as during the talks: the accusations said that his visit to Pale threatened the international efforts to put an end to the war and that his meetings with Karadzic gave legitimacy to a tyrant.

Thus, the Canadian Toronto Sun wrote:

Again in Bosnia, as in North Korea and Haiti, Carter seemed to embarrass the U.S. government and violate U.S. policy. He fawns on some of this world's most loathsome people.

As a former president and a neutral figure, and unlike almost any other diplomat, Carter – personally involved in the Bosnian negotiations – could claim his sensitivity to the burdens of leadership. Finally, Carter proved his fundamental belief that all sides in a conflict must be included in peace negotiations. When Karadzic became part of the talks, most of Bosnia's artillery kept silent during the first two months and a half of the year 1995. And ire was not resumed until the Bosnian Serbs were excluded from the peace talks again.

On their way home, Carter's team made a stop-over in Belgrade where the former U.S. President had a scheduled meeting with Slobodan Milosevic. Serbia's President was eager about lifting – by the United States and the United Nations – of the international sanctions against the F.R. of Yugoslavia. Also, he was extremely frustrated by Radovan Karadzic's resistance to his control over the Republic of Srpska. He was aware of the fact that at the moment the opinion in the West prevailed that Karadzic was the greatest bene iciary of the deal, for his spectacular comeback to the world's media scene had pushed Slobodan Milosevic aside.

During the reception in Belgrade, Slobodan Milosevic made a solemn address to Jimmy Carter wherein he said:

Let me express my great pleasure for the opportunity to welcome President Carter and his spouse Rosalynn here in Belgrade. Over the last few days, various assessments of President Carter's visit to the region have appeared. Some of these are very negative, some reservedly positive; however, it is my strong impression that President Carter is here with one and only goal – to sincerely contribute to peace. The success of the mission should not be judged by the private character of President Carter's visit. His presence undoubtedly re lects America's and President Clinton's commitment to peace. That commitment of America and her President – to achieving peace in our region – deserves our full attention. Serbia, too, shall endeavor – as it has so far – to make its own full contribution. I am grateful to President Carter and his spouse Rosalynn for this visit and for the extremely open and exhaustive discussion we had about all crucial issues that are of signi icance to the Yugoslav crisis.

In his conversation with Carter, the resourceful Milosevic promised to support Carter's peace efforts, thus clearing some terrain for embargo lifting. Milosevic knew well enough that to persuade the Bosnian Serbs and the Bosnian government to take on obligations to make peace was one thing, but that persuading them into implementation of the agreements was quite another thing.

Aboard the plane on the way home from Belgrade, Carter wrote letters to President Bill Clinton and Secretary of State Warren Christopher respectively; he reported on the content of his negotiations in Sarajevo and Pale: the Bosnian Serbs had accepted the language formula proposed by the White House and the Contact Group, but the Bosnian government did not. In these letters, Carter additionally suggested that – provided the Serbs honored the cease ire and manifested good faith in the peace negotiations – the economic sanctions imposed on them should be lifted. The agreement brokered by Carter appealed on the United Nations to monitor the cease-fire and the negotiations in order to achieve the complete cessation of hostilities scheduled to begin on December 23.

The negotiations about the four-month cessation of hostilities were to be completed by Januray 1, 1995 and – in all likelihood – include some representatives of the United Nations, although the latter had not been written down in the agreement. Besides, the Bosnian government withdrew from the demilitarized zone in Mt. Igman, based on the existing agreement with the U.N. conditioned by the deployment of the U.N. peacemaking troops in the area.

On December 20, the day when Carter left Sarajevo, it seemed that just some less important details had to be elaborated by the Bosnian sides in conflict and the United Nations. While these three parties were trying to agree upon the details, implementation of the cease-fire was one day late. On the eve of December 23, the date envisaged as the beginning of cease-fire, Karadzic summoned Yasushi Akashi to Pale in order to ix the details concerning the interpositioning of the U.N. troops referred to in Carter-brokered agreements. The next few months showed that there were many obstacles to successful implementation of the agreements signed in Sarajevo and Pale.

Jimmy Carter, Harry Barnes and Joyce Neu were kept intensely involved in the process. They made pressures on both sides to bring them to fulfill the conditions of the agreements they had signed. Likewise, the Carter Center continued with the appeals on the sides in conflict to make difficult decisions. The Bosnian government changed its attitude re the clause of the Carter-brokered agreement which concerned the exchange of detainees: they insisted on pre-establishment of the facts regarding all of the missing-in-action, but the Serbs were not willing to accept it.

  And yet the avenue toward a four-month cease-fire and commencement of negotiations seemed clear enough. Each side had signed the agreement with Carter in the belief that it appropriately ensured the beginning of such talks. Although both sides were reserved, assuming the difficult character of the talks, there was hope. But in spite of difficulties, the implementation of the agreement began. From time to time, Carter would himself intervene in the implementation process. He would call Karadzic at times to advise him on broadening his chance of entrance into fruitful negotiations. Similarly, he would at times contact the Bosnian-government side, too, and a few representatives of the Contact Group member-countries.

  The reports which reached Carter were the results of extensive talks of his associates Harry Barnes and Joyce Neu with Tom Hanley and myself as representatives of the Bosnian Serbs, with the Bosnian-government delegates Ganic and Silajdzic, with the U.S. delegates Chris Hill and Richard Holbrooke, as well as with the representatives of the UNPROFOR and the United Nations.

  From my point of view, the real problem of the peace in Bosnia were the Muslims and not the Serbs. For, the Muslims proved unwilling to demilitarize Mt. Igman. In return, Karadzic was unwilling to open the 'Blue Route' to the Sarajevo airport. The Americans, that is, to be precise, Richard Holbrooke, immediately accused the Bosnian Serbs of disobedience and threatened by excluding them from the negotiations with the Contact Group. Karadzic's references to the clauses of the *Agreement on Complete Cessation of Hostilities* and the agreement on Mt. Igman as demilitarized zone were in vain; Holbrooke was siding with Alija Izetbegovic. That is what I heard from Robert Bobby Frasure, new American representative in the Contact Group.

Besides, Joyce Neu called and asked me to inform Radovan Karadzic on Holbrooke's threat re his exclusion from the talks with the Contact Group. It was then that I made a statement for the CNN: I said that the Bosnian Serbs would open the 'Blue Routes of transportation' by the end of the week, in compliance with the *Agreement on Complete Cessation of Hostilities.*

It is noteworthy that Jimmy Carter, in accordance with good political manners, sent special letters of thanks to Dr. Radovan Karadzic, Slavko Lazarevic and myself, expressing his feelings about the welcome and the peace talks at Pale. On January 5, 1995, he sent his special messages to us from the States. Jimmy and Rosalynn sent their sincere good wishes for a Happy New Year 1995. Carter announced that he was working on lifting the sanctions imposed on the Republic of Srpska, which was a truly emboldening piece of information. Therefore, to maintain the cessation of hostilities was a primary task.

Karadzic initiated signing (on January 23, 1995) of a protocol on the implementation of the *Agreement on Complete Cessation of Hostilities* with the Muslims, and this was done. According to the Protocol, peace was ensured along the roads to Sarajevo, Visoko, Grbavica bridge, the roads to Dobrinje, Butmir, Lukavica and Ilidza (they are all parts of the of Sarajevo's metropolitan area). Signing of the Protocol took place at the Sarajevo airport on the abovesaid date.

Karadzic thus honored his own pledge. What ensued was the visit to Pale by a couple of Contact Group representatives, the first such visit after a five-month pause.

*

The Carter Center was often used as a communication channel for the exchange of information between the Bosnian Serbs and the representatives of the U.S. Administration, whereby it played a key role in keeping the peace process 'live'. Yet Carter himself refused some appeals for his intensi ied involvement in the peace process in Bosnia.

January 6, 1995

To Dr. Borko Djordjevic

Thank you for your assistance in the negotiations with Dr. Karadzic during our visits to Pale and for your continuing assistance. I am following the situation with great interest and was pleased to learn that both parties have signed a four-month cessation of hostilities agreement. I hope that the Contact Group negotiations will resume without delay.

Rosalynn and I send you our best wishes for a happy and peaceful new year.

Sincerely,

Jimmy Carter

Dr. Borko Djordjevic
924 Anacapa Street
Santa Barbara, California 93101

ONE COPENHILL · ATLANTA, GEORGIA 30307 · (404) 331-3900 · FAX (404) 331-0283

Jimmy Carter letter

Karadzic and I asked Carter if he would possibly replace the Contact Group as the prime negotiator on the Balkans. Carter did not accept the option, for he firmly believed that the American commitment via the Contact Group was the key to the peaceful solution. When the problem arose concerning the passage of humanitarian convoys – for speci ication was lacking on who could and who could not travel by the opened roads – Gen. Michael Rose called Jimmy Carter who then rang up Radovan Karadzic to tell him that only registered convoys could be allowed to pass across the Bosnian Serbs-held territory. Other disputes concerned the exchange of prisoners, local exchanges of ire here and there, attacks by Abdic's rebel troops on the Muslims and the Bosnian blockade of the city of Tuzla.

It is noteworthy that – by the U.N. Security Council Resolution No. 943 which had been adopted earlier, on September 23, 1994 – the state border between the F.R. of Yugoslavia and Bosnia-Herzegovina had been closed for 100 days; the worst damage thereof was suffered by the Republic of Srpska. The issue was also a point of Karadzic's complaints to Carter who then wrote letters to Clinton, Christopher and U.N. Secretary-General Boutros-Ghali asking for alterations in the proposed Resolution. Carter suggested lifting of the sanctions, but the White House refused entry of a corresponding phrasing into the pending renewed Resolution.

During the negotiations with the Contact Group, the Bosnian government vacillated: now they take it (a proposal discussed), now they don't. This was a source of difficulties in the implementation of one part of the *Agreement on Complete Cessation of Hostilities*. Namely, the Muslims insisted that the Bosnian Serbs must "accept" the Contact Group plan, while the Bosnian Serbs "accept the basis of negotiations as proposed by the Contact Group".

From the very beginning of his talks with Jimmy Carter, Karadzic had claimed that the *acceptance* of the Contact Group plan – if his Serbs heard of such a thing – would mean his political suicide. I relayed Karadzic's request to Harry Barnes and the Carter Center. The talks to the Contact Group were scheduled for early February 1995. And it was then, however, that Richard Holbrooke, Bill Clinton's envoy, showed his frustration: his readiness to support

Carter's mission was decreasing, and he threatened by exclusion of Karadzic from the negotiations. Holbrooke said:

– There is no point in shuttling up the hill from Sarajevo to Pale to listen to the kind of crap which was dished out by Karadzic.

The talks aimed at a restart of the negotiations continued when the Contact Group decided to stop proposing various political formulations. In the exchange of proposals, the representatives of the Bosnian Serbs and of the Contact Group usually relied on the Carter Center as a communication channel. Barnes and Neu kept in touch with me all the time, and I did the same with Radovan Karadzic. We were eager to restart vitally important negotiations – in any way possible.

In mid-January 1995, Tom Hanley and I – together with the Atlanta-based Carter Center staff – presented yet another alternative to the Contact Group plan. We submitted a new map of Bosnia-Herzegovina, one that Radovan Karadzic and the leadership of the Republic of Srpska were prepared to accept; it maintained the previous partitioning into 51% to the Serbs and 49% to the Muslims and Croats jointly. The related discussion never took place, because Croatia's President Franjo Tudjman officially demanded termination of the UNPROFOR's mandate in his country, thus opening prospects for a war offensive against the Serbs in Kninska Krajina and part of Herzegovina.

In response, Slobodan Milosevic stepped in as *the* patron of Krajina's people, which diverted the attention of the Contact Group from Bosnia-Herzegovina to the problems between Croatia and Serbia.

The disputes involving Croatia, Yugoslavia/Serbia and the Contact Group worsened the position of Radovan Karadzic, whose opportunity to create an independent state of the Republic of Srpska would have been jeopardized if Slobodan Milosevic had recognized Bosnia-Herzegovina. Tom Hanley and I complained to Jimmy Carter, to the U.S. Ambassadors Robert Frasure and Charles Thomas, and even straight to the Department of State.

The four-month *Agreement on Complete Cessation of Hostilities* in Bosnia basically came to an end on April 30, 1995, when the war lared up between Croatia, the army of Bosnia-Herzegovina and the Serbs of Croatia and Bosnia respectively. The Bosnian government forces launched a limited offensive onto the positions of the Bosnian Serbs in northern and central Bosnia, justifying the action as a preventive one: it was to forestall re-armament of the Bosnian Serbs and fortifying of their positions. In return, the Serbs intermittently shelled some positions of the Bosnian-government and some 'safe areas'. Again, the Contact Group discontinued the talks with Karadzic, giving priority to Milosevic. There was an evident danger of increased war hostilities in both Bosnia-Herzegovina and Croatia.

In early April 1995, foreseeing an end to the *Agreement on Complete Cessation of Hostilities*, Jimmy Carter wrote letters to Alija Izetbegovic and Radovan Karadzic respectively, offering the two leaders his return to the area for quiet yet private meetings/talks which should lead to the commencement of meaningful negotiations.

CARTER'S NONACCEPTANCE

THROUGH HARRY BARNERS AND MYSELF, Jimmy Carter and Radovan Karadzic started an active correspondence on April 4, 1995. In his letter to the leader of the Bosnian Serbs, the former U.S. President wrote: He had been monitoring the developments in BH since the December visit; the short time within which the agreed cease ire and cessation of hostilities had been accomplished had encouraged him, and he hoped – as said in their talk on the phone toward the end of January – that more could have been done in the continuation of the talks according to the recommendations of the Contact Group. Over the following weeks, there had been regular contacts between Ambassodors Crickmore and Barnes with Dr. Djordjevic and Mr. Hanley; there were also close contacts with the U.S. Administration, the United Nations and Professor Ganic; in addition, attention was given to the discussions with President Milosevic regarding the recognition of Bosnia-Herzegovina. Jimmy Carter added that he understood how the ongoings in Croatia made the situation even more complicated to the U.N. and that there was still a lot to be done before the settlement of the matter. But he was discouraged by the increasing degree of fighting in Bosnia over the past few weeks.

The former U.S. President then referred to the Last of Karadzic's letters, the one of March 8, 1995, which emboldened him to continue his mission, but through Dr. Djordjevic he had sent a message about his reluctance to answer before clarifying the further steps by the Contact Group and the American government. Jimmy Carter explicitly said in this letter that he never gave up his hope for peace coming to Bosnia, which had earlier guided his decision to visit Pale. Now he thought about Karadzic's reassurance about his aspiration to peaceful settlement, without violence, and readiness to negotiate on the basis of just and well-balanced arrangements.

Carter expressed his belief that the Carter Center could be relied on in the search for ways of recommencing meaningful negotiations that would include Karadzic's consent to organizing the state in the form of two entities, so a new encounter should focus on the principles re such organization.

What Jimmy Carter had in mind were quiet, private meetings with Karadzic and Izetbegovic without any statements made for the public, for that would allow a search for some new approaches which could prevent resumption of sanguinary hostilities and open way toward a permanent resolution on the existing differences and creation of a federal state structure acceptable to all parties in Bosnia-Herzegovina. The ensuing bene icial ideas would then be shared with the United States and other governments represented within the Contact Group –as a basis for further peace efforts.

Finally, Carter said in this letter that he would with pleasure revisit BH on behalf of the Carter Center, but only with the approval by the American officials. Harry Barnes was expected to register Karadzic's response to the proposal which was also sent to President Izetbegovic. Carter was hoping that both leaders were to accept it, and that they were going to take steps for the Agreement on the Cessation of Hostilities to be honored by the end of that month [April 1995].

President Radovan Karadzic answered this letter (brought to him by me, Dr. Djordjevic) as soon as on April 6, 1995:

Karadzic shared Carter's feeling of discouragement re the recent combats; however, the cease-fire owed to the U.S. President was the most ef icacious one throughout the conflict, for many lives had been saved; yet the Agreement on Cessation of Hostilities was dead at the moment just because of the recent Muslim offensives. While the Muslims used the peaceful period for regrouping and re-armament –sometimes with the help of the U.S.A. – the Serbs were languishing under the international commercial, political and other sanctions, which cannot be taken as equal attitude to the parties in conflict. New chances for the Muslims, who opted for the war path, were unacceptable to the Serbs who had to defend themselves; therefore, a prolongation of the Agreement on Cessation of Hostilities could not be allowed. "I am deeply convinced" that a permanent peace settlement was needed, as soon as possible, and President Carter could help thereby making a breakthrough which the efforts of the international community failed to produce thus far. The proposed peace treaty would put an end to the war and disable the parties to restore hostilities. As to the constitutional arrangements, the Serbs had to get a state of their own, one based on the principles of democracy and market economy. The Serbs planned to distance themselves from and surpass the hard consequences of communism and socialism, and they could achieve that only as an individual subject in terms of international law. Actually, there already existed three states in Bosnia, and that was an irrevocable status quo. Any attempt at creation of one state out of three would imply a warfare longer and on a larger scale than the present one. Moreover, if we were not a state with an international border to the Muslim state, the Muslim extremists from all over the world were going to hope they could enslave us and establish a strong Muslim country in the heart of Europe. An international border would be the sole guarantee that no new conflicts would arise between us. Some foundations for such solution already existed in the Serbian-Muslim Declaration of September 16, 1993, which allowed to the Serbs independence from the "Union of Bosnia-Herzegovina" in accordance with the referendum of our people. But if the international community was keen upon saving its face, we could accept a union of two or three sovereign and independent states – until our own independence referendum. But such a union sould only follow the model of the European Union, i.e. a union of sovereign and independent states. Such a union, consisting of three states, or "constitutive entities" headed by a Union Council mentioned in Carter's letter, could be accepted, and we would respect the full scale of human rights and fundamental freedoms de ined by international instruments that would be enlisted in the Constitution or agreed by the Union Council. We would like to see you here as soon as you make an agreement with Mr. Izetbegovic.

In somewhat more than two weeks, on April 24, Jimmy Carter wrote back to Karadzic:

The former U.S. President thanked for the af irmative response re his revisiting Bosnia and helping the peacemaking process, but President Izetbegovic had said that he could not accept the offer; therefore, despite appreciation of Karadzic's suggestions, he could not see any accomplishment if the Bosnian government were not ready to talk. Carter regretted the threats to the four-month cease ire, for resumed war meant human loss, devastation of many more families and a new amount of despair and hopelessness. He had hoped that the cease-fire could consolidate the Agreement on Cessation of Hostilities and prioritize diplomatic over military option. The said Agreement had not been implemented completely due to the uncompromising stance and distrust on both sides; combined with the international attempt at mediation which produced no effect, this led to the current crisis. Although frustrated by the current state of affairs, Carter expressed his preparedness to assist in peace negotiations as soon as better prospects emerged; he would continue to keep in touch through Dr. Djordjevic and offer any assistance possible to further negotiations which would lead to peace.

The above letters show that Karadzic did want to be back into the peace process; he instantly accepted Carter's offer, yet Izetbegovic refused it. From the point of view of the Bosnian government, a visit by Jimmy Carter or the prolongation of the cessation of hostilities would 'legalize' Serbian control of more than 60 percent of Bosnia-Herzegovina's territory. It was following Alija Izetbegovic's negative response that Carter refused Radovan Karadzic's invitation to return into the peace process in Bosnia.

However, both personally and publicly, Carter remained involved in the peace efforts after the *Agreement on Complete Cessation of Hostilities* had expired. In May 1995, Carter received a request for help by the family of Jonathan Knapp, an American citizen who worked for the French organization *Pharmaciens sans frontières* (PSF)/Pharmacists without Borders). Knapp was one of the four activists of the said humanitarian organization held in detention by the Serbs since February. The man's family had contacted several organizations, including the American government, in order to secure his release.

Carter wrote a letter to Radovan Karadzic asking him to order the release of these humanitarian workers and pointing out the negative perception of the Bosnian Serbs by the international public due to such detentions. Later in May, all four PSF activists were released.

*

Saudi Arabia used to effect payments of 50 million dollars monthly to Alija Izetbegovic, the money lowing in through the American *Chemical Bank*. gThe bank was oywned by gJames Bakger III, former U.S. Secretary of State in the George Bush Sr. Administration. The 'relay' was Muhamed 'Mo' Sacirbey, Bosnia's first ambassador to the United Nations who was in May 1995 appointed foreign minister. My partner Tom Hanley worked for a law irm that represented another bank, *Indosuez*, which was yet another member of the Muslim network that financed Alija Izetbegovic, the prime champion of Islam on the Balkans and Europewide. As Hanley's company, which payed him $ 50,000 per month, found that he – as a representative of the Serbs – worked against the irm's interests, the man was dismissed from his job.

The above case shows that the Americans would do anything for money. And, moreover, that it was owing to Saudi Arabia and the U.S.A. that the Muslims surpassed the Croats sponsored by the Vatican and the Serbs – snatching Bosnia away for themselves.

Despite the fact that both the Muslims and the Croats were adding fuel to the warfare and expelling the Serbs, Jimmy Carter and the Carter Center experts continued their commitment to the search for peace settlement, co-working with representatives of the international community and of the three Bosnian sides. During the summer, Carter kept private correspondence with Bill Clinton, Warren Chrostopher, Carl Bildt (EU Special Envoy to the Former Yugoslavia from June 1995), the leaders of all the Contact Group member-countries, as well as Karadzic and Izetbegovic.

As early as in 1995, American political analysts and media saw Carter's mediation in Bosnia between Radovan Karadzic and Alija Izetbegovic as 'fragile peace', i.e. – in literal Serbian phrasing, 'glass-made peace' – one which could break at any moment. This may have been true, but the crucial fact is: peace *was* accomplished. The Catholics and the Orthodox in Bosnia had a peaceful Christmas. The Muslims lived in peace as well. This is to say – in answer to the often-raised question 'Did Carter succeed in Bosnia?' – Yes, he did!

HOLBROOKE'S JIGGERY-POKERY

CARTER'S MISSION IN BOSNIA came forth as a straightforward consequence of his unique position – that of a former U.S. President enjoying the well-earned reputation of a mediator dedicated to peace and human rights. Logically enough, Carter's mission relied on his connections with the U.S. government, which opened to him access to the information of the State Department, NSC and CIA. Likewise, his links with the United Nations and governments of many other countries were of considerable importance, too. The mission was well-designed and eficiently conducted; its goals were somewhat limited yet reachable, and they were achieved. In his own country, the missioner Jimmy Carter was often denigrated by slanderers because of his alleged readiness to "legitimize tyrants".

Since the American government and international organizations were forbidden to meet revolutionary forces that were their ideological opponents, Carter clearly stated from the beginning that his objective was not to substitute the Contact Group or seek the inal solution to the conflict, but to provide enhancement toward an eficient negotiation over the four-month cessation of hostilities which, he hoped, could open a road to a comprehensive peace settlement. The fact that Carter's line of activity shifted the American focus from Milosevic to Karadzic and from the Muslims to the Bosnian Serbs cannot overshadow another fact: the former U.S. President contravened the Contact Group policy of isolating the Serbs. In that sense, his effort underlined the lack of unity and the law in the international approach to the war conflict in Bosnia-Herzegovina.

Carter himself and the Carter Center staff almost exclusively relied on the American interests within the Contact Group, rarely consulting the other members of the Group. The delegation mistakenly assumed that the U.S. representatives spoke on behalf of the Group as a whole. Hence, they literally took over the stance of the American government and put it into the wording of the Group's request from the Bosnian Serbs, failing to consult the representatives of the other member-countries in the Contact Group.

The relationship between Carter's endeavor and the permanent U.N. mediation in Bosnia differed completely from the relationship between Jimmy Carter and the Contact Group. While the Contact Group aspired to create a comprehensive peace plan which could put an end to the war in the whole of Bosnia, Yasushi Akashi and other international figures usually pursued some less comprehensive solutions, including short-term cease-fires on just regional or all-Bosnian scale. Representing the United Nations in the field, Akashi was moving among the people and staffers in Bosnia, working tirelessly with all the parties involved, in an attempt to lessen the burdens of war and lay foundations for the Contact Group-led negotiations over the inal peace settlement. The task was extremely frustrating and difficult. For, nearly 30 short-term cease-fires had been signed in the year 1994, but almost each of these would be broken before the ink was dry.

*

During some six months preceding the Carter mission, Yasushi Akashi had been making attempts to ensure a lasting cease-fire for entire Bosnia. Despite his praiseworthy efforts, the attempts would as a rule fail. It was only after Carter's endeavor that Akashi signed the *Agreement on Complete Cessation of Hostilities* with all the warring parties. As a person of great international stature whose presence on the political scene was still quite seeable, Jimmy Carter resorted to an action which should have impelled the parties to call a halt to hostilities, which was the goal Akashi had not managed to accomplish; yet one has to admit that the previous work of the U.N. representative on the ground provided a solid basis to Carter's success.

Carter found himself in a role that no other U.S. representative could play. His critics in Washington used to say that Carter was not known as an expert in the Balkan affairs, that he was armed with – as a D.C. envoy put it – "a mad smile", "casual clothing" and "imperfect grasp of the issues"; there was also an opinion that he had let Karadzic manipulate him by talking him into the promise about lifting sanctions against the Bosnian Serbs if they demonstrated their preparedness for peace. I shall allow myself the modesty-lacking claim that it was me who did most in assuring Carter of Radovan Karadzic's earnestness and the honesty of the Bosnian Serbs.

The initial reaction of Washington to Carter's positive statements about the Serbs at Pale was quite unfavorable.

Dee Dee Myers, press secretary in the Clinton Administration, harshly disputed Carter's assessment that the Bosnian Serbs opted for peace, repeating the U.S. view of the Bosnian Serbs as aggressors.

Unlike many other western politicians, Jimmy Carter did not shrink away from the 'dangerous Serbs'; neither did he scare the Americans with the Serbs, as had been the practise of a number of politicians in Washington. Carter showed his full respect for the Serbs. Unfortunately – and I am saying this with full responsibility – it was that attitude on his part which led to his removal from the American game on Bosnia's political scene and the political map of Bosnia-Herzegovina.

Truth is, the United States in the time of Bill Clinton, speci ically in mid-1995, no longer cared much about the Serbs. The country needed one anchor-point on the planet Earth whereon it could defend the Muslims' interests. The situation in Bosnia-Herzegovina was grist to the mill. Such U.S. policy was getting impetus and lavor from Richard Holbrooke, who also had some personal lucrative motives to act as he did. The reality in Bosnia could have been quite different, if Cyrus Vance or Ambassador Robert Frasure (who died tragically later on) remained as protagonists in the Bosnian arena.

Ambassador Frasure was the chief American architect of the peace in Bosnia, while Richard Holbrooke was just a participant in the process. Frasure repeatedly negotiated with Milosevic in Belgrade.

Behind the tightly closed door, in Belgrade and Karadjordjevo[12], secret negotiations between Milosevic and Frasure were in progress. Frasure was the U.S. representative in the Contact Group and, as diplomatic sources referred to him, an expert in "savage tribal" clashes. The American ambassador to the Contact Group and Milosevic were secretly seeking a peaceful solution to the war crisis in the former Yugoslavia. Frasure tirelessly endeavored to de ine the American approach to the conflict solution and proved invaluably helpful to the mission of Jimmy Carter.

However, this kind of politician was an obstacle to the belligerent groups in the U.S.A. and part of Europe. The remotion of Jimmy Carter from Bosnia was accomplished in a way which cost Ambassador Robert Frasure his life. The accident in which Frasure was killed is thought by many to have been a staged homicide. Prior to his death, Ambassador Frasure had – together with Tom Hanley, Karadzic's lawyer – signed a memorandum which supported the negotiations of the President of the Republic of Srpska toward a peace settlement for Bosnia-Herzegovina. The date the memorandum was penned read: August 19, 1995.

In this document, Robert Frasure – as the U.S. Ambassador to the Contact Group – recognized the formation of Bosnia-Herzegovina, but also of the Republic of Srpska. Which – to my mind – was the reason why he was "driven to death".

I expect Jimmy Carter to unveil the American secret: Who and why did drive Rober Bob Frasure to death? The man had been Carter's confidant. During Carter's presidential term he was U.S. Ambassador to Nigeria, Ethiopia and South Africa. During the Carter mission in Bosnia, Ambassador Frasure officially reported to the Secretary of State Warren Christopher.

The armored vehicle slid off the Mt. Igman road to Sarajevo on August 19, 1995. Three U.S. officials were killed: State Department Deputy Assistant Secretary and member of the Contact Group Robert C. Frasure, Advisor to the Secretary of Defense (for European affairs and NATO policy) Joseph Kruzel and Air Force Colonel Samuel Nelson Drew, NSC Advisor. In the aftermath of Frasure's death, Ambassador Richard Holbrooke took over the prime control over the peace initiative – at the moment when Bill Clinton was invigorating the role of the United States on the Balkans.

In hole-and-corner conferences one could hear that Ambassador Richard Holbrooke stood behind Frasure's death, eager to remove the 'Carter man'. For, upon Holbrooke's takeover in the place of the chief American negotiator in Bosnia-Herzegovina and Yugoslavia, Warren Christopher, then Secretary of State, and the Contact Group with three U.S. representatives became directly involved in the negotiations. Holbrooke's operative on the ground and in the negotiations was Michael Steiner, German diplomat from the Contact Group (later advisor to Carl Bildt, European negotiator for Bosnia). Steiner initiated a major change in the Carter-Karadzic agreement, proposing that the Serbs get 49 percent of the territory instead of 51%.

One point appeared clear to me: The Muslims did not want peace, for they had been promised an entirely Islam-ruled state of Bosnia-Herzegovina. In 1994, they behaved like a boxer knocked down. Instead of beating them up, the Serbs offered them peace. Like a defeated boxer, the Muslims took all the starch out of themselves and tried to maintain fighting, and also to beastly retaliate by killing Serbian civilians in villages. They committed horrible crimes against the Serbs, but the West kept silent, for what was needed was an Islamic and not a Serbian Bosnia.

Thus, as Slobodan Milosevic was advocating one and unitarian Bosnia-Herzegovina and Karadzic was urging for BH plus Republic of Srpska, Ambassador Holbrooke was strongly pushing Slobodan Milosevic toward luring Bosnian Serbs into concessions by offering relief of the sanctions against the F.R. of Yugoslavia. The so-called 'Holbrooke initiative' was rooted in the Contact Group plan but allowed the Bosnian Serbs to keep control over Srebrenica and Zepa. Only from time to time would Holbrooke deal with the Bosnian Serbs through the Carter Center. Late in August 1995, he agreed to visit Pale and include Radovan Karadzic in the peace process under his management –provided the Serb leader had revised his formula presented to Jimmy Carter earlier that month.

Namely, after the agreement between Serbs and Muslims had been accomplished, the Americans were to install Radovan Karadzic as the leader of all Serbs Balkanwide. They judged that Karadzic was a 'softer' politician than Slobodan Milosevic, that he could be "worked with" and that the Bosnian Serb leader was prepared to make concessions in order to reach his own goal – recognition of the Republic of Srpska as an independent state. That is to say: Slobodan Milosevic was advocating the creation of Bosnia-Herzegovina as one and independent state; on the other hand, Radovan Karadzic was arguing for the creation of two states – Bosnia-Herzegovina and the Republic of Srpska.

Slobodan Milosevic complained officially to Richard Holbrooke: it was him who formally represented all of the Balkan Serbs, while Radovan Karadzic was a rebel who refused to obey him. Holbrooke favoured Milosevic and ordered NATO air strikes against the Republic of Srpska, forcing Karadzic to sign an agreement with Slobodan Milosevic which is referred to as 'Patriarch Agreement'. Signed under the auspices of the Serbian Patriarch Pavle, it authorized Slobodan Milosevic to negotiate on behalf of the Bosnian Serbs. As a follow-up, Holbrooke personally signed an arrangement with Radovan Karadzic whereby the President of Srpska resigned his post and retired politically in exchange for Holbrook's promise – on behalf of the United States – to let him live in peace.

On the crest of a wave following the triumph, Richard Holbrooke prepared his peace initiative and the truce of October 5, 1995. This further led to the peak of American policy – the Dayton summit. In the Wright-Patterson Air Force Base at Dayton, Ohio, Holbrooke 'detained' Slobodan Milosevic, Alija Izetbegovic and – at some moments – Franjo Tudjman until they completed negotiations of the peace settlement and signed the Dayton Peace Accords which put an end to warfare in ex-Yugoslavia. The "proximity talks" took 17 days in the month of November 1995. The outcome was the post-Dayton Bosnia: the Republic of Srpska was recognized as an entity within the unitary state/country of Bosnia-Herzegovina. The Serbs were given 49 percent of the country's territory, while Croats and Muslims took 51 percent for the other entity, the Federation of Bosnia-Herzegovina.

---

[12] **Karadjordjevo** is hunting ground near the village of the same name (in the Municipality of Backa Palanka, some 80 miles northwest of Belgrade) where late Yugoslavia's President Josip Broz Tito built a residence. Some of historic decisions and meetings took place there, including the controversial encounter of Serbia's and Croatia's Presidents Slobodan Milosevic and Franjo Tudjman in March 1991 when they reportedly discussed and sketched the partitioning of Bosnia-Herzegovina. – *Translator's note.*

THE BULLDOZER DIPLOMAT

IN THE UNITED STATES, but also in Europe, Richard Holbrooke used to be referred to as the 'Balkan Kissinger', for he comprised agglomerated virtues and faults that perfectly complemented one another. Brilliant and ambitious, egocentric and vain, irascible once he felt the sweet taste of power. His abrasive manner earned him nicknames such as 'Wild Bull', 'Bulldozer', 'Pirate of Diplomacy'. A cynic, he could resort to bluffing, threats, promises, charming – following the model of Henry Kissinger. What the two men shared in common were Jewish-German origin, enjoyment in public attention and conduction of the aggressive domineering policy of the United States. Richard Holbrook was a tall, burly man with dark hair, sparkling eyes and 'hanging' belly. His frequent visits to the Balkans resulted in gaining 10-kilo weight (some 20 pounds) owing to roast lamb consumption.

Dick Holbrooke was born into a family of German immigrants in New York City in 1941. His grandfather was a Jewish merchant in Hamburg who had, as a soldier in World War One, been awarded the Iron Cross. His parents Dan Goldbrajch and Trudy nee Moos had been born in Hamburg, where from they emigrated to America in 1933, together with grandfather. Their last name was established upon arrival in the United States. The young Richard Holbrooke entered foreign service upon graduation from Brown University. In 1963, the service sent him to Vietnam where he spent three years at Saigon as an American diplomat specializing in the country's economic recovery. As early as in those days – as his colleague Frank Wisner recollects – young Holbrooke gained one quality that would launch him into the top ranks of the American political scene: he passionately strived for the company of prominent persons and, for that purpose, used to reschedule his daily duties or get his name inserted in the invitation lists for solemn occasions.

His indisputable diplomatic knowledge and sycophantic skills led Holbrooke into Lyndon Johnson's negotiation team: the crown of his Vietnam adventure was presence at the 1969 peace negotiations in Paris. As the Pentagon was impressed by Richard Holbrooke's reports from Vietnam, the government assigned him the duty of the Peace Corps Director in Morocco in early 1970's; since his success there proved questionable, he left the Foreign Service in order to pursue journalism.

Holbrooke became managing editor of the diplomatic magazine *Foreign Affairs*, then also publishing director of the Carnegie Endowment for International Peace and editor of the magazine *Foreign Policy*. In mid-1970's, the agile diplomat joined in the election headquarters of Governor Jimmy Carter as campaign coordinator for national security affairs. When the peanut farmer was elected President, he thanked Holbrooke by appointing him the youngestever Assistant Secretary of State for East Asian and Paciic Affairs. Showing off, he told the press that he found Asia to be the most appealing part of the world.

It was then that he personally got introduced to Henry Kissinger, the man he had written odes to in his magazines (which earned him the nickname of 'Little Kissinger'). They soon proved to be very much like each other, so Ambassador Donald F. McHenry once said of the two men: "They are both wiley, bright, ambitious. They have an ability to decide where they are headed and doggedly pursue their goals. Both have reputations for manipulativeness, for not always telling the truth."

Ronald Reagan

In the times when Ronald Reagan and George Bush ruled the United States, Holbrooke had been in business for 12 years. He was a foreign-policy commentator, advisor to Walter Mondale as presidential candidate, author of the biography of Clark Klifford, Minister of Defense. He offered his commentator services to *The New York Times*, which was declined. From 1985, Holbrooke became a senior adviser to Lehman Brothers with an annual salary of $ 900,000. As he could not do without politics, he joined in the presidential campaign of Bill Clinton, little-known governor of Arkansas.

> **BORKO B. DJORDJEVIC, M.D., Ph.D., F. I. C. S., F.A.A.C.S.**
> **Cosmetic Plastic Surgery Center**
>
> Palm Springs Office:
> 1091 North Palm Canyon Dr., Palm Springs, CA 92262
> Office: 760 325 7777   Fax: 760 325 7474
>
> E Mail: CSCps@aol.com ••• Website: www.djordjevicMD.com
>
> **FACSIMILE TRANSMISSION**
>
> To: US Dept of State — Robert Holbrook   Date: 12/31/03
>
> Fax #: 213-894-0914   Total of Pages: 2
>
> From: Dr Djordjevic
>
> Subject: _____
>
> Message: Dear Robert,
> Here is direct connection with the information I gave you which apparently got to Hague – Carla Del Ponte which she's accussing Mr. Amfilohije of hiding Karadžica in the monestary.
> Have a Happy New Year and hopefully we can make progress next year.
> Best,
> Borko

The Author's fax to R. Holbrooke

Bill Clinton having moved into the White House, in 1992, Richard Holbrooke was back into diplomatic service – as Ambassador to Tokyo first, then to Bonn. He then repeated his favourite sentence about the most appealing part of the globe, now naming Germany to be the one.

Loyal to his habit of befriending only famed and prominent figures, Holbrooke decided that in Germany Helmut Kohl was going to be his friend. This enraged Klaus Kinkel, Vice-Chancellor. He opened the White House door to the Chancellor and a channel to Bill Clinton for himself. As early as in those days, Holbrooke bore the nickname of 'Grand Ambassador' owing to the fact that he was the sole person who – in addition to the Mayor of Boston and the Vatican's envoy – had the right to enter the right wing of the White House (President Clinton's office) unannounced. For this trustworthiness he was rewarded in 1994, when he became Assistant Secretary of State for European and Canadian Affairs (1994-6), the strategist for the Balkans and head of the 'shuttle team' for Bosnia.

At that time Holbrooke had already visited the Balkans, and Bosnia especially, as a Red Cross missionary and an intelligence officer, in order to get familiar with the situation on the ground. He imposed himself by aggressive manners and, also, by his views taken over from Henry Kissinger and his friend Anthony Lake about the imperative that the U.S. retakes the supremacy in the West, for Europe has not proved capable of such leadership.

One half of the Washington staffers hated Dick Holbrooke, while the other half was avoiding to meet him, owing to his ferocious temper. Most Americans, however, believed that it was nothing else but his abrasive character which made Holbrooke an ideal negotiator in the Balkans. He had a personal experience of the war: as a U.S. intelligencer working with a humanitarian mission at Banja Luka in August 1992, he eye-witnessed "an insane asylym, with all these half-drunk Serb paramilitaries and middle-aged men going and raping and killing young Muslim women". It was at that moment that he already advised the White House to start a military action against the Serbs. He wrote to President Clinton describing these as criminals and show-offs who could be stopped by a couple of military strikes.

Some people from Holbrooke's milieu reveal his opinion of his major partners in the talks in ex-Yugoslavia: from the very beginning, and disregarding diplomatic language, he had seen them as a small and provoked "combative forest menagerie". In his eyes, Izetbegovic was "a balky and difficult mule, with only his stubborness and victim status as negotiating tools". Franjo

Tudjman was – Holbrooke claimed – exceptionally vain, "but politically determined to lift Croatia from Balkan poverty to West European affluence".

He refused to shake hands with Karadzic and Mladic. He called Arkan[13] a murderer. As Milosevic enjoyed his respect, Holbrooke chose this man as his co-worker and ally once he realized he could not defeat him. It was with the help of Serbia's President, who struggled for peace, that Richard Holbrooke got the Dayton Accords signed by Izetbegovic and Tudjman in November 1995; the settlement put an end to war operations in Bosnia. The Accords were veri ied in Paris, and the Americans see them as Bill Clinton's greatest diplomatic achievement.

Foreign observers, especially those in Europe, have not forgotten that it had been Richard Holbrooke who, with Anthony Lake, ordered the bombing of the Serbs, and who took part in the secret armament of the Muslims. They remembered his yelling and banging ists on the table. The manners were called "bulldozer diplomacy", for Holbrook had a habit to raze every obstacle to the ground. In post-Dayton days he would justify his behavior as befitting the situation, for at the negotiations on Bosnia he had to deal with dodgers, sometimes killers, traditions, so one had to be harsh. *The New York Times* wrote that the negotiations on Bosnia worked because Richard Holbrooke knew the Balkans were a 'snake nest' where he decided to be 'the python'. But one could say that Richard Holbrooke himself acted like a snake.

In his letter to Bill Clinton, Richard Holbrooke wrote that those were "the worst war crimes in Europe since the Holocaust". In that way he talked Washington into pressing and sidelining the Bosnian Serbs within the political negotiations over Dayton-taylored Bosnia. He had contemplated removal of Karadzic from the scene and gone as far as to offer General Ratko Mladic (as a "brave military leader") to become a politician and take over leadership in the Serb-held part of Bosnia. Mladic declined the offer point-blank.

At Dayton, Holbrooke reached success. Not only because he would roar and bang his hand against the table, but also because the bang symbolized the world's most powerful country and because the warring sides were cornered into compromise. He yelled at Sacirbey, Buha, Koljevic, Milosevic... Holbrooke himself said that those were the toughest negotioatians in the history of contemporary diplomacy, but also the moment when a new world policy was born after the Cold War.

Holbrooke admitted that Dayton Accords were not lawless, yet it was the best outcome one could get in the Balkans. The war operations were brought to an end, the Serbs withdrew behind the lines agreed upon, Sarajevo got united under Muslims' control. Following his 'recipe', Bosnia-Herzegovina was partitioned 51:49 percent. NATO was saved and enabled to reach out 'as far as Russia's windowsill'. In military terms, Dayton was a total success. In civil terms, however, it was not.

*

Richard Holbrooke was later sent back to Bosnia/Yugoslavia twice –to remedy his Dayton mistakes and to strengthen the American belief that Bill Clinton was a worldwide peacemaker. On both of these occasions, he pinned all blame on the Serbs. During the summer of 1996, Holbrooke left his Wall Street banking business in New York City and visited Sarajevo and Belgrade in order to eliminate Dr. Radovan Karadzic, President of the Republic of Srpska, and General Ratko Mladic, Commander of Srpska's Army, from politics.

He threatened the two men by arrest and detainment at The Hague Tribunal. He additionally threatened them by the economic sanctions on both the Republic of Srpska and Yugoslavia. As he himself admitted, the mission was *partially* successful. In the presence of Slobodan Milosevic, Karadzic and Mladic signed a statement of resignment from their respective posts in the Government of the Republic of Srpska and the Serbian Democratic Party (in Bosnia), as well as their withdrawal from political life. All of that proved to be sheer formality.

The President of the Republic of Srpska and the Commander of the Republic of Srpska's Army were not arrested. Neither any sanctions were imposed on the Republic of Srpska. Following the will of Washington, elections were held and Dr. Biljana Plavsic became President. It was a significant triumph for Bill Clinton which the once-again presidential candidate dangled before his voters. Boasting, Holbrooke would often say that the best support possible was provided by Washington at all levels, starting with the President.

And he had in just one week got over the death of Robert Frasure and two other men in the accident in Bosnia. Their substitute was Wesley Clark as the head of NATO. After this triumph on both sides – in Bosnia and in the United States – President Clinton sent Holbrooke back to New York to resume the banking business. It was then that Holbrooke, Clinton's special envoy, sent word to the Serbs that they were never going to see him again!

Consistent to his habit, he deceived us. Intoxicated by the glory, he was happily expecting Nobel Peace Prize and announced his nomination for a senator. As he had not won the Nobel Prize (there were 104 candidates), he went back to New York and the business of banking which had proved to be a productive school of bargain.

*

The Dayton-tailored Bosnia, Holbrooke's political creation, never came into sound operation. The Muslims and the Croats are still quarreling and fighting. They have had discrepant views on ambassadorial posts, so Holbrooke was there in the first week of August 1997 to reconcile them and dictate the diplomatic destinations of the Serbs/Muslims/Croats from the newly-created Bosnia-Herzegovina. The refugees have not returned to their homes, and the economic aid for the reconstruction of the country has been lowing in at a slow pace. For all of these failures, the White House put blame on the Serbs, i.e. on Radovan Karadzic and his Serbian Democratic Party. Though himself a creator of the aggressive U.S. diplomacy, Professor Henry Kissinger called the Dayton Accords 'a deception', proclaiming all those who think the Dayton-created Bosnia was tenable – 'dreamers'.

Holbrooke found Kissinger's view rather rigid, but got comfort in the belief that the whole area of Yugoslavia presents a history of unresolved issues. In private life, the year 1995 was quite upsetting for the Holbrooke family, for Richard broke off with his longstanding partner Diane Sawyer and married Kati Marton, a journalist and author. At the same time, the Metropolitan Police of New York threatened to detain him for unpaid parking ine. Richard Holbrooke passed away in mid-December 2010, to be buried in Washington D.C.

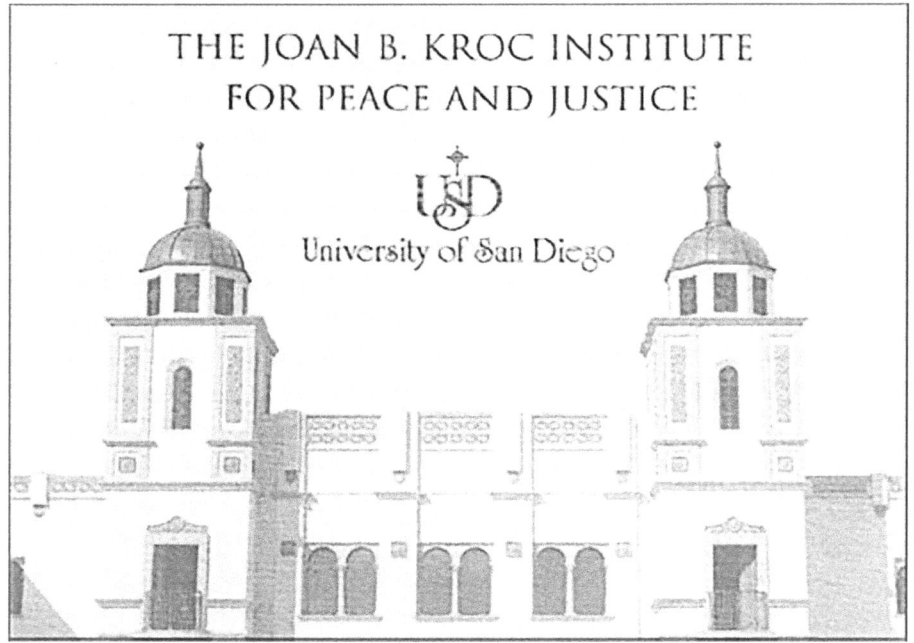

Joyce Neu's card om Joan B. Kroc Institute for Peace and Justice which recommended establishment of The Hague Tribunal branch division in Belgrade.

*

Dayton Peace Accords terminated the war which had lasted from 1991 to 1995. Milosevic was celebrated as "the guarantor of peace and stability in the region", while Radovan Karadzic was designated as a war criminal. The International Criminal Tribunal for the former Yugoslavia in The Hague was established under the American mantle of authority.

Political analysts and the individuals who were directly involved in the Bosnian crisis have different views of the in luence of Carter's peace initiative in Bosnia upon the geopolitical climate worldwide, and particularly upon the Dayton Peace Accords. In the opinion of Ambassador Harry Barnes, the cease-fire signed by the Serbs and Muslims "provided the longest pause in the fighting up to that point", that is, the end of 1994 and beginning of 1995. "But" – as he added –each side was not totally respectful of its terms".

Thus, Barnes wondered: "Just because we may have come up with certain ideas first, does that mean that's why they were accepted in Dayton?" He himself answered the question: "I don't think that you can necessarily make that leap."

His opinion was shared by Paul Shoup, political science professor at the University of Virginia who studied the situation in Bosnia in detail: "I thought the work Hanley and Carter did was important at the time, but you have to admit that the negotiations in Dayton didn't have anything to do with it." Yet there is something else Shoup would admit: as a result of Carter's peace efforts, "we now have a map that makes more sense. That's the map the people in Dayton were working with."

My personal opinion – and I was one of the organizers of Carter's peace mission to Bosnia – is that the mission was forerunner and the basis of the settlement reached at Dayton in November 1995. Had there not been the cease-fire Carter accomplished for Bosnia, Holbrooke's peace would not have been forged either.

*

When Milosevic, Tudjman and Izetbegovic initialed the Dayton Peace Accords in November 1995, the war was officially over, but it was only the beginning of a long journey to real peace.[14] It was difficult to complete it, for the warring parties waged political battles as if the war had still been going on. As the Dayton Accords was being put into practise, Jimmy Carter and the Carter Center were decreasingly dealing with Bosnian affairs. Early in 1996, Carter offered to help Carl Bildt, the Swedish politician and diplomat who had been co-chairman of the Dayton Peace Conference in November 1995, whereafter he was appointed High Representative for Bosnia Herzegovina in charge of implementing the Accords in the political and civil domains. The clauses regulating the latter were extremely hard to put into practise.

Jimmy Carter offered assistance in terms of his own and the Center's experience in the fields of conflict resolution, human rights and elections monitoring, but the offer did not lead to any engagement of the Carter Center in the period which followed.

Although he was excluded from the signing of the Dayton Agreement and, moreover, accused of war crimes, my friend Radovan Karadzic remained in the office of the President of the Republic of Srpska. Exposed to great international pressures aimed at his withdrawal from public life, he refused to abandon his post as the Bosnian-Serb leader, which was interpreted as a "slap across the face of the international community".

Karadzic was declared 'guilty' and an obstructive element in the implementation of Dayton Accords and reconstruction process in the Republic of Srpska. In the spring of 1996, Jimmy Carter sent a letter to Radovan Karadzic appealing on him to surrender to the International Criminal Tribunal for the Former Yugoslavia (ICTY). Unwilling to offend Carter by declination, Radovan did not respond at all.

Late in June 1996, Carter's assistant Joyce Neu visited Bosnia-Herzegovina to assess if there were some possibilities for a new involvement of the Carter Center in the processes of reconciliation between the three ethnic communities and the reconstruction of the country. In order to avoid duplication of the efforts by other organizations, the Carter Center reduced its activities to just monitoring of the events in Bosnia. During the visit, Ambassador Joyce Neu suggested that I should meet Carl Bildt so that we could find ways to get Karadzic step down and leave public life.

Carl Bildt rejected any compromise that could enable Karadzic to escape the appearance before the ICTY. Radovan Karadzic, often spotted but never captured by the international troops/officials, relinquished his presidential office to Biljana Plavsic on July 19, 1996. According to Ambassador Joyce Neu, Jimmy Carter was pleased with the principled conduct of Dr. Radovan Karadzic.

– He is a man of dignity – Jimmy Carter said.

*

My last contacts with Richard Holbrooke took place in 2006 and 2007. The mediator in the correspondence was Joyce Neu, then Director of the University of San Diego's Institute for Peace and Justice. Namely, in 2004 I renewed the initiative to allow Radovan Karadzic and Gen. Ratko Mladic to surrender to Serbia for a trial in Belgrade. I enjoyed the support by Joan B. Kroc Institute for Peace and Justice, run by the wife of the founder of McDonald's (at the time, its value was estimated to 50 billion dollars). This Institute was ready to provide 30 million for the establishment of a branch division of The Hague Tribunal in Serbia where Karadzic and Mladic would undergo trial.

The Institute for Peace and Justice insisted that Richard Holbrooke should be involved in this new campaign, for – as a worldfamous politician – he would lend it international legitimacy. So I asked Holbrooke for his support and view. Although he was just a lawyer at the moment, I suggested to Holbrooke that he could help me about the solution for Karadzic's destiny. Holbrooke, who had once signed the non-agression agreement with Karadzic, rejected my initiative.

Reportedly, as a U.S. civil citizen, Holbrooke was a bitter opponent to Radovan Karadzic and all other 'dangerous Serbs'. That is how my new mission of saving Karadzic and Mladic failed.

---

[13] **Arkan** was the nickname of **Zeljko Raznatovic**, leader of the paramilitary force 'Serb Volunteer Guard' (nicknamed "Tigers") that fought in Croatia and BH during the wars of 1990's. – *Translator's note.*

[14] The full name of the document/event reads: *General Framework Agreement for Peace in Bosnia and Herzegovina,* but is most often referred to as the Dayton (Peace) Accords, or Dayton Agreement. It was reached at Wright-Patterson Air Force Base in Dayton, Ohio on November 21, 1995 and initialed by Slobodan Milosevic (Serbia), Franjo Tudjman (Croatia) and Alija Izetbegovic (Bosnia-Herzegovina). The full and formal agreement was signed in Paris on December 14, 1995 – hence the other two names: *Paris Protocol or Dayton-Paris Agreement.* The document was co-signed by the most prominent international witnesses: Bill Clinton (President of the U.S.A.), Jacque Chirac (President of France), John Major (U.K. Prime Minister), Helmut Kohl (German Chancellor) and Viktor Chernomyrdin (Russian Prime Minister). –*Translator's note.*

A DANGEROUS SERB

THE CONFLICT BETWEEN Slobodan Milosevic and Radovan Karadzic was an epic and historic quarrel, a political clash of two Serbs over their personal interests. Each fought for himself and not for the Serbian people or the Serbian state. Slobodan Milosevic and Radovan Karadzic had no sound system of action or a vision of progress – either their own or the state's. They both acted like the old-time Serbian hajduci[15]. They undertook their activities from day to day, hardly ever thinking of the day after tomorrow or the future in general.

The Americans truly held Radovan Karadzic in high esteem, for, in principle, they respect winners. And in 1994, Karadzic controlled 72 percent of the BH territory. Yet as much as they respect winners, the Americans disparage losers. And Karadzic had disappointed them and became a loser because he feared Milosevic and curried favor with him. As soon as in the spring of 1995, Slobodan Milosevic managed to push Karadzic away and impose himself as the sole player on the Serb side in the peace process. He promised the Americans that Bosnia-Herzegovina would stay whole, that is, that he was not going to create a 'Great(er) Serbia'[16].

Vojislav Seselj, who behaved like a paramilitary commander, Jovica Stanisic, chief of Serbia's secret police, Arkan's 'Tigers' and Seselj's

'White Eagles'[17] frequented Pale and met with Karadzic much too often. This created an impression of the Republic of Srpska growing into the center of 'Great Serbia'. The impression was wrong but the Bosnian Serb leader's respectability and legitimacy began to decline in the American eyes. Therefore, the U.S. excluded Karadzic from all peacemaking options; Jimmy Carter did not. Carter believed that Karadzic was a man of honor, that he was a better choice in the peace settlement than Milosevic. He deemed Radovan Karadzic not to be a 'dangerous Serb' and

Slobodan Milosevic to be very dangerous, even fatal to the Serbs themselves.

For that reason, Carter sent a warning to Karadzic when he learned of his scheduled meeting with Slobodan Milosevic and Patrairch Pavle:

– Don't go to Belgrade. The meeting with Milosevic is a great scheme!

Carter personally informed me that, the moment Karadzic crossed the Serbian border, NATO was going to bomb Pale following Holbrooke's order. And that is what happened on August 30, 1995. As soon as Radovan crossed the Drina river by the town of Loznica, NATO attacked Pale.

Bombs were hitting all administrative buildings of the Republic of Srpska. Karadzic's personal secretary Jovan Zametica quailed. I found shelter in the basement of the Bistrica Hotel. I sent my girlfriend (now wife) Sandra to Belgrade and thus saved her life. There, in the shelter, I heard of two Spaniards from the Contact Group using locators to direct the bombers to the Serb capital Pale and the house of Radovan Karadzic. Officially, NATO attacked the Republic of Srpska because of the carnage at Sarajevo's Markale Market of August 28; 37 civilians were killed therein – allegedly – by Serbs' shells. By September 14, NATO used 15,000 tons of ammo and explosives filled with depleted uranium.

The news about a 'Serbian bomb' killing dozens of Muslims at Markale in Sarajevo was a U.S. message 'addressed' to Radovan Karadzic, yet one he proved unable to decipher. Instead of apologizing to the Muslims and dismissal of the commander in charge of Sarajevo, he ordered that the Army of the Republic of Srpska and the Army of the Republic of Srpska Krajina (Croatia) should unite into a single army force. Milosevic 'smashed' the plan into pieces. I called Radovan and told him about Carter's message: he should give a statement, via CNN, that he had ired the commander of Sarajevo and that he apologized to the Muslims. This was necessary for him in order to preserve his credibility. A CNN crew was waiting for him at Loznica, but Karadzic failed to give such a statement. In other words, Radovan failed to follow the advice of his sole American friend – Jimmy Carter.

Milosevic was blackmailing Karadzic while negotiating peace terms with Holbrooke at Karadjordjevo, Tito's hunting residence.

The wily Richard Holbrooke neutralised all of Karadzic's activities: he obtained President Clinton's authorization to invite the Serbs for peace negotiations at Dayton, Ohio. Holbrooke had opted for Milosevic, although aware of the fact that the man could not leave for Dayton without Karadzic's consent. So Karadzic headed for Belgrade, convinced that through Milosevic he could win a good status for the Republic of Srpska at Dayton. And that Patriarch Pavle was going to help him reach the goal.

– I *am* going. Milosevic cannot attack me, with Patriarch Pavle there! – That is how Karadzic responded to Carter's word of advice.

Karadzic was wrong. He did not know that Milosevic held the head of the Serbian Orthodox Church in control, pressing slowly and fatally, 'like a snake killing a frog'. He threatened the Patriarch with taking away the Church from Him, and without the Church His Holiness could not protect the Serbian people. Three months before, he had banned candle-wax imports from Bulgaria, thus signalling the Patriarch that coping with inancial pressures awaited him. So Karadzic danced attendance on Milosevic, before the lineup of Sloba's generals and before the obedient Patriarch Pavle. Actually, both Radovan and the Patriarch were 'taken hostages' by Milosevic, yet unaware of their positions. Karadzic was taken to the nearby hunting residence in the suburb of Dobanovci where he was practically detained until he signed an authorization for Dayton agreement.

By this signature, Radovan Karadzic allowed Milosevic to bargain with the towns of Brcko, Tuzla and Gorazde, plus two percent of the Serb-held territory. In other words, Karadzic lost control and command over the Republic of Srpska. The leader of all Serbs turned into the greatest Serb loser.

*

Subsequently to the Dayton Peace Accords, Slobodan Milosevic grew from "the Butcher of the Balkans" and "the last of Communist dictators" into a favorite "factor of stability in the Balkans". Richard Holbrooke was really fascinated by the man, they feasted and had good time together; as to the Serbian opposition, Holbrooke never found time to meet with them. Nevertheless, Milosevic miscalculated his own role and importance. Holbrooke had gone to see Milosevic fully biased. And then he was taken by surprise: the man facing him was neither a communist nor a nationalist nor an Oriental-style dictator. The man was absolutely none of it.

Milosevic was no slave of any ideology, or any principle, except that these were useful to manipulate unsparingly. As it happens with any other opportunist who defends his own power, Holbrooke found him quite appealing, despite all his point-blank speech and inconsideration.

Not for a minute did Sloba protect Radovan Karadzic or the Serbian people in Bosnia-Herzegovina. He sold Karadzic to Ambassador Holbrooke and defamed him before Americans as a bad man and an appallingly inferior politician. On the other hand, Milosevic aspired to charm and fascinate Holbrooke at all costs. He could not imagine being outdone after his theatrical bravura display in a production wherein he was – for a short while – the leading star. That Serbia had right to fight for her national interests and to resort to military force in defense was never disputed. Even in November 1994, when the Serbs entered Bihac, the U.S. Secretary of Defense William Perry stated that the fact that the Serbs had won the war had to be accepted, adding that the "friends in Sarajevo" had to be persuaded to accept the peace agreement, which was the best solution for them at the moment.

Milosevic demanded from Karadzic that the Serb army withdraw from Bihac. He was convinced that the American bombs were a proper remedy for the Serb hotheads in Bosnia. Richard Holbrooke boasted in front of his staff about Milosevic welcoming him kindly while NATO was bombarding the Serbs. He had assumed that Milosevic would have denied the reception and sent him back to where he had come from.

– Dick, I've got great news for you! – Slobodan stepped forward and hugged him, and Holbrooke felt totally baffled.

As soon as they took their seats, Milosevic pulled out the paper with the authorization given him by the Bosnian-Serb leadership to negotiate – on behalf of Radovan Karadzic – on the peace settlement for Bosnia, at Dayton. Holbrooke could not help expressing openly his wonderment by the tolerant welcome at the moment when American bombs were ruthlessly hitting the Serbs in Bosnia.

– What's the wonder about it? Dick, they needed some

bombardment to come to their senses and become reasonable, for those are all head-strong hotheads.

Historical events have meanwhile revealed that Milosevic did not need the Serbs in Croatia, BH, Montenegro or diaspora. That is what he used to tell the Americans, but his words to Radovan Karadzic and Jovan Raskovic[18] during their secret encounters suggest otherwise:

– You, the Serbs outside of Serbia, you'd better stay where you are. Stay away from Serbia!

– We don't want to live with the Muslims and Croats! We want to be with Serbia – they would respond.

A little later, Milosevic "sold and surrendered" them all to Alija Izetbegovic and Franjo Tudjman respectively. Falsely pretending to be the leader of all Serbs, in order to remain in power. He just acted being a great Serb, and the role implied deliveries of arms to Bosnia-Herzegovina and sending his commanders and paramilitary/parapolice formations there. With Americans, he claimed he did not know anything about these.

*

In that fateful year, 1995, both Milosevic and Karadzic demonstrated their hotheaded characters: the former – in his triumph over his unfavorite Serb, the latter – in his getting defeated by his favorite Serb. They were both so preoccupied with their personal struggles for power that they failed to notice that they were losing their state. While the Serbs triumphantly waited for others to recognize their victory, the Muslim and Croat armies expressly consolidated themselves. Milosevic's preference was to reach/stick to a secret agreement with Tudjman; thus he was prepared for the promised peace and lifting of the sanctions. For these purposes, he was willing to sacrifice the territories in Bosnia and in Krajina (Croatia).

What followed was the Croats' Operation Storm: backed up by the Americans, the Serbs were driven out of Krajina, and there was also danger of losing Banja Luka (Bosnia). Obrad Kesic, political analyst from Washington, D.C., wrote down in his chronicles that Richard Holbrooke was boasting about personally preventing the fall of Banja Luka to the Croatian hands after the Storm. Interestingly, at a meeting closed for public Holbrooke divulged:

he had indirectly suggested to Milosevic that the Americans would approve of his attack on the Croats and the Muslims.

– Mr. President, the fall of Banja Luka would be most unwelcome! That would not be in either your interest or even in ours, for it would trigger off new conflicts and delay the peace solution for a long time, the solution which is now at hand! – That is what Holbrook said to President Slobodan Milosevic.

It was only when it became evident that Milosevic would not venture into any action that the Americans restrained Tudjman from further triumphant expedition on Banja Luka and saved the city from Croatian occupation in August 1995. Milosevic was in America's favor for less than two years. He could do literally anything against the so- called 'internal enemy', i.e. the opposition in Serbia. The attitude encouraged Milosevic to rashly steal the local elections of 1997, for he took it for granted that the tolerance included such an act.

He relied on the messages of the smooth-talking Nebojsa Vujovic, chargé d'affaires at the Embassy in Washington, D.C., who kept telling him that America was full of thankfulness to him and admiration for his historic mission. On the very day the first NATO air strikes were launched, March 24, 1999, the man informed Milosevic that such a thing was not going to happen. The attack did happen, and – following the 78 days of war against the United States and Europe – the Serbian people in Serbia, too, suffered a political and military defeat.

---

[15] **Hajduci** (Sg. *hajduk*) were groups of outlawed men whose social pro ile varied in different periods and/or areas – from bandits (either notorious criminals or poor people's benefactors like English folklore hero Robin Hood) to more or less organized guerrilla that fought against the Turks and for the liberation of the country. In the latter case, *hajduci* were often leaders of peasants' or regional rebellions against the Ottoman authorities, respected as heroes and sung about in the Serbian epic poetry. – *Translator's note.*

[16] The term **'Great Serbia'** or 'Greater Serbia' (*Velika Srbija*) has usually been (ab) used by the non-Serb political figures of ex-Yugoslavia who advocated distancing from, or confrontation with, the Serbian people by interpreting Serbian politics as dangerously based on claiming the territories of other Yugoslavia's nation(alitie)s or even neighboring countries in order to dominate one big country that incorporates all territories with Serbian population. –*Translator's note.*

[17] **Arkan's Tigers** were Serbian paramilitary that fought in Croatia and Bosnia-Herzegovina during the wars of 1990's, led by Zeljko Raznatovic Arkan. They named themselves as 'Serb Volunteer Guard'. The **'White Eagles'** (not to be confused with those of World War II that bore the same name) were another paramilitary organization in the said period and the said territories, usually associated with Vojislav Seselj, founder of the Serbian Radical Party. –Translator's note.

[18] **Dr. Jovan Raskovic** (1929-1992) was Croatian-Serb psychiatrist, academic and politician who founded Serbian Democratic Party in Croatia toward the 1990 elections; perceived by the Croat leadership as a serious leader of Croatia's Serbs worth negotiating with. Soon, however, he was moved from power and political life by radical Serb nationalists. – *Translator's note.*

DOUBLE-DEALING IN THE ARMY

ACCORDING TO SOME INFORMATION that were available to me, Slobodan Milosevic wanted to enter a war with NATO and therefore did his best to defy this western alliance to the point of bombarding his country and his people. To this day I have not been able to account for his reasons. Did he really believe that NATO would not attack, that he was too strong with his army or his Russian friends? Or, did he want to invigorate his own position among the Serbs by acting out the victim of Western democracy, that is, of military aggression? Whatever his motives, the air campaign against Serbia and Montenegro ensued as punishment for Slobodan Milosevic's attempt at cheating the western military alliance and the peacemakers from the United States and Europe. At the same time, Milosevic deceived the Supreme Command of the Yugoslav Army, passing the buck on the conflict.

What was going on in the Army prior to the NATO raid of March 24, 1999?

As my friends among the Serbian generals told me, the NATO Headquarters had warned Slobodan Milosevic requesting the end of the military operation in Kosovo-Metohija against the Albanian terrorists; they objected the excessive deployment of tank units which endangered broad population. He was ordered to resort only to the force adequate to counter-strike the terrorists of the 'Kosovo Liberation Army' as the ethnic Albanians referred to their paramilitary organization[19]. Milosevic did not follow the advice, so the Command of the Alliance issued a "Solemn Warning" preceding an attack on the F.R.Y. unless Milosevic withdrew the tanks, aviation and troops from Kosovo-Metohija.

Instead of shrinking back from the possible NATO retaliation, the Serbian 'Vozhd' resorted to hoodwinking, jeopardizing the destiny of his army and his nation. While dividing the top ranks of the military into the 'pro' and 'con' officers with regard to their attitude to him (the latter were also labeled 'pro-NATO'), Slobodan Milosevic incorporated paramilitary and smugglers into the Army. In the times of international sanctions, their task was to supply the F.R.Y. Army with stolen kerosene and oil, plus aircraft missiles and bombs of suspicious origin and often defective. They were abusing the Army for oil and cigarette smuggling from Macedonia, Bulgaria, Greece, Turkey and – via Yugoslavia – further to Italy. In Montenegro, for example, the cigarette smugglers used the vessels of the Yugoslav Navy Force.

These civil and military criminals were run by a parallel/secret HQ of Milosevic's army. That is how a military mafia came into being, and it never surfaced as a subject of discussion in public; what is more, since the fall of Milosevic, the mafia has never been exposed to political or judicial condemnation.

In October 1998, Milosevic officially composed his team for the negotiations with NATO: General Momcilo Perisic, Chief of the General Staff of the Yugoslav Army, and General Ljubisa Velickovic, Commander of Air Force and Anti-Aircraft Defense. During the talks with General Michael C. Short, Commander of Allied (NATO) Air Forces Southern Europe and his team, an agreement was reached about aerial monitoring of the situation on the ground in Kosovo-Metohija being done jointly by the Yugoslav Air Force and the NATO Air Force, whereby they should coordinate the light schedules of their respective aircraft; the reports on the situation should be sent to the NATO Headquarters in Brussels and the General Staff of the Yugoslav Army in Belgrade.

As a sign of mutual trust, a team of Yugoslav Air Force officers and pilots should be sent to visit the NATO air base in Vicenza, Italy, while such a team of NATO should be received at the Batajnica military airport near Belgrade.

This draft agreement, composed on October 12, 1998, should have provided the basis for a military agreement between the F.R. of Yugoslavia and NATO to be signed by Gen. Momcilo Perisic and Gen. Wesley Clark, Supreme Allied Commander Europe. The envisaged next step implied adoption and signing – by Ambassador Richard Holbrooke and President Slobodan Milosevic – of a political agreement between the international community and the F.R.Y. An hour-precise schedule was prepared for the Belgrade light/landing of Gen. Wesley Clark and the Holbrooke-Milosevic meeting.

– When the papers of the accord between the two Armies were ready for the signatures of the parties, i.e. of General Short and General Velickovic, the Serbian Air Force Commander refused to sign. He found refuge at Dedinje, in the residence of Slobodan Milosevic, so as to escape signing of the agreement with NATO which prevented air strikes on Serbia and its people. Instead of Velickovic, Gen. Momcilo Perisic signed the agreement – this is how General Blagoje Grahovac, witness to the event, described the circumstances.

Having signed the agreement, Generals Short and Perisic went to see Milosevic; Gen. Wesley Clark and Ambassador Richard Holbrooke came there, too. Without any mention of Velickovic's boycott performed by his own order, Milosevic himself signed the military accord on aerial reconnaissance lights in Kosovo-Metohija and restricted deployment of tanks and aviation.

Two days later, on October 15, 1998, Milosevic performed another act of deception: Without the knowledge of the Yugoslav Army's number one, Gen. Momcilo Perisic, he ordered Air Force Commander Ljubisa Velickovic to cancel the reception of the NATO officers and pilots at the Batajnica airport. It was at that moment that the chiefs of NATO grasped Milosevic's duplicity by which he sacrificed his loyal generals. While signing the said F.R.Y.–NATO accord, he was secretly ordering his generals not to comply with its requirements.

The event was 'accompanied' by a triumphal shout of Gen. Velickovic:

– NATO and I, together – never ever!

Chief of the General Staff of the Yugoslav Army, General Momcilo Perisic, behind whose back the whole scheme was run, issued commands that honored the military accord; he ordered his subordinates to welcome and accomodate the NATO officers and pilots at the Batajnica airport.

As Milosevic's obedient servant, Gen. Velickovic spent the next three days in hiding, thus stonewalling the planned visit of the Serbian Air Force delegation to the NATO air base at Vicenza. Working behind the scene, Gen. Velickovic appointed another Milosevic's sycophant, General Spasoje Smiljanic, his successor as Air Force and Anti-Aircraft Defense Commander.

In December 1998, displeased with the failure of his NATO-boycott, Serbia's President ired Gen. Momcilo Perisic and installed his successor in the post of Yugoslav Army Chief of General Staff – Gen. Dragoljub Ojdanic. Ojdanic was yet another admirer of Slobodan Milosevic, blindly obedient, and also opponent to the cooperation between Yugoslavia and NATO. In other words, he opposed the efforts to spare Serbia the bombardments.

Air Force Major-General Blagoje Grahovac, a protagonist of the above-described episode, wrote the following notes in his war diary: *When NATO began sending warnings to the F.R.Y. Army and Slobodan Milosevic referring to their failure to comply with the military accord by intensifying the tank attacks on the Albanians in Kosovo-Metohija, and when Gen. Wesley Clark came to Belgrade to talk about the compliance with the accord, Chief of the General Staff General Dragoljub Ojdanic rejected all of his objections. At that moment, Wesley Clark knew what Milosevic's duplicity game was and openly said to Ojdanic: 'You'd better realize the gravity of the situation. If I get an order to launch air strikes, it will be executed. What if we use cluster bombs?' When Clark had left, Ojdanic uttered a chesty comment before Milosevic's adherents: 'He got his comeuppance!'*

Subsequently to the encounter of Gen. Clark and Gen. Ojdanic, Yugoslav media reported on "the victory of the Serbian Army in Kosovo". The F.R.Y. Army rewarded its generals with higher ranks and offices. The war against NATO was imminent. The Army was aware of that, yet in spite of the clash with NATO forces, it was secretly preparing – following an order by Milosevic – to attack Montenegro in order to overthrow the government of Milo Djukanovic. Since the negotiations at Rambouillet in February 1999 did not calm down Milosevic's desire for a war against the West, NATO was readying its bombers for an air campaign against Yugoslavia.

Slobodan Milosevic did not believe that his quite recent allies were going to attack him; and yet, he ordered the political and military leaderships to retreat into the Karas Bunker at Topcider Hill, near Belgrade's downtown.

The first missiles of NATO aviation hit ground on March 24, 1999 at 7:45 p.m. The first targets were the military air fields in Pristina (Kosovo), Podgorica (Montenegro), Batajnica (near

Belgrade), as well as spots in Kursumlija, Novi Sad, Pancevo, Kragujevac and Lucani. When Milosevic saw the report on bombarding in Montenegro in the morning of March 25, he grinned with pleasure and said:

– The Montenegrins thought they would not be attacked! As the devastation of Serbia and Montenegro was under way in the spring of 1999, pro-Milosevic media reported on as many as 79 aircraft of the western alliance downed and about the successes of the Yugoslav Army. Milosevic, however, fearing a strike on Karas Bunker, moved to a secret shelter by the village of Simanovci (Srem, Vojvodina). The 78 days of NATO air campaign resulted in the defeat of both the country (F.R.Y.) and its Army; official reports tell about mere three western airplanes downed by the latter. In spite of the obvious disaster and ruins across the country, Slobodan Milosevic declared victory over NATO.

*

By letting his nation become victim of the bombardments and killings, Milosevic demonstrated the fact that he was the worst of the Balkan rulers. The presidents of Slovenia, Croatia and Bosnia-Herzegovina, i.e. Kucan, Tudjman and Izetbegovic respectively, had meanwhile done for their nations much more than Milosevic had for his people. Thinking of himself as an irreplaceable partner of the major powers, he could not grasp the reality: the result of his 'roleplaying' was – giving all for nothing.

Paradoxically enough, Milosevic's negotiation position was far stronger in the time he had been labeled 'the Butcher of the Balkans' while controlling one third of Croatia and 70 percent of Bosnia-Herzegovina than after his rash cession of these had earned him the courtship of "a factor of stability in the Balkans". If he did not put the Serbian national interests into practise, he did so for the American ones. He definitely brought the United States into the Balkans, possibly against its conscious will, to ensure a total revival of NATO as a consequence of the air-strikes against Serbia. His defeat gave rise to the credibility of the United States and the Clinton Administration.

As the political analyst Obrad Kesic claims, and I agree with him, Slobodan Milosevic was far from being "an American man" as he himself pretended to be. Milosevic used to spread the story about his awareness of the effects of his acts, about these acts as parts of some great global strategy. It was only after he had lost everything that his policies proved to be nothing but a big bluff and self-delusion which irreparably impaired the Serbian national interests and betrayed the American interests in Yugoslavia. The United States never threatens in vain; in most cases, it does resort to force. Only totally obedient politicians and the allies are in high esteem with the Americans. Milosevic attempted to double-cross them, and the punishment ensued through the killing of his people and his own death at The Hague's Detention Center.

---

[19] The **KLA** uses the Albanian acronym UCK (*Ushtria Clirimtare e Kosoves*), while the Serbian one is OVK (*Oslobodilacka vojska Kosova*). – *Translator's note.*

SLOBA'S BIRD

SLOBIDAN MILOSEVIC was aware of the fact that I, Borko Djordjevic, "a vagabond-doctor" – as his gossips labeled me, was Radovan's man, plus "an American spy and traitor". He had leafed through my police record received from Serbia's state security police and erased the information on my M.D. degree acquired at the Belgrade University, despite the checking done at the Faculty of Medicine on his request. Namely, Slobodan Milosevic took my CV from Dr. Grbic, Dean of the Faculty, as well as my Party-created biography from the Yugoslav League of Communists, and composed a dossier on me. He, who had been a close collaborator with the Americans for a while, proclaimed me, Dr. Djordjevic, an American spy.

Richard Holbrooke and Slobodan Milosevic

From the year 1995 in which Milosevic marked me as his adversary, whenever I was entering or leaving Serbia, the border police would make special inquiry or take me into custody for questioning. As I always carried with me my documentation (records of my correspondence with Jimmy Carter and photos of the former U.S. President and myself), Milosevic's police officers con iscated these.

Slobodan Milosevic personally engaged the police in his witchhunt for me, for he thought that I had fooled and betrayed him. He ordered his cops and criminals to kill me. In Serbia, the bounty amounted to $ 400,000. Tomislav Pejovic, the artist who used to sculpt Tito's busts and was a close friend of the President's spouse Jovanka Broz, sent me a tip-off about a criminal nick-named Pomorandza ('Orange') who had decided to kill me and thus earn the $ 400,000. I found a bodyguard, but the man requested $ 400,000 to save my life from this liquidator. I declined such payment for his protection services.

To Milosevic, that did not suffice, so he repeatedly ordered Radovan Karadzic to kill me:

– Dr. Borko is an American spy and traitor of the Serbs! Wipe him out!

Karadzic did not wipe me out, but he left me to contend with the Milosevic family by myself.

*

During the witch-hunt, at the whims of life, I happened to meet all the members of the Milosevic family.

Slobodan's daughter-in-law and wife of Marko Milosevic, Milica Gajic, had come to see me at the Igalo clinic after – as she said – I had appeared in an advertisement with Ruska Mulina Jakic; however, she left Igalo all of a sudden and hurried back to Belgrade.

Her husband, Marko Milosevic, had been injured in an accident meanwhile and, with a spinal trauma, was hospitalized at the Military

Medical Academy in Belgrade, on the 14th loor. His wife Milica was with him. It was then that I met Milosevic's son. We shook hands. 'Little Marko' (*Mali Marko*), as everybody referred to him, felt the need to present to me his view of the situation in Yugoslavia:

– We've got a disaster here. All's in a shambles. Communism has collapsed, now's the time of capitalism. That is what we should strive for – Marko Milosevic was saying while his own parents were trying to save communism from crumbling.

Through her daughter-in-law Milica, Professor Mira Markovic began to apply her political and police-way 'carrot and stick' treatment. She asked how she could "touch up her belly and thighs" in a re ined way, by liposuction. My answer was that the best way to do that is to use the scalpel. She declined my offer outright, which I was actually up to. That is, I did not want to risk my life for ten pounds of fat on the belly of Slobodan Milosevic's wife, the most powerful and most dangerous woman in Serbia during the 1990's. I witnessed this kind of her potentials myself – to some extent.

In mid-1990's I sold my house at Dedinje[20], at No. 13 Majke Jevrosime Street, for 700,000 Swiss franks. Reportedly, the buyer was a cop whose nick-name was Zica. The story was that he needed a building site for the residence of General Pavkovic. A couple of days later, three men kidnapped me to hold me in a cellar for three days. A man with hoarse voice, who identi ied himself as a war veteran, was yelling at me, putting the barrel of his handgun into my mouth and threatening:

– I'm gonna kill you if you don't gimme the money. I've got throat cancer so I'm gonna die anyway. I lose nothing. And you stay alive if you pay me!

I payed 200,000 German marks to the kidnapper and he let me go. Later I found out that the kidnapping was done by some guys from JUL[21], some adherents of the party from the *Duga Industry,* including their director Batalovic.

The letter written by Dobrica Cosic to R. Karadzic after Carter's visit to Pale

Slobodan Milosevic was soft on his wife Mira. He used to speak in a low voice and with some caution so that she would not make out his words. Mira Markovic was the secret ruler of Serbia and the F.R. of Yugoslavia. She fancied herself as a daughter of Josip Broz Tito which to her implied that she was the 'heiress' of Tito's Yugoslavia. She grew upon the Brijuni Islands[22] among the members of Yugoslav elite. And she aspired to become another Tito, which is clearly noticeable from her political activities, her letters and her books. Intimately, Slobodan Milosevic shared Mira's phantasy and supported her idea that they should become the new Tito-and-Jovanka couple.

The two-word 'recipe' for their political career was once revealed by Mira Markovic herself: *money and political power*. She admitted that she had been arranging Slobodan's life so as to place him in a milieu where he could gain power, and money as well. Thus, he worked at *Tehnogas* Company which availed of big money, then at *Beobanka* from which he made a leap and seized power by knocking out his closest friend, Ivan Stambolic. Subsequently, Milosevic turned the whole of Serbia into his personal/private bank.

During a dinner at Belgrade's *Hyatt* Hotel, one of the Milosevic family's security staff, who was then dating Slobodan's daughter Marija Milosevic, had the following piece of conversation:

– I am the only man who's toppled Milosevic twice: each time I made love with Marija, Milosevic's picture fell down.

A question followed:

– Hey, doc! Do you have some medicine for Mira's husband? His 'bird' wouldn't 'fly'!

I took the question as a blatant provocation, and an opportunity for him – provided I gave any answer at all – to turn it into a hearsay that "Sloba wouldn't have a bone stiffy" which I, Dr. Djordjevic, reportedly spread around Belgrade. It could spell doom for me.

Medically speaking, I might have been right, for it is a wellknown fact that people with fluctuating blood pressure and high blood-sugar (Milosevic was one of those and, due to his crimson cheeks, often referred to as *Rumenko*/'Red-Face') had a persistent problem with penile blood- low and rigidity.

In the aftermath of the dinner with Mira's security agent-provocateur and as soon as possible I took light to the States, in order to escape getting beaten with a 'stick'/club along the sweet 'carrot'.

A while before the above-described event I had met Mira's daughter Marija and realized that she was as dangerous for the Serbian people as her parents. Marija Milosevic was going out around Belgrade with a guy from the state security police who – as a secret agent – always carried two handguns. Marija was fond of shooting from guns in public places. In some villas of the Dedinje quarter she organized midnight parties during which she demonstrated her cowboy-and-gunman-like skills.

Milosevic was dangerous for the Serbs because he was using them for his personal bene its. He thus used the great writer Dobrica Cosic for raising his own reputation among the people – temporarily at least. Cosic was the first President of the F.R. of Yugoslavia (June 1992–June 1993). When I met Dobrica during his presidential term, I asked him why he failed to rule in compliance with the Constitution, and he responded:

– I don't know, I'm a writer. I can't understand why they installed me in this post to rule.

At the same time, President Cosic knew why he asked me to bring some Golden Kent cigarettes for his wife.

Milosevic also capitalized on Milan Panic, an ex-Yugoslavia's émigré

taken to him by Dusko Mitevic[23] so that he could – without the blessing from the White House – be installed as the first Prime Minister of his newly shaped country, the F.R.Y. As it proved later on, Panic was only working for his personal gain. As a true sel ish American, Milan Panic used to gossip with the Americans about Slobodan Milosevic. In the near future, Panic double-crossed Milosevic, turning the United States against him. Although toppled, Panic made his fortune in Serbia as the owner of the pharmaceutical company *ICN Galenika*.

Panic was an egomaniacal person, and Cosic was a political profiteer, a dissident of yesteryear and a loyal Serb with communist pedigree.

Both men found a confidant and a capable executive in the figure of my friend Dr. Ljubisa Rakic, Member of the Serbian Academy of Sciences and Arts. Having 'dethroned' Panic and Cosic, Slobodan Milosevic ordered that his goons beat up Dr. Rakic, medical doctor, because he self-confidently and out of free will abandoned the Serbian 'Vozhd'[24]. I personally treated the wounds which the men of Slobodan Milosevic had inflicted on the Vice-President of SASU.

---

[20] **Dedinje** is an urban neighborhood of Belgrade with stately mansions and villas, considered to be the city's wealthiest part. – *Translator's note.*

[21] **JUL**, acronym of *Jugoslovenska (udruzena) levica,* i.e. 'Yugoslav (Allied) Left', a coalition of 23 left-oriented parties which merged into one in 1994. Mirjana-Mira Markovic, wife of Slobodan Milosevic, was its leader. At its peak, following the 1997 general elections, the party won 20 seats in the National Assembly of the Republic of Serbia. The party was dissolved in 2003. The leader, Mirjana Markovic lives in Russia. Serbia's authorities issued arrest warrant on fraud charges, extended (2006) with charges for ordering the murder of the journalist Slavko Curuvija. – *Translator's note.*

[22] The **Brijuni** (Brioni in Italian and Serbian) is a group of 14 small islands off the northern coast of Croatia where Marshal Tito established his State Summer Residence after World War II. The top ranks of Yugoslavia's authorities and the Communist Party would spend parts of the year there. Tito died in 1980, and in 1983 the archipelago was declared a National Park of Yugoslavia (now of Croatia). – *Translator's note.*

[23] **Dusan Mitevic** (1938-2003) was a journalist, director of Radio-Television Belgrade and a key player in Milosevic propaganda until forced resignment during the large-scale opposition protests of March 1991. – *Translator's note.*

[24] **'Vozhd'** means 'leader'; the word usually pertains to Djordje Petrovic – Karadjordje ('Black George'), leader of the First Serbian Uprising against the Ottoman Empire (1804-13). When referring to Milosevic, it bears ironical or even ridiculing undertone. – *Translator's note.*

BATTLING FOR BILLIONS

THE NERVOUS AND THREATININGLY intolerant Milosevic's attitude to his own adherents whom he installed to high positions and then, at some point, hated, attacked and got rid of – that was something I had first noticed while still in the United States. In late 1980's, in Washington D.C., I met a smart and enterprising man, Yugoslavia's Ambassador Zivorad Kovacevic. He instantly told me that Slobodan Milosevic, then President of Serbia, could not stand him, what is more, he pursued him. That, however, never hindered the behaviour of His Excellency: he acted as a loyal Serb. Namely, it occurred to Kovacevic that we, the Serbs, should establish a Serbian representative office. Gathered around the project, we started some activities in order to implement it.

The plan implied concentration of Serbian diplomats, businessmen and artists from Serbia in one building, and the choice was the 17-storeyed building of the former Embassy of Argentina in the Fifth Avenue. In the same avenue, there was another available building – the guilded mansion where Tito used to stay overnight while in New York City, once occupied by a member of the Vanderbilt family.

There were two options with regard to the Argentinian building: either to rent it for $ 50,000 or to purchase it for 16 billion dollars. The annual rent payed by our representative offices and state institutions in NYC was well above two million per month. This meant an obvious and enormous saving! The money was abundant at the time, in 1988: Yugoslavia was negotiating sale of aircraft and arms to Venezuela in exchange for crystallized oil and payments to the Serbian/Yugoslav company *Jugoimport SDPR*.

The whole transaction, handled adroitly by General Jovo Popovic, was three billion dollars worth. The deal was under way beyond the insight of the IMF and OPEC, organizations that controlled the low of money, weapons and oil. General Popovic promised to supply us with 16 million dollars intended for the purchase of the New York building we would name the *Serbian House*. However, as soon as he heard of Zivorad Kovacevic 'handling something', Slobodan Milosevic threatened by his dismissal from the ambassadorial office. The federal Minister of National Defense, Admiral Branko Mamula, did not sign the arms export permit of Yugoslav weapons to Venezuela. Reportedly, Mamula found himself in a conflict of interests, for he was supposed to receive $ 300,000 commission for another deal.

*

In that same year, 1988, I happened to make another deal for the Socialist Federal Republic of Yugoslavia. At the Miami Florida Gun Show I came across General Andjelkovic of the Yugoslav National Army who was selling CZ pistols made in Kragujevac, Serbia. He was up to buying the Sikorsky electronic system from the Americans, needed for a new type of Yugoslav-made helicopter. The chopper was to be produced by *Ivo Lola Ribar Factory*. I helped the *Jugoimport* SDPR and the YNA purchase the American Sikorsky program. Unfortunately, the production of that type of Yugoslav combat chopper never began. Following my efforts in the deal, Ambassador Kovacevic – as he later confessed to me – wrote in his diplomatic report to the Yugoslav Ministry of Foreign Affairs: "Dr. Djordjevic is a very capable man. He has strong connections in the American top-rank politics and business. Caution in relation to him is recommended!"

Borko Djordjevic, Vice-President of Serbian Government Slobodan-Buca Prohaska and Dragan Tomic, Director of Jugopetrol

Slobodan Milosevic and Guido Scmidt-Chiari, Vice-President of the Austrian bank Creditanstalt

From the year 1994, and especially after 1995, I permanently resided in Belgrade. Those were the years of the mad civil war and international economic sanctions. Silently moving about, I was observing the situation in healthcare services and in politics alike, seeking a chance to get involved in a business. I did not work much at first, for nothing of importance was happening in the medical field in Serbia.

So I decided to get a doctoral degree. I defended my dissertation at the Faculty of Medicine, Belgrade University. It was entitled *Secondary Lipoplastics*. Thereafter, I wrote books (five volumes) on plastic surgery in order to pass my experience to students and to provide something the young people could learn from. I met Professor Isidor Papo, a famed doctor, and asked him why he failed to write students' text-books, for they still studied from some old scripts. He answered with arrogance:

– I haven't written text-books because I didn't want them to find out my way of work!

*

Whenever I could, I was helping Serbia. Until mid-nineties there were a great many people in the diaspora who were trying to help Serbia. I was not the sole example. Some of the Serbian patriots living abroad pursued activities aimed at political change in Serbia, but I insisted on economic reforms. There were émigrés who tried to transact business while emphasizing the issue of their own fee: "What do *I* get from it?"

Such people made their fortunes by selling their patriotism to their fatherland. They never cared about their people and the country.

As for myself, I represented American capital as a beginner in both business and (Serbian) politics. I served both the United States and Serbia as a man who gets things done – efficiently enough.

General Jovo Popovic

The protagonists of the business of arms purchase for the reduced Yugoslavia were Generals Jovo Popovic and Zivota Panic, Nikodin *Jovanovic* as CEO of SDPR and Dragan Tomic, Director-General of *Jugopetrol*. The weapons secretly dispatched to the Serbheld territories in Croatia would be decomposed, wrapped up appropriately and sunken into Jugopetrol's tanker trucks for concealment. One of those men was a confidant of Milosevic's wife Mira Markovic, so I assume she was aware of the secret purchases and deliveries of weapons, including the money earned thereby. The confidant used to do shopping for *drugarica* ('Comrade') Mira (fur, shawls and other gifts) amounting to 50,000 Deutsche Mark.

Jovan Zebic, Borko Djordjevic, Slobodan-Buca Prohaska and Schmidt-Chiari

When Texaco Inc. and *Shell Oil Co.* wanted to buy *Jugopetrol*, Mira Markovic did not allow the transaction, probably because it would have deprived her of the habitual fur, shawls and other precious presents.

I recall that Dragan Petronijevic of the *Jugoimport SDRP* company was trying to purchase some modern weapons abroad. The story was going about imported arms arriving in *Jugopetrol's* tanker trucks as if it had been oil. At one moment, real oil coming from Iran to Yugoslavia was stopped in Sisak, Croatia; it happened when the war broke out and the Croats con iscated the shipment.

I engaged Guido Scmidt-Chiari, Vice-President of the Austrian bank *Kreditanstalt* and son-in-law of the wealthy international banker Prince Philip of Liechtenstein, to broker the business transaction. I took him to Slobodan Milosevic and *Jugopetrol* Company. It was through him that I obtained 12 million dollars for *Jugopetrol* to buy off the oil stuck at Sisak.

JIMMY CARTER

October 24, 2002

To Dr. Borko Djordjevic

It is a great honor to be awarded the Nobel Peace Prize, and I am touched by your warm congratulations. Rosalynn and I appreciate your support for The Carter Center's work to promote peace, health, and human rights around the world. In a very real sense, you share this tribute with us.

Sincerely,

Jimmy Carter

Dr. Borko Djordjevic
American Academy of Plastic Surgery
1091 North Palm Canyon Drive
Palm Springs, California 92262

Letter by Jimmy Carter

Miodrag Jaksic, Director of PTT "Srbija"

Likewise, I brought about a dozen American congressmen, senators and owners of multinational companies to Serbia/Belgrade so that they could get an insight into the current circumstances and get involved in the privatization process in Serbia's economy. *Philip Morris* (with my mother-in-law as member of the management) wanted to buy the tobacco manufactures in Nis (*Duvanska industrija Nis,* southern Serbia). The envisaged investment amounted to 200 million dollars. Slobodan Milosevic did not allow for it.

His wife Mirjana Markovic declined the offer by the Italian SEPTA Company to privatize Serbia's mobile telephony. General Jovo Popovic managed Mira Markovic's businesses. He financed *Radio Kosava,* the broadcaster run by her daughter Marija Milosevic. In one case, I brokered a deal between the French and Jovo Popovic;

as the General failed to effect payments, the foreigners charged me for the loss of as much as 800,000 Deutsche Mark. They could not know that it was owing to Gen. Popovic that I was left without my red Volkswagen Golf –someone from his team had stolen and resold it.

Miodrag Jaksic, Director of PTT Srbija, did not want to have the state company privatized. In 1991, I brought the Motorola company with the purpose to introduce mobile telephony. This had taken place before Bogoljub Karic did that in Belgrade. The Milosevices turned down *Motorola*. For instance, *Sony* – during the company's peak performance
- wanted to buy *El Nish* (electronic industry).
- No! You can't! You're not offering enough money! – That was the answer by Milosevic-ruled Yugoslavia. He feared losing power once the foreign companies enter the domestic economy. The local Party officials were afraid, too, for *Sony* could deprive them of the power and authority they had enjoyed. In consequence to all those refusals on the part of Slobodan Milosevic, troublesome economic sanctions were imposed on Serbia/Yugoslavia. It was then that I left Serbia and went to the United States.

The five biggest American companies turned down by Milosevic included *Westinghouse, Honeywell* and *General Electric*. He behaved like a racketeering mobster, requesting cash payments to him for his good will to let them do business in Yugoslavia/Serbia.

Many of my own business arrangements failed, too, for I did not want to fall victim to the manipulations by Yugoslav politicians and managements. I wanted to escape compromising myself and involvement in criminal transactions. Whenever I felt a breath of mafia and/or crime, I would cut and run.

*

During the international sanctions imposed on Yugoslavia, the country's economy and the markets exploited in the Balkans, the non-aligned countries (the Third World) and Europe's East just vanished. Despite the embargo, however, the Americans wanted to keep the Serbian economy alive and revive it with fresh and direct investments, through privatization and exports from Serbia.

Milosevic did not show interest. For, he only strived for power and his own survival as a ruler. Obviously, the Serbian 'Vozhd' failed to learn the lesson 'delivered' by Tito, whom the townspeople of Valjevo often called the greatest "Serbian Tsar". Josip Broz democratized Yugoslavia by taking credits/loans and business arrangements from the Americans. He was providing profit to the Americans, and they, in return, gave him decorations and worldwide respectability. Slobodan Milosevic did not want to act likewise; what is more, he was not adroit enough to do so.

Milosevic was a political chameleon. He would change the course of his politics depending on current situation in Serbia and current circumstances on the international scene. He was doing so because he had to struggle for his voters. He was losing control over the people and over the voters, so he resorted to electioneering. The old Party system (Communist/Socialist)[25] which implied governance in enterprises through their directors loyal to the Party had fallen apart, and a new system had not been established to replace it. I was a witness thereof personally.

What I suggested to Slobodan-Buca Prohaska, member of the SPS and Vice-President of Serbian Government, was to launch a campaign and explain to the people the necessity to carry out political changes, privatization and democratization; that was the way to win over the electorate in Milosevic's favor.

– Are you insane? The people won't give up their self-management position and property rights in state-run enterprises – Prohaska said.

At that moment, I realized that the control exerted on the people and property of Yugoslavia was the key to Slobodan Milosevic's power. For that reason he did not accept economic transition and change of ownership over the state possessions. Any success of such processes would lead to his inability to control the people and hold power. What was lacking in Serbia for implementation of a transition by 'bypassing' Milosevic, and which had existed in Slovenia, were independent businessmen and companies.

---

[25] The **Socialist Party of Serbia,** SPS, was founded in 1990 as a merger between the League of Communists of Serbia (led by Slobodan Milosevic) and the Socialist Alliance of the Working People of Serbia (led by Radmila Andjelkovic). – *Translator's note.*

A SCHEME TO TRICK THE NATION

WHEN MILOSEVIC had meanwhile centralized Serbia, introduced police control and para-criminal groups, and developed the largescale/state-run business of smuggling and black market, the American Ambassador Warren Zimmerman informed President George Bush Sr. thereof. He wrote a 'White Book' about Serbia and sent it to the White House. Zimmerman, who spoke Serbian very well and knew the mentality of the Serbs (for he had formerly worked as a secretary in the American Consulate General in Zagreb), portrayed the figures surrounding
Milosevic – from Sainovic to Zebic[26] – as "little Slobas", cloned nationalists and arrogant politicians.

Ambassador Zimmerman was right. In the midst of the country's collapse and devastation of the nation, Slobodan Milosevic got the idea how to trick the Serbs giving himself the appearance of a pronounced nationalist. He uttered the famous sentence, whispered to him by Kosovo-Metohija's Serbs:
– Nobody should beat you!

The message, uttered in Kosovo Polje, was taken as his political creed, i.e. as a symbol of the protective role of the Socialist Party of Serbia spreading on the Serbs all over the region. That is how Milosevic earned the trust of the Serbs in Serbia, Bosnia-Herzegovina, Croatia, Montenegro and diaspora. The people were not aware of the fact that he was not a nationalist but only a manipulator playing on their nationally marked sentiments.

*

On the other hand, however, the United States was preparing to carry out the first successful transition in the Eastern European countries. America wanted the start of the process to take place in Serbia as the economically strongest and politically most receptive in the region. The 72 billion dolars promised in 1992 for the transition of ex-Yugoslavia's biggest companies were still available; in exchange, the economic sanctions imposed on Yugoslavia/Serbia would be lifted. The offer reached the table of each of Serbia's successive prime ministers.

– The Boss has banned and stopped it all! – Vladimir Stambuk[27] told me. He was a man trusted by Slobodan Milosevic.

– Which boss? Slobodan Milosevic or Mira Markovic? – I asked this friend of mine.

– Well, Milosevic – Stambuk was trying to persuade me, although I thought that the communist heroine Dr. Mirjana Markovic was to be blamed for all of it.

Milosevic was a banker, but one who knew nothing about real business. He only proved to be a good manager of black market and smuggling. In early 1990's, he had refused to sell the *Nish Tobacco Industry* to the Americans at normal price, because during the sanctions cigarette-smuggling provided inancial resources to his Party and the Administration.

Some media and some Serbian officials used to claim that *Philip Morris* organized illegal tobacco trade worldwide during the sanctions, the base being in Rotterdam where the company's largest factory operated. Also involved were their plants in Russia, Macedonia, Turkey, Italy, Montenegro and Serbia. The cigarettes would, with changed packaging and bar code, travel round the globe. Newspaper articles about cigarette smuggling claimed that the routes began in Turkey, ran via Macedonia and further to Montenegro and Italy. The production price was 25 percent packet, while the selling price amounted to $5. The profit was enormous. It served the American tobacco lobbies to finance the war in Yugoslavia.

There are people who believe that – provided Milosevic had allowed for the privatization of the – the smuggling business would not have lourished and, consequently, the war would not have erupted. The involved in the cigarette business included the Military Security Agency, State Security Service, the weapons and military equipment manufacturer *Jugoimport* SDPR, military and civil collaborators of the secret police, and even some respectable businessmen, physicians and Swiss dealers. The names mentioned by the media included Vucurevic, Sekulic, Radovanovic and Subotic. A great many people in Belgrade were profiteering on war and cigarettes.

I could see sacks filled with money going to Slobodan Milosevic and his family. *JAT* (Yugoslav Airline) carried these to Cyprus and delivered to *Cyprus Popular Bank*. Rumours operated with an amount of 15 million dollars. I dare claim that the amount was far larger. In order to rule without obstacles, Milosevic needed really big money. The staffers around him were instrumentalized, that is assigned to make money and transport it out of Serbia or take for themselves. For instance, the money seized from state-controlled companies was sent and deposited all around – in Cyprus, Russia, China, even Austria. Doing that, Milosevic acted like a fireman and not a ruler. He kept extinguishing political and war fires yet failed to build a system of state/national protection against disaster.

As swayers of the Serbian state and people, Slobodan Milosevic and Mirjana Markovic feared that the transition by privatization would deprive them of state-controlled factories and state-run communist property which lay at the base of their political power. To Milosevic, loss of money would mean loss of power. In my opinion, Slobodan Milosevic – as the leader of Serbia and head of the F.R. of Yugoslavia –was waging war not to save his country and fellow-nationals, but to save ex-Yugoslavia's billions. Jimmy Carter and Bill Clinton failed to bring peace (in cooperation with the U.N. and European Community/Union) to the territory of the former S.F.R. of Yugoslavia because Milosevic kept waging the war in order to protect his personal power and political authority.

It was in Vienna, Moscow, Singapore, Tokyo, China and Cyprus that Slobodan Milosevic and Mirjana Markovic deposited the capital accumulated in the F.R. of Yugoslavia. One of the Serbian tycoons invested some of that money into purchases of artworks by the greatest Serbian artists and made a collection worth at least a billion euros today.

The famed banker and financial expert Mrs. Borka Vucic phoned to me in 1995 asking for my assistance in the attempt to release four billion dollars of Yugoslavia's profit kept in American banks. The money had been earned by exports of arms, cars, food and movies to the States. She repeatedly told me about the 47 billion German marks of state money in the possession of Slobodan Milosevic and Mirjana Markovic. She deemed it hazardous to safeguard the money in the state treasury and state banks, so she planned to transfer it to Cyprus and further to a Serbo-Russian bank she planned to establish in Moscow. There are still some public figures, including a number of those who used to occupy high posts, that claim Borka Vucic's death in a 2009 car crash to have been a murder; the motive was her familiarity with the hidden locations of the money taken out of the country by the Milosevic family. She was killed by Milosevic's successors from the ranks of DOS[28]. I would not know if she had managed to found a bank in Russia and deposit Serbia's state money therein, but I do know that Dr. Mirjana Markovic has fled to Moscow. The choice of destination was by no means a random one.

The story goes that Dr. Mirjana Markovic, Milosevic's wife, used to buy diamonds in Japan, Singapore and China – for the money of the Serbian state and people. The purchases were carried out by individuals who enjoyed her full trust. Vlada Stambuk could testify on that in public, if he is willing to[29]. As far as I am aware, Mirjana Markovic enjoys the right to political asylum granted to her by Russia; she lives there spending the money from the sale of diamond pieces once bought in Japan, Singapore and China.

Truth is, Milosevic had no vision as to how to exit from the war crisis and carry out the transformation of Serbia into a democratic and capitalist country. Sloba was well aware of the fact that he could win the war and protect his family solely by availing of tremendous amounts of money. When his wife Mira Markovic realized that the goal could not be reached by Milosevic alone, she founded a party of her own, and that was – JUL, i.e. *Jugoslovenska (udruzena) levica*, 'Yugoslav (Allied) Left'. The membership, her comrades, included many directors of Yugoslav/Serbian companies, and they were requested to pay her using the company resources.

According to some voices from political circles, Mrs. Markovic entrusted two men to make money and protect it: they were a Batalovic, director of *Duga Paints and Varnishes Industry*, Mira's sympathizer, and Zoran Todorovic Kundak ('Ri le-Butt'), her favorite. During a business trip to Macedonia, Kundak confessed that he wanted to leave Mira Markovic and JUL because they were forcing Party-led and family-run centralism. Kundak was killed in 1997, and the shooting is said to have been ordered by Mira Markovic, angered by his "betrayal". The story has never been confirmed or proved.

Other 'money-makers' included the Serbian secret police and Special Operations Unit (*JSO – Jedinica za specijalne operacije*), popularly referred to as the 'Red Berets', which co-worked with the Zemun-based drug cartel: they were selling 60 kilograms (132 pounds) to Serbia's youth monthly.

Sloba did not understand that – by organizing the state as a machine that produced private capital – he was actually losing both power and the state. His ruling competences were threatened by the violence into which his wife was drawing him. The people who resisted them most seriously, Vuk and Danica Draskovic, were beaten up. Ivan Stambolic, Sloba's likely competitor in the upcoming 2000 election, was murdered. Thus, it was by his own practise of political violence that Milosevic began to undermine the F.R. of Yugoslavia/Serbia from inside. The couple aspired to have full political control of Yugoslavia and the parties in the country.

The Milosevic-Markovic duo was also accused of triggering off the liquidation of Serbia's Prime Minister Dr. Zoran Djindjic on March 12, 2003; for that purpose, they are said to have engaged the above-mentioned Zemun cartel and some members of the Special Operations Unit.

The opposition led by Zoran Djindjic enjoyed the support of Germany and had the task to overthrow Milosevic. Backed up by the United States and Germany, Djindjic succeeded in doing so, on October 5, 2000. Soon thereafter, he had Milosevic arrested and, not in compliance with the domestic law, extradited to the International Criminal Tribunal for the Former Yugoslavia in The Hague on St. Vitus' Day (*Vidovdan*)[30] of 2001. Slobodan Milosevic died there in 2006. The opposition claimed that the murder of Djindjic was carried out as an act of revenge on the part of Mirjana Markovic.

*

Money was the cause of the disintegration of the Socialist Federal Republic of Yugoslavia: the wealthier republics of Slovenia and Croatia were no longer willing to provide for the less prosperous and underdeveloped regions – Macedonia, Bosnia-Herzegovina and Kosovo-Metohija. Slovenia and Croatia wanted transition, independence and political sovereignty. As President of Serbia,

Slobodan Milosevic – for financial reasons – was not ready to give up Yugoslavia's resources, so he opted for a war. Declining partners from abroad and giving rise to belligerent feelings, the former Yugoslavia was left without three large markets – those in Europe, Russia and the Third World (African and Asian countries, members of the Non-Aligned Movement). Once deprived of the market, you have no production and, consequently, no exports and no profit in foreign currencies.

Milosevic was neither Serbian nor American man. He was a communist, a man lacking national consciousness, one without religious faith/identity. Money and political power – that was all he was interested in. He had renounced the Serbs in Bosnia-Herzegovina and the Serbs in Croatia in order to grab Yugoslavia's property and strengthen his authority in the F.R. of Yugoslavia.

As early as in 1992, Milosevic promised to the Americans that they would privatize the whole of Yugoslavia and Serbia, but then got scared that he himself could lose power once the capital was gone. So he gave up the transition process. He double-crossed the Americans.

It was too late when he understood that NATO was America's and Europe's instrument for the protection of capital and investments of multinational companies all over the globe. When Sloba rejected the investment plan of the New World Order for Yugoslavia/Serbia which was to amount to 70 billion dollars, NATO launched a 78-days' air campaign against us the Serbs.

Owing to the personal avarice of Slobodan Milosevic, Mirjana Markovic and their clique, the Serbian nation was defeated militarily and politically in 1999. Thousands of people were killed and/or wounded by the bombs filled with depleted uranium. Serbia's soil was contaminated to the extent that even today people keep dying of lethal uranium radiation and cancer. Slobodan Milosevic died in the American detention center in The Hague in 2006. His wife, Dr. Mirjana Markovic, had taken flight to Russia in 2003.

Serbia has been turned into an American colony which has been undergoing a process of tearing apart and plundering by way of criminal privatization by individuals who made excessive profits on the war and through state-organized smuggling.

[26] f**Nikola Sainovic** (b. 1948) was one of the leaders of the Socialist Party of Serbia, Serbia's Prime Minister (1993-4) and Deputy Prime Minister of the F.R. of Yugoslavia (1994-2000).

Jovan Zebic (1939-2007), former Vice-Governor of the National Bank of Yugoslavia, was Vice-Premier of Serbia and Minister of Finances (1993, 1994-6) and Vice-President of the Federal Government (1998-2000). Member of the Socialist Party's leadership. – *Translator's note.*

[27] Dr. **Vladimir Stambuk** (1942-2016), professor at Belgrade University, Faculty of Political Sciences, one of the founders of both the Socialist Party of Serbia and Yugoslavia's Left. Friend of Dr. Mirjana Markovic. Member of Serbia's negotiation team at Rambouillet (1999) which preceded the NATO air campaign against Yugoslavia later that year. – *Translator's note.*

[28] **DOS** is the acronym of the Democratic Opposition of Serbia *(Demokratska opozicija Srbije)*, an alliance of 18 parties which defeated Slobodan Milosevic and his Socialist Party in the 2000 general election. Its winning presidential candidate was Dr. Vojislav Kostunica. – *Translator's note.*

[29] Dr. Vladimir Stambuk died in 2016, when the Serbian edition of this book was already in print. – *Translator's note.*

[30] ***Vidovdan*** (St. Vitus Day) is a national holiday and religious feast day in Serbia, celebrated on June 28 (June 15 by Julian calendar) in memory of the Holy Prince Lazar who led the Serbian army in the Battle of Kosovo (1389). More recent historical events of signi icance took place on that day, to mention but a few: the 1914 assassination of the Austro-Hungarian Archduke Franz Ferdinand in Sarajevo which triggered off World War I; the Cominform condemnation of Yugoslavia's communist leaders (1948); Slobodan Milosevic's Gazimestan Speech (1989) within the observation of the 6th centenary of the Battle of Kosovo; Croatia reduced the constitutional status of the Serbs in the Republic to one of an ethnic minority (1990). – *Translator's note.*

THE FRIGHTENED SERB

IN THOSE DAYS OF WARFARE, Dr. Radovan Karadzic was a healthy Serbian nationalist, poet, intellectual... but, like Milosevic, a *hajduk* in politics. Aggressive, often intolerant, much too stubborn, conceding only when cornered. Radovan Karadzic was under constant control by Slobodan Milosevic. He would try to break free now and then, yet unsuccessfully. He was so scared by Milosevic that after meeting the man or a phone talk with him he would literally tear his hair out of despair. And chew his nails. He feared Milosevic, for the man humiliated him whenever they talked.

It was out of personal vanity that Milosevic came into conflict with Radovan. For, at Pale he had been taught a lesson in democracy. Namely, Slobodan was present at the session of the Republic of Srpska Assembly when the membership of this body discussed Vance-Owen Peace Plan (VOPP) to reject it in the end. He had been persuading Radovan to discontinue the debate, for he could see that the delegates opposed the plan. And Radovan told him:

– Slobodan, these delegates have been elected by the people and they are saying what the people think. And so they shall vote. That is democracy!

In the night of May 5-6, 1993, the Parliament of the Republic of Srpska rejected VOPP, in spite of the previous (May 2) consent of Karadzic who had in Athens initialed the paper "with reserve". Together with the whole political leadership of Yugoslavia and the Greek PM Konstantinos Mitsotakis, Milosevic came to Pale in person to af irm the plan. However, the rejection was incited by Ratko Mladic rather than Karadzic. It was through a back door and morning fog that Milosevic left the place of his greatest humiliation. That is why on this occasion the President of Serbia called the President of the Republic of Srpska "a drunken gambler".

Via the Government of Serbia and Zoran Lilic[31], Milosevic sent Karadzic a message that "the citizens of the F.R. of Yugoslavia shall not be taken hostages by any leader". Karadzic was not prepared for the new form of a struggle. Deprived of Milosevic's backup, he did not wish to lose the approval of the nation:

– I think that the people in Serbia accurately feel what is going on –in their hearts. We are not angry. You know, there is a saying about mother's right to slap her child while the child is forbidden to slap the mother. Though, some stupid stories have been heard over there about the Bosnian Serbs rising against the Serbs of Serbia. We would rather hang ourselves committing suicide than turn against Serbia. – That is what Radovan said.

*

After his first encounters with Milosevic, Karadzic held Serbia's leader in high esteem. Some claim, because he was one of Milosevic's 'yes-men' for a couple of years. Joseph Biden (Chairman of the Senate Judicial Committee 1987-95) shared with me his recollections of his first encounter with Dr. Radovan Karadzic which had been facilitated by no one else but Slobodan Milosevic:

The first time I went there was in April 1993, for a long, three-hour meeting with Mr. Milosevic. At one moment he said:
- Would you like to talk to Radovan Karadzic?
- Well, I thought you don't control him.
- I don't.

This was happening at 11 p.m. He dialed his phone and ifteen minutes later a man appeared on the staircase with hair I wish I myself had, with a mind I'm happy not to have and a demeanor I wouldn't wish anyone.

Karadzic was literally dashing. He came into the room, sat beside Milosevic and said:
- Mr. President, I apologize for being late.
And I glanced at Milosevic, saying:
- No control, eh?

On the wall of Karadzic's office, a picture of General Draza Mihailovic[32] was hanging. They both looked like losers. Karadzic's demeanor was like that whenever Milosevic rang him up. I personally heard – over the speakerphone – Slobodan's threats addressed to Radovan:

– I'm gonna take your army. You won't have what you need to wage a war and defend the people! You're undone!

He called him names, telling him that he, Doctor Karadzic, was a shame for the Serbian people. Radovan would just nod and say:

– Yes, Boss! I understand, Boss!

In his relationship with Milosevic, Karadzic had two acute problems he was not able to solve.

Firstly, there was the issue of inancing the Republic of Srpska and its president, i.e. Karadzic. As Milosevic was the one who provided money for Karadzic and the Serbs in Bosnia-Herzegovina, the President of the Republic of Srpska was dependent on him. What is more, Milosevic was spreading the rumor about Karadzic being a gambler who was losing hundreds of thousands of Deutsche Mark in Belgrade's casinos, especially the one at the *Intercontinental* Hotel. The gossip was supposed to depict Karadzic as a figure incapable of leading the Republic of Srpska either economically or politically.

Secondly, there was General Ratko Mladic who did not represent the Republic of Srpska but the (former) Yugoslav National Army. The general was not under Karadzic's command, so he led an army of his own waging a war of his own – following the orders coming from Belgrade. Milosevic's threat about taking over the army in Bosnia was terribly painful to Karadzic. Karadzic did not lead the army, so he depended on the vulgar Milosevic and the impulsive Mladic. Radovan had planned to create an army force of the Republic of Srpska, but Ratko Mladic 'took it away' from him, for the General wanted to revive his version of the YNA.

There was a period when Karadzic and Mladic did not talk to each other. Karadzic did not issue any military commands. And Mladic, as a quick-tempered man, committed crimes which have led to The Hague Tribunal where President Radovan Karadzic and the Serbian people on the whole have been put to trials. Moreover, Ratko Mladic was trading the ammunition from the YNA arsenals and handling huge amounts of money.

Owing to Milosevic and Mladic, the number one of the Republic of Srpska lost authority with both the military and the people, for he was not the commander of his army. Radovan truly hated Ratko Mladic.

When overwhelmed with anger, he would throw Biljana Plavsic[33] and Nikola Koljevic[34] out of his office. It was his fear speaking. Momcilo

Krajisnik[35] was the only one spared of his yelling.

It was only after the year 1994 that Karadzic managed to (re)organize the Army of the Republic of Srpska, install his own trustworthy men therein and take over the control over the armed force. General Mladic was marginalized therethrough.

Financially, Karadzic and the Republic of Srpska gained independence only in 1994, when aid came from the Serbian Orthodox Church in diaspora, the Greek Orthodox Church, the (Serbian-American) Serbian National Defense Council *(Srpska narodna odbrana)* and the Serbian National Federation *(Srpski narodni savez)* in the U.S.A..

*

On three occasions (in 1994, 1995 and 1996) Karadzic authorized me in writing to represent him and the Republic of Srpska – politically and in business affairs – in the United States, United Nations and The Hague Tribunal.

As I owned the *Atalanta* Company in Switzerland, I resorted to its inclusion in the imports of medical equipment and pharmaceuticals to the Republic of Srpska. In 1995, I brought a group of Americans from the KPMG trust to Pale headed by the Director of KPMG for Europe, and Mr. Jim Triguero, Washington's prominent inancial advisor. They ascertained what was suitable for privatization, enlisting the tobacco industry at Banja Luka, oil refinery, lumber industry, state-run postal services and agroindustrial combines.

As early as in 1994, I brought the *Motorola* Company in order to have them introduce mobile telephony in the Republic of Srpska. It had been before Radovan's younger brother Luka Karadzic made an arrangement of his own at Pale. The program of the cellular telephone network envisaged a growth in the number of subscribers from current 10,000 to 100,000 within the first five years, and a revenue of 454 million Deutsche Mark in the same period. The investment costs deduced, Srpska would have gained a profit of 234 million marks.

РЕПУБЛИКА СРПСКА
ПРЕДСЕДНИК РЕПУБЛИКЕ
САРАЈЕВО

12 October 1995

TO WHOM IT MAY CONCERN

This is to confirm that Borko Djordjevic, MD PhD, passport no.: 035192453, USA, singly, and Atalanta S.A., of Geneva, jointly, are authorized by the Republic of Srpska to, exclusively, arrange with a foreign partner or partners, a joint venture licence for paging and cellular telephone system in the Republic of Srpska.

Dr Radovan Karadzic
President, Republic of Srpska

Karadzic's authorization of Dr. Djordjevic re the cellular telephony

I was telling Radovan that the country which completed transition process on the Balkans *first* was to be very welcome with Americans and able to establish excellent political relations and cooperation with the United States of America. I tried, with Radovan, to carry out privatization in the Republic of Srpska. In 1996, the conditions were suitable, for Srpska had its Directorate for Privatization and Development, while a draft Company Privatization Bill was under way.

As a sign of good will and good intention, the Americans presented the Karadzic family with a 50,000-dollar worth watch. But that did not suffice to carry out privatization in the Republic of Srpska. Like Milosevic, Karadzic too declined the offer made by *Motorola* and –through his brother – started business in the field of mobile telephony with some double-dealers from the United States.

I had the authorization by the Republic of Srpska to bring companies that would build the paging system and develop cigarette production and distribution. I never charged any brokerage to Radovan Karadzic. Except that Karadzic 'sold' me a building site for a weekend-cottage at Pale, but I never set my foot down on it.

It seems that such inancial and political arrangements failed to suit the Karadzic family which at that time ruled the Republic of Srpska.

Alija Izetbegovic

The last authorization issued to me by Radovan Karadzic was dated July 1, 1996; it concerned cooperation with The Hague Tribunal and the American jurist Alan Dershowitz whom he wanted to hire as his defence attorney. If Serbia had payed $ 3.000,000 to Alan Dershowitz for the defense of Radovan Karadzic, the Bosnian-Serb leader and the other Serb detainees in The Hague would have been saved.

*

In the capacity of the President of the Republic of Srpska, Dr. Karadzic asked – via the Serbian lobby – Bill Clinton, head of the United States, to gather all the leaders involved in the Bosnian War in a conference room in Washington, D.C. for a peace agreement. Karadzic believed that – at a meeting with Clinton, Tudjman, Izetbegovic, Yeltsin and Milosevic – a solution to all problems could be reached, one regarding not Bosnia only, but also the Republic of Srpska Krajina in Croatia.

РЕПУБЛИКА СРПСКА
ПРЕДСЕДНИК РЕПУБЛИКЕ
С А Р А Ј Е В О

REPUBLIC OF SRPSKA
PRESIDENT OF THE REPUBLIC
S A R A J E V O

Power of Attorney

I, Radovan Karadzic, hereby authorize and empower Allen Dershowitz in fact to make a special appearance before the International Criminal Tribunal for Former Yugoslavia (the "ICTY") to challenge the validity and sufficiency of the rules and procedures of the ICTY.

Radovan Karadzic
Dated: July 1, 1996
Pale, Republica Srpska

Karadzic's authorization of Alan Dershowitz for the ICTY

– Clinton still considering the proposal – that was a piece of news headlined across the United States in the fall of 1993.

The several most prominent members of the Serb community in the United States who provided greatest support to Karadzic included Slobodan Pavlovic, Michael Djordjevic, Milan Panic and Branko Tupanjac. They were all 'rewarded' later by the right to develop their respective businesses across the Republic of Srpska. Expectedly enough, the Americans were aware of the Serbian Americans financially supporting the Bosnian-Serb leader, yet this was tolerated and controlled by the CIA and the U.S. Embassy in Belgrade.

Like Milosevic, Karadzic too was involved in black market deals, selling of the YNA's weapons, oil smuggling and cigarette trafficking. He offered me to get into the oil and cigarette business, but I declined repeatedly. I did not want to fall into disgrace with the U.S.A.; particularly, I would not have been happy with the FBI or the CIA inquiries/investigations, for the problems of the kind could have threatened my job of plastic surgeon in California.

Radovan Karadzic knew that I had once been 'Tito's Communist' and, for a while, adherent of Slobodan Milosevic. We did share something in common, and that was – Yugoslavia. We loved the country. And we lost it: I lost it while living over there, in America, and he lost it at home, in Bosnia.

– I wanted Yugoslavia to survive. Yugoslavia was a country one could comfortably live in – Radovan once told me in confidence, at Pale.

To what extent Radovan felt to be a Yugoslav can be seen from the fact that he dedicated his first collection of verse to Yugoslavia's lifelong president, Josip Broz Tito, whom he presented a copy of the book. At the same time, the episode testifies to his preoccupation with politics in youth. His high political ambition was affirmed in later years: he became President of the Republic of Srpska which officially stayed unrecognized for a long time yet highly visible as a state.

Our encounters at Pale during the war allowed little time for light or personal conversation. Each dialogue would start and end in political subjects. On one such occasion, I asked Radovan whether Yugoslavia could survive in Bosnia at least.

– The war could have been avoided if Izetbegovic had not been arming the Muslims. The real overture to the war was Izetbegovic's decision on general mobilization of April 4, 1992. According to the Constitution, he was not entitled to do that without consent of the Serbs, yet he did it. I phoned him and warned him that he was making a terrible mistake. I asked him: "Why have you done that, Alija? Do you realize what's gonna happen when the Muslims take up arms? The Croats will take up arms, too. And, do you realize what the Serbs' response is going to be?" Alija Izetbegovic agreed with my remark, but said, in cold voice, that it was too late to cancel the decision. On that night of April fourth-to- fifth 1992, violence spread across Sarajevo. The Muslims started the war and we could not stop it anymore – this is Radovan's account of the war's outbreak.

Then I asked more questions, referring to the Muslim claims that they had every reason to go to war, for they were frightened by the Serbs and the Yugoslav National Army, YNA.

– The Serbs didn't trust the YNA either. From time to time, the YNA would try to establish buffer zones between us and the Muslims, but it rarely supported us the Serbs. It was exposed to constant attacks by the Muslims. Its preoccupation was how to withdraw rather than how to help us. Worse even: the YNA saw the Serbs as nationalists and anti-Communists. To them, there was no difference between Izetbegovic and Tudjman and Karadzic. – Why didn't you struggle for peace? – I reformulated the question.

– We did our utmost to prevent the war in Bosnia from breaking out.

We have ample and hard evidence on that. We did accept the Lisbon Agreement[36], the European plan of partitioning. I did accept Vance-Owen Plan in Athens. True, our Parliament rejected it later, but the fact is, I'd accepted it.

Karadzic continued:

– Later, I accepted Bosnia's separation from Yugoslavia. That was the greatest risk I'd ever taken in my lifetime. That decision turned us, the Serbs, into a minority people in our own country. But I accepted that in order to avoid war. The most saddening thing of all is the fact that the Lisbon Agreement was to the geatest degree similar to the Dayton Accords adopted four years later. So what had we been fighting for over the four years? – Karadzic wondered aloud.

He realized that I reasoned as an American and that I was a good and soulful Serb. It was probably due to these qualities that he entrusted me with bringing Jimmy Carter to Pale. My first official contact with Karadzic had taken place as early as in January 1994. We became close in Geneva, where I lived with my family for a while and where he used to come for negotiations. Aware of my contacts around the United States, he asked for my help.

---

[31] **Zoran Lilic** (b. 1953) was President of Serbia's Paliament (January-June 1993), President of the Federal Republic of Yugoslavia (June 1993-June 1997) and Vice-President of the Federal Government of Yugoslavia (May 1998-August 1999). – *Translator's note.*

[32] *Dragoljub Draza Mihailovic* (1893-1946) was a colonel in the pre-second-worldwar Royal Yugoslav Army who, when the Axis forces overran Yugoslavia in 1941, tried to gather troops scattered in the mountains and organize guerrilla units under the name of "Chetnik Detachments of the Yugoslav Army" later renamed as the Yugoslav Army in the Homeland. The Communist regime of the postwar Yugoslavia put him to trial and sentenced to death for high treason and war crimes. After execution by a iring squad, the location of his grave was kept secret and has remained so to the present day. According to a ruling by the Supreme Court of Cassation, the highest appellate court in Serbia, on May 14, 2015, Mihailovic's verdict was annulled. The Serbs are still divided over General Mihailovic's military and ethical pro ile. Karadzic belongs to those who reject the communist interpretation (that Mihalovic was a Fascist collaborator) and emphasize his loyalty to the commissioned-officer oath and royal tradition of the Serbs/Serbia, accounting for his unwillingness to fight determinedly against the Germans by the fact that German retaliations implied killing of 100 civilians for a single German soldier dead, and 50 people for one wounded German - which Mihailovic tried to avoid by relative inactivity. The U.S. President Harry S. Truman posthumously awarded Mihailovic Legion of Merit for the cooperation in the 1944 Operation Halyard (successful rescue of hundreds of downed airmen of the Allies). – *Translator's note.*

[33] **Dr. Biljana Plavsic** (b. 1930) – A highly accomplished scientist and university professor (biology) in Sarajevo who succeded Radovan Karadzic in the office of the President of the Republic of Srpska (July 19, 1996-Nov. 4, 1998). Prior to the war and after the first multi-party elections, she was Serb member in the Presidency of the Socialist Republic of Bosnia-Herzegovina (1990-2). During the war, she was Vice-President of the Republic of Srpska (one of the two) and member of the Supreme Command of the RS Army. – *Translator's note.*

[34] **Dr. Nikola Koljevic** (1936-1997) – University professor, translator and essayist, one of the foremost Shakespear scholars in the former Yugoslavia. Like Dr. Plavsic, he was Serb member in the Presidency of the Socialist Republic of Bosnia-Herzegovina (1990-2), then (the other) Vice-President of the Republic of Srpska. – *Translator's note.*

[35] **Momcilo Krajisnik** (b. 1945) – Along Karadzic, co-founder of the Bosnian-Serb Serbian Democratic Party; first speaker of the National Assembly of the Republic of Srpska (1991-6); first post-war Serb Member of the Presidency of Bosnia-Herzegovina (1996-8). – *Translator's note.*

[36] **Lisbon Agreement** is another name of the Carrington-Cutilheiro Plan which envisaged division into Bosniak, Serb and Croat cantons; after tri-partite signing of it in March 18, 1992, Alija Izetbegovic withdrew his signature owing to Warren Zimmerman's promise that the United States would recognize Bosnia as an independent state. – *Translator's note.*

SECRET CORRESPONDENCE

The correspondence between Jimmy Carter and Radovan Karadzic –directly and with my help – included 44 letters/messages, while the correspondence through the lawyer Tom Hanley and Harry Barnes of the Carter Center counted an additional hundred – within just one year of our work.

I myself exchanged some 450 messages of all sorts and various content. I addressed the Bosnian Serbs in a familiar tone, for instance: "Dear Radovan, Dear Momcilo and other heroes of our time…" In most cases, my messages were sent through my medical offices at Santa Barbara, California, and Igalo, Montenegro, for these were open round the clock. Wherever worldwide I happened to be, I communicated with Karadzic via the two offices. I sent messages that concerned our peace-related activities, but also some confidential or publicly available information from Washington, D.C. about the American views of the situation and their preparations for some activities in Bosnia-Herzegovina.

These documents included the shorthand-taken testimony of Jimmy Carter before the U.S. Senate of June 14, 1995. He was interrogated by General John Galvin, former Supreme Allied Commander of NATO. Carter was answering him and ten other senators who questioned him, presenting an account of how the cease-fire in Bosnia had been accomplished and the course of his negotiations with Radovan Karadzic. These 35-page shorthand notes are now a historic document of the Senate about war and peace in Bosnia-Herzegovina.

A large portion of my information for Radovan Karadzic was classi ied as "confidential" or "in person" or "for your personal info only". The "confidential" papers included the letters Radovan Karadzic sent to Bill Clinton through my channel, as well as the indirect responses by the U.S. President when Bill Clinton supported Radovan Karadzic and his peace-aimed efforts, in July-

August 1995. The latter implied Clinton's principled recognition of the Bosnian-Serb leader, despite his criticism, yet I take them as a great success of my own.

Officially, I was introduced to Bill Clinton by a lawyer who sent in a letter to the White House. In late January 1995, I had an encounter with the former U.S. President Gerald Ford at Palm Springs whom I informed about the peace initiative and relaxing of the situation in BH. Though himself a Republican, he supported me and Jimmy Carter's peace efforts. Upon receiving an answer from Bill Clinton, I could boast contacts with five American Presidents.

As to the expenditures related to the engagement of the lawyer Tom Hanley and other associates, I was personally covering them. From November 1994 to April 1995, we only spent 150,000 Deutsche Mark on the following: 15 lights and business trips to the United States, three domestic lights inside the States, travels around Europe and visits to to the U.N. agencies in Geneva, telephone and fax contacts, printing of letters/brochures, documentation processing, plus various administrative/office activities.

The processes surrounding me in Bosnia/Republic of Srpska, Montenegro and Serbia absorbed me to a large degree, so I participated in historic events. I worked hard and did not expect or have any inancial and/or political gains. To me, all of it was 'spiritual food'. To help the Serbian people was my sole objective. For the sake of helping Radovan Karadzic and the Serbian people I established companies – in the United States (*Whitehouse Financial Co.)* and Switzerland (Atalanta S.A.) – on behalf of the Republic of Srpska, so that pharmaceuticals and medical equipment could be supplied for the wounded and the illness-stricken.

*

When the crisis over the French hostages emerged, in 1995, I happened to be in France. I called Carter to ask for his personal intervention in order to tranquillize the militant passions, but Karadzic was not willing to further politicize the issue. Radovan thought that the case was one of prisoners of wars and not hostages. I mediated for an interview with him by Roy Gutman of

Newsday (the daily collaborated with the Human Rights Watch). In May 1995, I arranged Karadzic's interviews for the CNN and Associated Press. In those days, I was still striving to keep Jimmy Carter involved in the BH negotiations and in contact with Radovan Karadzic. For, Radovan trusted Carter, seeking –through him – better understanding on the part of the Contact Group representatives, with regard to the peace plan(s). It was owing to me and Jimmy Carter (with whom Karadzic maintained regular correspondence until end of September 1995) that the American press published articles and news on their exchange of letters which was evidence of Radovan's resolution to work for peace.

On the other hand, Carter made some efforts to resume his role of a peacemaker in the negotiations, but for such an engagement he needed an approval by President Bill Clinton. However, the Americans were only buying time with Radovan Karadzic, for they had been preparing a peace settlement with Slobodan Milosevic and not the Bosnian-Serb leader – as was eventually seen at Dayton.

The other reason why Karadzic engaged me lay in his belief that I –with the American help – could release him from the ties with Slobodan Milosevic! As early as in the winter of 1994, Karadzic was emboldened enough to refuse some of Milosevic's proposals. At a moment of anger, he told Milosevic:

– Belgrade need not support me!

When Karadzic realized that Milosevic had controlled him, taking advantage thereof for his own political goals, he picked up steam and sought a road to peace by himself. During the negotiations with Jimmy Carter, he proved to be a genuine politician and diplomat. He was capable of conceding when necessary. Karadzic was the one who had mastered all the maps and data on the BH territories. He would stand in front of a map pointing with a stick towns and villages while imparting, with computer-like precision, data/percentages of their ethnic composition and numbers of the Serbs/Croats/Muslims. He proposed cantoning of Bosnia based on the ethnic structures. Radovan and I drew such maps together.

Visitors to Pale included most prominent figures such as Jimmy Carter, Carl Bildt, Yasushi Akashi... They would be welcomed by Radovan wearing a modest suit, and his wife Ljiljana in *Chanel* clothes. For the Karadzic family, visits by the world-renowned politicians were the only social occasions, for they themselves could not go abroad due to the economic and political sanctions.

President Carter's peace efforts earned Karadzic's extraordinary appreciation. There was much criticism addressed to Carter because of his visits to Pale and the guest status with Karadzic. Radovan was well aware of the risk for Carter's respectability the visits could enhance. One question deserves an answer: Why did Carter expose himself to the attacks coming from the U.S. Senate or the French Prime Minister Alain Juppé? Did he deliberately support an aggressor, tyrant and criminal? Certainly not! The simple explanation reads: Carter trusted Karadzic!

The encounter of the two men partially altered the attitude of the Contact Group and of the U.S. officials toward the Republic of Srpska, for before it took place they had completely ignored the Serbian leaders on the Bosnian side of the Drina river. Once such visits happened, the Americans relaxed their stance. Owing to Radovan Karadzic, a road to peace was opened.

It was only when he found himself facing the increasing intolerance of the official Belgrade and Slobodan Milosevic in person that the President of the Republic of Srpska sent an open letter to Milosevic. It happened toward the Dayton conference, on August 8, 1995. In the letter, Karadzic accused Milosevic of being a dishonest fighter for the Serbian interests, that is, of being a liar and a cheater. Yet aware of Milosevic representing the Serbdom internationally and at Dayton, Karadzic appealed on him to save the Serbs on both sides of the Drina river.

What Karadzic had achieved (opening an avenue to the United States and peace settlement) was taken advance of by Slobodan Milosevic: he pushed Radovan aside and himself set out to sign the Dayton Accords on the end of the war in Bosnia.

Noteworthy are the words I heard repeatedly by Zvonimir Trajkovic, who used to counsel both Milosevic and Karadzic:

– Karadzic is a man different from Milosevic. He is a great person, pro-West oriented, who always had a vision of his country and of the future.

To conclude, Radovan – at the time the United States and Jimmy Carter expected him to meet the related requirements – lacked the capacity to become the genuine leader of all Serbs. Deep inside, he was suffering of the 'Slobodan Milosevic syndrome'. The Americans sensed that and chose Milosevic to appear as the victor.

A loser in the game, he was soon (as soon as on July 24, 1995) accused by the same apparent patrons from the States – of alleged war crimes commited by his outlawed generals and other military commanders of the RS Army. He quarreled with Ratko Mladic when he realized that the general had committed crimes on his (Karadzic's) behalf. And he took an arrogant stance to The Hague Tribunal, saying:

- I'm not going before the kangaroo court!
- Do go there, Rasho, hire the lawyers, stand trial while free, tell the truth about the Serbs to the world – I was trying to persuade him.

At the U.S. Embassy in Sarajevo I started to negotiate about the Americans giving up apprehension of Karadzic. I talked to Carl Bildt about Karadzic leaving the presidential post in the Republic of Srpska but not being taken to The Hague. In the fall of 1995 Bildt was stricken by fever and I joked about contracting AIDS in Bosnia. Bildt did not respond at all. I repeated my suggestion:

– Let Karadzic resign from the presidency over the Party, too, but do not take him to The Hague.

A representative of Carter's attended the meeting, as did Robert Baer of CIA, Richard Holbrooke's man who supported my proposals. Carl Bildt answered brie ly:

– I'll see! I doubt that can happen?! – the European peacemaker for Bosnia and a Bosnian 'son-in-law' was pessimistic about it.

A group of us, Radovan's friends, were doing our best to get guarantees for his surrender. Karadzic gave me a written authorization to negotiate on his behalf. What is more, we made one more speci ic offer. And I will never be able to suppress the memory of that long, distressing conversation with Carl Bildt in the capacity of the High Representative for BH. He told me:

– Mr. Djordjevic, Karadzic's destiny has already been decided on!Instead of being saved de initely, Karadzic committed political suicide. Unable to withstand the pressures by Slobodan Milosevic and the international community, he gave in on June 26, 1996. On that day he submitted his resignation from the office of the President of the R.S. in a signed and seal-veri ied letter to the

High Representative Carl Bildt. The text read:

"In compliance with the provisions of Paragraph 3, Article 40 of the Constitution of the Republic of Srpska which entitles the President of the Republic to decide who of the Vice-Presidents of the Republic should substitute him in case of temporary inability to hold the office, I hereby appoint Vice-President Biljana Plavsic as of June 30, 1996."

In that year, 1996, I left for the United States, and Radovan Karadzic went underground. As has been known, he had signed an agreement of non-aggression with Richard Holbrooke. "Rasho from the Mountains" (Raso sa planine) was in hiding, and the Americans were not too eager to get him surrendered. From the States, I kept in touch with Radovan solely through his personal secretary Jovan Zametica. Although the Americans were aware of the fact, the FBI and the CIA invariably pressed me to dislose the exact whereabouts of Radovan Karadzic. They refrained from arresting Karadzic, yet all the time they wanted to know where he was and whom he contacted. I did not know that, and I did not want to know, for Radovan Karadzic was now a subject of high politics between the United States and Serbia. It was recommendable to take care and not go anywhere close to the man. Surplus information about him could endanger my life, my family and my job.

RAY CARTER PROTECTING RADOVAN

THE HAGUE'S ICTY and its Chief Prosecutor Carla del Ponte relied on three teams assigned to locate and capture Radovan Karadzic. One was headed by an American, one by an Englishman and the third by a Frenchman. Personally, Carla del Ponte was eager to have Radovan arrested, for that would ensure world fame to her, as well as political credibility. Her 'hunters' made about a dozen attempts to catch Karadzic. At one point, he was offered surrender under the conditions he himself would lay down.

Del Ponte's investigators from the Section for War Crimes came to see me, too, in order to interrogate me and thus find out Karadzic's hiding place.

– I don't know where Radovan Karadzic is. Ask those who are guarding him! – I answered.

Following his last appearance in public, on July 19, 1996, various media reported Karadzic being seen in a number of places: in front of a special bunker at Han Pijesak (small town in eastern Bosnia/RS), in Belgrade, in Montenegro – with his relatives, in Srbinje/Foca (southeastern Bosnia/RS) and the nearby Perucica virgin forest, at Pale, in the monasteries of the Holy Mountain/ Mt. Athos (Greece) plus some locations in Greece, Russia, Czech Republic. Prvoslav Davinic, a well informed diplomat at the U.N. (and Minister of Defense later), told me once:

Raymond Ray Carter

– While The Hague was chasing Radovan, I used to meet him in his own house. He was not on the run, he was at Pale all the time!

Interestingly, the CIA was pressing upon me in 1997 and 1998 demanding that I find Karadzic. At that time, the U.S. wanted Slobodan Milosevic 'dethroned' and Radovan Karadzic to resume his role of the all-Serb leader. Simultaneously, the Montenegrin leaders Milo Djukanovic and Vukasin Maras turned against Milosevic and thus became America's favorites.

The CIA also interrogated me concerning the activities and plans of Slobodan Milosevic, his family and ministers. Those were difficult questions I could not answer. For, sensing the end of his rule, Milosevic had 'built' a 'security wall' around him so that the CIA proved incapable of spying on him or surveillance/tapping. So they wanted some external sources of information on both Milosevic and Karadzic in hiding.

It was only five years later that I learned who had protected Karadzic against arrest. Namely, for three whole years, Karadzic used hiding places in the environs of Pale, protected by Ray Carter, spearhead of Carla del Ponte's Team One. As he himself told me, the U.S. gave him the task to "help Radovan Karadzic escape locationing".

In those years, Raymond Ray Carter was a security expert in high esteem. He was exterior security chief of France, owner of the *Homeland Security Agency,* advisor to Jacques Chirac. He was in charge of the security on French airports. His books include those on jiu-jitsu and on the chase for Radovan Karadzic. As he admitted to me, he was helping Radovan's wife Ljiljana Zelen meet the fugitive in secret or hide him so as to escape the actual chase by Del Ponte's agents. To put it clearly: Ray Carter protected Radovan against being caught, while chasing and capturing the other individuals wanted by The Hague Tribunal.

Raymond H.A. Carter was born in Rochefort-sur-Mer on April 17, 1955. He grew up and attended schools in France. After beginning a military career, he was awarded degrees that concern several scientific/scholarly domains: aeronautics (1989), criminology (Bordeaux), philosophy in public law (Nice) and philosophy in international penal law (Poitier). As a teenager, Carter began training karate and aikido to become certi ied teacher of the martial arts, self-defense and combat techniques and author of five books in the fields.

Carter's professional career as a gendarme began in the rank of a non-commissioned officer in 1973. Owing to his skills and education, he reached the rank of gendarmerie major in a task force brigade. In late 1990's, he commanded a mobile platoon securing the residence of President Jacque Chirac. Then he transferred to the air branch and went to work in Africa (airplane and helicopter pilot, light instructor and leader of airborne rescue missions and criminal investigations).

I met Ray Carter in France in mid-1990's, unaware of his upcoming mission in Bosnia-Herzegovina. He told me about his aikido instructorship in Sarajevo in mid-1980's. In late 1880's he met aikido master Ljubomir Vracarevic in Belgrade; with this famous martial artist he improved the techniques of knife attack and defense. So I appeared to be his third friend from ex-Yugoslavia with whom he cooperated and met for some time to come.

In the year 1999, just before the NATO campaign against Yugoslavia, Captain Ray Carter was appointed member of Foreign Operations Unit under NATO and got a duty in Yugoslavia. Subsequently to the bombardments of Serbia and Montenegro, he joined the U.N. Mission in Bosnia-Herzegovina. In 2000, he was commander of the international police task force with High Commissioner's cabinet in Sarajevo, where he was superior to 1647 cops from 46 countries.

Carter was the liaison officer of the SFOR[37] for the ICTY linked with the SFOR's task force in charge of apprehending major war criminals, their protection after arrest and delivery to the local office of the Tribunal before their transfer to The Hague.

When The Hague's Chief Prosecutor Carla del Ponte appointed Raymond Carter the head of TIFU, the Tribunal's international unit tracking the ICTY's suspects and undertaking anti-terrorist operations, fighting organized crime etc. Carter's duty was to plan and organize hunt for, locating and capture of Dr. Radovan Karadzic, Gen. Ratko Mladic, Momcilo Krajisnik and other Serb indictees.

The lying squad member Ray Carter has published his recollections of our encounter and talks with regard to Radovan Karadzic:

"At the time I headed the Tracking, Intelligence and Fugitive Unit of The Hague Tribunal which I had founded upon the request by Mrs. Carla del Ponte, I was informed that we could meet Dr. Borko Djordjevic who came from Serbia and lived in the U.S.A. in connection with Mr. Radovan Karadzic dossier. I was informed that he had earlier personally known him and got him introduced to President Jimmy Carter. This encounter with Doctor Borko took place in 2002. I lew to the United States in order to meet him. We did meet and discuss Dr. Radovan Karadzic dossier. Personally, I have nothing against Karadzic or any war criminal at large, but I was then required to search for him and a few other alleged Serb war criminals involved in crimes against humanity, genocide and war crimes within ex-Yugoslavia. We managed – with my team made up of men from different countries – to capture 15 of them within two-years' work and actions of my unit, but not Radovan Karadzic."

It appears he was very good in his cop role, for The Hague's Chief Prosecutor Carla del Ponte personally summoned him – through the French Minister of Interior Michèle Alliot-Marie – to be one of her staff in the ICTY. Carter was appointed Del Ponte's special adviser, who took care of her security, but also of the destiny of the detained indictees at the Tribunal.

As I have found out through my confidential source at Pale, during the period 2002-4, Raymond Carter located Radovan Karadzic in Foca (southeastern Bosnia).

He protected Karadzic against being located or caught by the Tribunal's 'hunters', Bosnian police or mafia, Croatian secret service, as well as the German and British intelligence (BND and MI6 respectively). Even the Italians sent out their own squads to attack and search Karadzic's house at Pale where his wife Ljiljana and the family of his daughter Sonja lived. It was a great trauma for Karadzic's family. Radovan was not caught, for Ray Carter had timely warned Ljiljana Karadzic to hide Radovan out of the house. Thus, he moved to Foca and lived in the outpatient clinic there.

However, Ray Carter does not want to admit this ever happened; his own account of the events is different:

"I have never met President Radovan Karadzic. I searched for him with the special squad of my unit. It was extremely difficult, on the ground especially, for the Balkans is so mountainous and impenetrable. Although I did try several times, I never came to know Mr. Radovan Karadzic. I did come to know some members of his family, particularly Mrs. Ljiljana. It was not my duty to save Radovan Karadzic from his pursuers or hired guns, but to protect him and let him stay alive so that he could appear in the International Court and plead his case and his role in the war. On this task I was exposed to life danger. Zemun's mafia clan was after me and Carla del Ponte, intent to liquidate us. Thank God, we have managed to stay alive and not fall victims to that mafia clan."

At that time, and not only due to the five-million-dollars bounty but due to his political signi icance for the control over the territory of Bosnia-Herzegovina and the former Yugoslavia, Karadzic was the number one fugitive and prey.

His guard Raymond Carter never personally told me who ordered and/or assisted him to protect Radovan Karadzic from detention and transfer to The Hague Tribunal, but I sense it was in the political interest of the United States and the CIA. The Americans saved Karadzic from being located and arrested – in order to hold him in control and exploit him as a major political figure in their diplomatic battles for global domination.

Obviously, the Bosnian-Serb leader Dr. Karadzic was not located and arrested over the three years (2002-5) during which Raymond Carter commanded the unit in charge of pursuing the indictees by The Hague Tribunal. Neither was he assassinated, although many – as Ray Carter himself said – wanted Karadzic dead.

– On the ground, many individuals had some reason to kill Radovan Karadzic! – Ray Carter said to me.

Upon the expiry of his contract with the ICTY in 2005, Carter, as a French lieutenant-colonel, took the post of the director of GTA *(Gendarmerie des transports aériens)*, introduced aerial transport police in France and set up an anti-terrorist detachment specialized in airport protection. Due to his accomplishments in the security-related jobs, Carter was promoted to the rank of colonel in 2006 and appointed chief of the French President's security division within the national security agency of France, thus for the second time taking care of President Jacques Chirac's safety. The two men were friends. His career on an upswing, Raymond Carter became a world-renowned figure. He owns a company that manufactures airport safety systems. Besides, he is an associate professor of international criminal law at Paris Descartes University, a lecturer at the Strategic and Diplomatic Study Center (CEDS), adviser of the European Commission and the United Nations on safety, security and police matters. His awards include: Legion of Honor, National Order of Merit of France, Order of Knighthood and many medals won in sports and martial arts contests.

Ray Carter still works on the improvement of the security system on airports. With a friend of his, he patented a novel system and asked me, in 2015, to help him commercialize it and bring it out onto the U.S. market, which I gladly accepted.

While Radovan Karadzic lived his clandestine life, I was working in the States. For full eight years we did not either see or hear from each other. Nevertheless, this great and persecuted Serb often came to my mind.

---

[37] **SFOR** is acronym for the **Stabilization Force for Bosnia-Herzegovina,** NATO-led multinational peacekeeping force established by the U.N. Security Council in December 1996 and operating under peace *enforcement* rules. The SFOR arrested 29 individuals charged with war crimes and transferred them to the ICTY in The Hague. The Force was disbanded in December 2004. – *Translator's note.*

SURRENDER YOURSELVES, SERBS!

IN THE WINTERTIME OF 2004, I found out – from some confidential sources in the U.S. Republican Party and the Congress – that America was preparing a new round of sanctions against my country. The former sanctions had been imposed by a resolution of the U.N. Security Council of May 30, 1992 due to Serbia's/Yugoslavia's interference in the domestic affairs of Bosnia-Herzegovina; they were abolished as late as on October 2, 1996, following the free multiparty elections in Bosnia. During the embargo, Serbia and its people lived in a chaos generated by black market, smuggling, illegal trade and other forms of criminal business.

Eight years later, the U.S. Congress threatened by imposing new sanctions on the State Union of Serbia and Montenegro from January 20, 2005 because of the country's failure to meet international obligations including those to The Hague Tribunal, that is, failure to deliver to the ICTY indictees Radovan Karadzic and General Ratko Mladic. The measures – as I was informed – were going to be joined in by the member-countries of the European Union. Such measures would have worsened the international position of the State Union and additionally set back the economy of Serbia and Montenegro, with further consequences to the living standard of the population and new political agony of my people.

I felt impelled to do something in order to prevent re-introduction of international sanctions. So I shared my concern with several American Serbs in California, and they suggested that we write an open letter to Boris Tadic, President of Serbia, and Vojislav Kostunica, Prime Minister. The letter should propose a direct contact of the two leaders with Radovan Karadzic and Ratko Mladic in order to persuade them to surrender; we – the former U.S. President Jimmy Carter and myself –would, as mediators between the state and the ICTY indictees/fugitives "establish straightforward communication with Karadzic and Mladic and ensure all necessary conditions for fair trials, not in The Hague but in Belgrade".

Such an open letter composed by the "Initiative Group of California's American Serbs" and signed by myself was sent to Serbia's President and Prime Minister. The message said that, toward the winter of 2004 Jimmy Carter and I had "already had some contacts with the U.S. Ambassador-at-Large for War Crime Issues Pierre Richard Prosper" who conveyed the consent of the American government to make all legal papers available to the indictees and ensure legal protection by world's best lawyers, as well as to inquire the possibility of The Hague Tribunal organizing the trial in Belgrade.

The White House number three in charge of 'the dangerous Serbs', Ambassador Pierre Prosper understood my proposals and advised me to make them official on behalf of the Serbian state and people. Prosper ran the Tribunal affairs on behalf of the U.S.A. The Serbian Minister of Diaspora Affairs Dr. Vojislav Vukcevic and his Assistant Vukman Krivokuca visited the United States and supported my proposal, accepting to relay it to Boris Tadic and Vojislav Kostunica in the form of the said open letter. Ambassador Prosper then accepted a telephone conference with at least ten participants. Our question was:

– Is the United States for or against this proposal: that Karadzic and Mladic surrender to the authorities in Belgrade and stand trial in Serbia?
– The U.S.A. has no objection – Ambassador Prosper answered.
– It will not exercise a veto. And who are you going to work on it with?
– With Tadic and Kostunica – Minister Vukcevic answered.
– Good luck to you! They are both distrustful and do not keep their word! – said Prosper and hung up.

The whole protocol had to be official in character, so we sent the letters to Serbia's President and Prime Minister respectively, and released it to the media. Minister of (Serbian) Diaspora Vukcevic took the original letter, the complete proposal and a plan for the mission, as well as the minutes of the conversation with Ambassador Pierre Richard Prosper – in order to hand them in to

Boris Tadic and Vojislav Kostunica respectively. My intention was to spare Karadzic and Mladic humiliation and the Serbian people embarrassment. For, it would have been embarrassing should the brave members of the nation be treated like notorious convicts and deprived of the right to tell the truth about their struggle for freedom. America, the U.N., the E.U. and the whole western world had turned against the Serbian people. As many as 80 Serbs were indicted and condemned as criminals.

The list of the most dangerous Serbs worldwide included the names of Zeljko Raznatovic, Dr. Vojislav Seselj, Slobodan Milosevic, Dr. Radovan Karadzic and Gen. Ratko Mladic. Raznatovic Arkan ended dead (killed) that year (2004), Vojislav Seselj had voluntarily surrendered himself to the Tribunal in The Hague, Milosevic had been delivered to the ICTY by the new, democratic government of Premier Zoran Djindjic, while Karadzic and Mladic were on the run. Jimmy Carter – the man who had been acquainted with Radovan and Ratko in 1994, and whose wife Rosalynn had found the two appealing enough to offer them invitation to the 1996 Atlanta Olympics – backed up my proposal and agreed to join in the action of getting Karadzic and Mladic surrender.

To my mind, Radovan Karadzic should have surrendered himself so that he could tell the truth about the struggle and aflictions of the Serb people in Bosnia-Herzegovina. If he had been caught as a fugitive, he would have become a man deprived of human rights and a convict; if he had surrendered himself, he would have enjoyed all human rights in The Hague as a Serb hero and champion of the truth about the Serbs. At that moment, the work and life of Radovan Karadzic belonged to the Serbian people rather than his family. In my opinion, the issue of further destiny of Radovan Karadzic was a national issue of the Serbs and the Serbian lands.

Moreover, Karadzic and the members of his family were under serious threat by the Americans and the Prosecutor's Of ice in The Hague. The SFOR and EUFOR had repeatedly searched the houses/apartments of Radovan's wife Ljiljana, son Aleksandar and daughter Sonja, for they were suspected of not only cooperating but also maintaining contacts with him. The CIA task force even con iscated some intimate personal effects of Ljiljana and Sonja Karadzic in order to submit them for forensic analyses which hopefully could detect Radovan's presence in his house or his daughter's apartment at Pale.

The Americans offered a five-million-dollar bounty to the person(s) providing useful information or locating Radovan Karadzic. Tracking of Radovan Karadzic cost the United States about three million dollars yearly. With Radovan surrendered, the budget entry could be cancelled.

*

At this point, the reader should be reminded of the change in the American attitude which took place in 2001, when Bill Clinton was succeded by George Bush Jr. in the White House. The newly elected President annulled the agreement between Radovan Karadzic and Ambassador Richard Holbrooke which allowed the Bosnian Serb leader to live in peace and seclusion without fear from attacks. The annulment implied a hunt for Karadzic and Mladic alongside pressures on the official Belgrade to deliver the two to the ICTY as soon as possible. Serbia's refusal to positively respond was in Washington D.C. taken as Serbian disregard for the international community, the country's failure to meet its obligations and, moreover, damaging of the good relations with the United States.

Therefore, the Americans accepted my initiative, yet under the condition that the authorities in Belgrade, i.e. Boris Tadic and Vojislav Kostunica, authorize me as a plenipotentiary representative of the State Union of Serbia and Montenegro in the mission of Karadzic's and Mladic's voluntary surrender. Larry Burns, special advisor to Ambassador Pierre Richard Prosper, composed the text of the authorization to be signed by the highest officials of the State Union which was the sole subject of international affairs, and also by the representatives of the Republic of Serbia as memberstate that solely could offer guarantees to the indicted Karadzic.

Radovan was not supposed to surrender himself to the authorities of the Republic of Srpska, for it was not recognized internationally and lacked the opportunities to address or rely on international political and legal institutions in the matters related to the negotiations and trial concerning the former President of the RS. While holding the office of the President of the Serb-run state within Bosnia-Herzegovina, Radovan Karadzic was deprived of the chance to round off the constitution of the Republic of Srpska; for, he had been banned from Dayton 'proximity talks' by the Americans and Slobodan Milosevic, so in November 1995 he could not accomplish the desired legal/international status for the Republic of Srpska.

Awaiting the responses on the part of Boris Tadic and Vojislav Kostunica (and I kept inquiring daily by calling Dr. Vojislav Vukcevic, Minister of Serbian Diaspora), some politicians individually confronted the idea of allowing me the authorization to represent the country in the mission. Adviser to the PM of Serbia Aleksandar Simic said for Belgrade's daily *Blic* that "according to the Constitution, authorization can be issued to an official negotiator by the Government of Serbia solely, or, possibly, the Ministerial Council of Serbia and Montenegro, while the President of Serbia is not entitled to do so". Minister of Justice Zoran Stojkovic, however, said for the same newspaper that "the negotiant authorizations can only be given by the State Union of SM, that is, the National Council for Cooperation with The Hague Tribunal".

They did not read the Open Letter to Tadic and Kostunica which contained the claim that "the inclusion of Prof Dr. Borko Djordjevic in this process implies that he is given the status of authorized negotiator" and that "the Department of State, upon a request by the State Union of Serbia and Montenegro, issues a consent therefor bearing in mind that he, apart from the citizenship of SM, has the citizenship of the U.S.A."; hence, they failed to comment on that. They just proclaimed Serbia as unqualified to issue a negotiant authorization to me.

Expecting to hear the related views of President Tadic and Premier Kostunica, I was – together with Jimmy Carter – planning to involve the Atlanta-based Carter Center in the project, as well as some influential U.S. congressmen and senators, politician Henry Kissinger, Dr. Joyce Neu as the director of the Joan B. Croc Institute for Peace and Justice, former Chief Prosecutor of the ICTY Hon. Judge Richard Goldstone, and Mr. Alan Dershowitz as one of the most renowned lawyers worldwide.

The San Diego-based Institute for Peace and Justice was willing to put 30 million dollars in the implementation of the action, which implied commissioning of some of the world's best lawyers – Ed Medwin, Thomas Hanley and, as head of the team, Alan Dershowitz, Harvard Law School professor.

Karadzic had already had three American lawyers who in 1996 proved him not guilty of the allegations put forward by the U.S. and The Hague Tribunal. The plan was that a five-member judicial panel carry out the trial to Karadzic and Mladic in Belgrade, four of whom should be judges from Serbia and the presiding judge should come from the European Union. The arrangement envisaged that Radovan Karadzic would – provided he voluntarily surrendered himself – stand the trial undetained.

In the Republic of Srpska and in Serbia, many a response to my proposal was encouraging and approving. Nearly all of the political parties in RS welcomed the appeal for Karadzic's surrender, while the Serbian Democratic Party refrained from comments under the official excuse that "to interfere with a family with such problems as the Karadzic family is facing would be misplaced and overbold".

The majority of Srpska's citizens – if one believes the press there –thought that Radovan Karadzic should have surrendered himself. The opinion was shared by Ostoja Barasin, a military/political analyst of Banja Luka and once member of the Presidential Of ice of RS. The EUFOR Commander Gen. David Leaky and Stephen P. Schook, NATO HQ Commander at Sarajevo, expressed their approval of my proposal. They both insisted on Karadzic and Mladic's surrender:

– We shall aggressively continue to search for the individuals indicted of war crimes, expecting the surrender of Karadzic and Mladic for two convincing reasons: first, for the sake of their families, and, second, for the bene it of Bosnia-Hercegovina.

In Serbia, we enjoyed the support of the Ministry of (Serbian) Diaspora of the Government of Serbia and nearly all of the Serbian media.

During an international conference in Budapest, Minister of Diaspora Dr. Vojislav Vuckovic said:

– I am completely familiar with the initiative and support it. I find it to be very serious. That is the sole and the best solution for the Serbs. Anyway, the initiator of the idea, Dr. Borko Djordjevic, has already gained full trust of the leading representatives of the

Serbs in Bosnia-Herzegovina, and of Radovan Karadzic in the irst place, which is testi ied by the letters and correspondence between them that give evidence of Dr. Borko's familiarity and close relationship with Karadzic. Djordjevic came to know Karadzic and Mladic during the last war, when he was helping the wounded as a doctor. In mid-nineties he took part in the negotiation mission in Bosnia with Jimmy Carter, which Karadzic himself was very pleased with.

ON PAIN OF DEATH

Expectedly enough, and normally among the Serbs, there were different views as well. Miroslav Michael Djordjevic, one of the leading figures of the Serbian Unity Congress in the United States, talked to some Belgrade media claiming that the whole story was lacking logics and "roots in reality", that "nobody in the Serbian diaspora" knew Borko Djordjevic who had first become known when he visited Pale with Jimmy Carter in an attempt to mediate between the Republic of Srpska and the Contact Group; inally, he said that "the operation proved a complete iasco".

Radovan's brother Luka Karadzic was another opponent to the plan, who made the following statement for the media:

– The story about Borko Djordjevic finding Radovan Karadzic and negotiating with him, with the help of Ambassador Prosper and Carter's staff, is naive. Doctor Djordjevic does not represent the Serbian diaspora but only himself, and I do not believe that he will be able to find my brother Radovan Karadzic! A trial before The Hague Tribunal –may it be in its 'af iliate' in Belgrade – is unacceptable to Radovan! That is not something my brother would agree to either. If he really knows my brother, and if he has been in touch with him, Dr. Borko should be aware of that. I'm afraid that, if Radovan does surrender himself, a new revolt of the Serbs and a new war in BH could break out.

I had to answer him indirectly, for there were other people among us who claimed that the Bosnian Serbs would rise up if Radovan surrendered himself voluntarily and if he was to sit in "The Hague's prison in Belgrade":

– In my opinion, there's no threat of a political or people's rebellion of the Serbs in the Republic of Srpska, Montenegro or Serbia if Radovan Karadzic surrenders himself today, for there are many other Radovans in these countries. However, if our authorities in Belgrade lack the political will, or the capability, to defend the Serbian national interests embodied in the figure and accomplishments of Radovan Karadzic, they should insist that the former President of the RS stands trial in America. The United States of America is a country where the principle of being not guilty unless proved otherwise is honored.

Miroslav Toholj, the former Minister of Information in the Republic of Srpska Krajina (now Croatia) detached himself from me then and said that he did not take my whole story seriously.

– I met Borko Djordjevic during a New Year's celebration, I guess it was in 1994. He was in the company of a prominent lady from our diaspora. The celebration took place in the *Bistrica* Hotel, at Mt. Jahorina. I remember Predrag Zivkovic Tozovac singing. There were some other ministers of ours, but Radovan was not present. According to what I have heard, I believe all of this is but someone's self-promotion and self-advertizing. Sort of: somebody's going to mediate and get Radovan Karadzic surrendered. It's all nonsense. Surrender himself – who to? The Hague and the Americans – Toholj said.

In Bosnia-Herzegovina and the United States, the mission of getting Karadzic and Mladic surrendered and stand trial in Belgrade was dangerous to my life. For, my task was to save the face of America, re-examine the work of The Hague Tribunal and ensure peaceful surrender of the two men. Many disliked the idea – both in the States and in the former Yugoslavia. It was me, who had a close and deep relationship with Radovan Karadzic, that became a target to headhunters such as Naser Oric[38]. He wanted to catch Radovan Karadzic by himself, deliver the man to the Americans and take the five-million-dollars bounty. In order to succeed, Oric imagined he had to capture me so that I disclose Radovan's hiding place. On pain of death, I had to leave Bosnia rather often.

On the other hand, Radovan's brother Luka Karadzic persisted in his criticism, going as far as to call me a deceiver:

– If Djordjevic refers to the support and cooperation by the former American President Jimmy Carter, I'm not sure of the power this Democrat enjoys in the Republican Administration of George Bush. Especially so if we are aware of the statement given by Pierre Richard Prosper, Ambassador for war crimes, who has already detached himself publicly, in the name of the White House, from that initiative of Dr. Djordjevic. Henceforth, this is but one in a series of deceits offered to the Serbian people. Deceits which, following an old recipe, should imply a repeated demand that the Serbs cooperate and meet all the requests by the international community. The American President Bush is attacking Radovan Karadzic in order to win the favors of Islamists and demonstrate American readiness to cooperate with the Muslims. They have filled up Scheveningen with the Serbs, just Karadzic and Mladic are missing there. And that should be the price of the Americans being at peace with the Islamists. On the other hand, the U.S.A. and the NATO are destroying the Republic of Srpska and supporting the Muslims who are increasingly aggressive – said Luka Karadzic in a categorical and angry tone.

That Ambassador Prosper tried to deny his cooperation with me is true:

– We have never asked Dr. Djordjevic to mediate or negotiate, and such claims are inaccurate. Simply, the whole story is entirely untrue –Prosper said for Belgrade's Beta News Agency. The U.S. Ambassador-at-Large also said that the statement of the Serbian Minister of Diaspora Vojislav Vukcevic was absolutely unfounded, referring to the statement that there was some possibility that Karadzic and Mladic stand trial in Belgrade.

I did not want to argue with Ambassador Prosper and the White House, for they themselves knew the reasons why they changed the whole story and denied whatever we had jointly figured out and began to work on. Instead of from myself, the answer to Ambassador Prosper came from the Minister of Diaspora, professor of law Vojislav Vukcevic who testi ied for the daily *Vecernje novosti* ('Daily News'):

– I was in Palm Springs with Mr. Borko Djordjevic, witnessing the phone talk between Mr. Prosper and Dr. Borko Djordjevic's lawyer, also Prosper's acquaintance, Larry Barnes. After the conversation, Barnes explained to Djordjevic that he could not carry out his plan as a self-initiative but had to obtain adequate authorizations by the state. Barnes composed the authorization text which should be signed by the officials of the State Union of Serbia and Montenegro and the representatives of Serbia's Government. Ambassador Prosper said that the two of them, himself and Barnes, had to go to The Hague, but that the American

Administration would agree to the trial being held in Belgrade, provided The Hague Tribunal itself approved of that.

– Prosper's lying – Larry Burns told me discreetly.

Eight people had talked to Prosper. He had agreed about our plan, but somebody at the White House persuaded him to discard it all, and he uttered the lie about never having met us!

In Serbia, the United States exerted its in luence through Vuk Draskovic[39], then Minister of Foreign Affairs, in order to stonewall the story of Radovan Karadzic's surrender and standing trial in Belgrade. This caused some conflicts inside Draskovic's party, the Serbian Renewal Movement, for Draskovic opposed the plan while the Minister of Diaspora Vukcevic approved of it.

I had to release a public statement on December 16, 2004 which said that Ambassador Pierre Richard Prosper's refusal to admit any awareness of these ongoings in the cases of Karadzic and Mladic was understandable, for it was required by the diplomatic tradition to have "secret negotiations before public disclosure".

I repeated that Prosper had promised – on behalf of the U.S.A. and the White House – that it would be "quite possible, provided Karadzic and Mladic surrendered themselves, that they stand trial in Belgrade". And that I had obtained the consent of President George Bush. Thereafter, Prosper denied all of it and said that we had never met and that the Serbs had to stand trial in The Hague. The White House changed their mind, and so did Ambassador Prosper.

Both Minister Vukcevic and the attorney Larry Burns testi ied to my credibility, but Ambassador Pierre Richard Prosper came out as a winner in the game of lying, whereby he enjoyed the backup of both the United States and Serbia.

The media in Washington, D.C. supported Prosper. They wrote that the activities of the Carter Center for Peace and Justice, headed by Jimmy Carter, and Dr. Borko Djordjevic had actually set a trap to catch Radovan and Ratko and throw them into The Hague's prison.

The Serbian public was up on the information about the project and was able to choose whom to believe: either the denial of an American ambassador or the testimony of a Serbian minister and another American official. I would say that they chose to believe

Vukcevic and Burns, for nobody – including the United States – repeated or supported Prosper's disclaimer thereafter.

The spokesperson of the Tribunal Florence Hartmann rejected any chance to have the cases of Karadzic and Mladic adjudicated before a domestic/Serbian court of justice.

– Domestic courts already face too much workload in the lawsuits they themselves have launched – Hartmann said for the daily newspaper *Blic*.

She was reluctant to comment on my initiative, that is, on the possibility that a branch division of the ICTY is established in Belgrade where Mladic and Karadzic could stand trial.

– The arrest of Mladic and Karadzic is the legal obligation of the State of Serbia and Montenegro and not an issue of negotiations. Many member-states of the United Nations, including the U.S.A., demand their detention, saying that although on the run they could not escape justice – Florence Hartmann emphasized.

In the Presidential Of ice of Boris Tadic, a reporter of the newspaper *Vecernje novosti* ('Evening News') got a confirmation of their familiarity with the initiative by a group of American Serbs and Dr. Djordjevic; they emphasized that any help was welcome. Professor Vladeta Jankovic, foreign affairs adviser to PM Kostunica, just told me that "no signals came on the part of the U.S.A. with regard to the initiative, that is, the Government of Serbia expected an official confirmation from Washington and, provided we get one, we shall act in accorcance with the circumstances".

Srdjan Djuric, head of the Government's office for the cooperation with the media made a brief statement:

– No one from the Government of Serbia is involved in the reported negotiations with Radovan Karadzic and Ratko Mladic on their surrender.

Nothing else was said. As President and Prime Minister of Serbia, Boris Tadic and Vojislav Kostunica never responded, officially and in writing, to either Minister Vuckovic or me, in answer to our Open Letter and proposals as to how to save the honor and face of Radovan Karadzic, General Ratko Mladic and the Serbian nation.

– They are probably making an assessment of the situation, considering whether such an action could cause some damage to the country. They only told me they were going to think about everything and give me an answer – Minister Vukcevic complained to me.

When I realized that the Serbian leaders kept silent, unwilling to respond, we sent the proposal/request to Svetozar Marovic, President of the State Union of Serbia and Montenegro. I had known Sveto Marovic from an earlier time and believed he would not ignore me. He received us in the Serbia Palace. I officially appealed on President Marovic for an improvement of the Yugoslav-American relations through the said proposal which could also free us from the pending sanctions and create a positive climate in the Federal Republic of Yugoslavia. In order to accomplish the goals, we should create adequate conditions, reach a concensus, give necessary guarantees to The Hague Tribunal and obtain consent from Radovan Karadzic and Ratko Mladic. I handed in to him the text of my state authorization for the White House. But Sveto Marovic failed to help. He did not respond, either.

Then I called Minister of Interior Vukasin Maras to advocate and push my proposal with the Montenegrin politicians and Svetozar Marovic, and also my friend Misko Jeremic; at that moment (2004), however, they were all fudging the issue of "dangerous Hague indictees and fugitives", Radovan Karadzic and Ratko Mladic.

I was appalled by the fact that none of the officials of Serbia and Montenegro wanted to deal with the freedom of the two Serbs proclaimed by the international community as the most dangerous men worldwide. To them, it was more convenient to have Karadzic 'out in the forest' than before The Hague Tribunal.

The situation being as it was, Radovan was distrustful of the idea of surrender and trial held in Belgrade, for he could not be certain about the effects of his surrender and/or the trial in Serbia. Perhaps he was afraid that some parts of the Army (YNA) and State Security Agency could break loose from state control and assassinate him, for, to these, Karadzic was a dangerous man.

Therefore, Karadzic's answer took me by surprise, for it implied that he did not want to be free. My 'liaison' with Karadzic were the writer Miroslav Toholj and Radovan's adviser Jovan Zametica, who gave him my letter with the appeal for his surrender:

– That does not depend on me – answered Radovan Karadzic. I told Jimmy Carter about the situation, and he gave me a friendly piece of advice:

– Borko, give it all up. You alone can't change the state of affairs in Serbia!

The former U.S. President and seasoned politician was right. Tadic and Kostunica had refused our proposal in silence, for they held Radovan Karadzic and Ratko Mladic in control owing to the secret police *(BIA – Bezbednosno-informativna agencija)* and the military intelligence *(VBA – Vojno-bezbednosna agencija)*. To both Tadic and Kostunica it was more convenient to keep Karadzic as a fugitive than imprisoned and in the courtroom, for in that way they could keep bargaining in the negotiations on the two men's surrender with the U.S.A., E.U. and Russia.

The military and police lobbies in Serbia disapproved of Karadzic and Mladic's surrenders, for they could testify on war crimes perpetrated by their fellow-troops and units. They feared the accounts of the two men of what had really been going on in Serbia and among the Serbs in Croatia and Bosnia-Herzegovina. They feared disclosure of the Serbian war criminals who were members of the YNA, generals from the memberships of the Socialist Party of Serbia (SPS) and Yugoslav Left (JUL), commanders of the Special Operation Units (JSO) and other special forces.

Hence some of them were ready to liquidate Radovan Karadzic and thus prevent him from testifying on their crimes. That such threats were genuine I learned from some anonymous witnesses who were willing to help about the voluntary surrender of Karadzic and Mladic yet feared Serbia's belligerent clans.

– We're scared to help you, they'll kill our children!

---

[38] **Naser Oric** (b. 1967), from 1992, Commander of the Army of the Republic of BH for the sub-region of Srebrenica. In 1992-5, he led the troops which assaulted some 50 Serb-settled villages in the vicinity of Srebrenica and the Municipality of Bratunac, killing the local population massively and non-discriminatorily. Oric was evacuated from Srebrenica by a chopper prior to the seizure of the town by the Army of the Republic of Srpska (1995). First (2006) sentenced to 2-years' imprisonment by the ICTY, then (2008) acquitted of all charges. *–Translator's note.*

[39] **Vuk Draskovic** (b. 1946) Serbian writer and leader of Srpski pokret obnove - SPO (Serbian Renewal Movement), most popular of the opposition leaders in Serbia during 1990's. His posts in state administration included Deputy Prime Minister of Yugoslavia (January 18 – April 28, 1999) and Minister of Foreign Affairs of Serbia and Montenegro (March 3, 2004 – May 15, 2007). – *Translator's note.*

MOMCILO KRAJISNIK'S AMERICAN DEFENSE

AT THE TIME WHEN I was sending messages to Karadzic and Mladic appealing on them to surrender themselves in order to stand a fair trial in Belgrade, Momcilo Krajisnik was in The Hague, awaiting the beginning of his own trial. He is the former President of the National Assembly of the Republic of Srpska. In April 2000, he was arrested in his house at Pale by the French troops of the SFOR who transferred him to the ICTY Detention Center at Scheveningen. As Serbian reporters used to put it, "Krajisnik was waiting for Karadzic" there, for they were seen as sitting in the dock together, under charges of genocide and war crimes perpetrated in Bosnia-Herzegovina.

As in 2004 I was working on the commissioning of the world's best lawyers to defend Radovan Karadzic – Ed Medwin, Thomas Hanley and Alan Dershowitz (the latter being professor of international law at Harvard University) – I was rung up by Mirko Krajisnik, brother of the defendant Momcilo Krajisnik. He asked me to help Momcilo summon Alan Dershowitz to defend him at The Hague Tribunal. Upon my advice, Momcilo Krajisnik wrote to Derschowitz on September 26, 2003:

Though absolutely innocent, I am well aware that indictment is a serious matter, because if there is possibility to make baseless accusations, anything can happen. Some of my friends and associates, who are well informed about my work in the period 1990-2000, recommended that I should address you and ask you to take active part in my defense. I was told that you are humanitarian and a brave person, and a great fighter for justice, so that is why I took the liberty to ask you to help me.

My family lost all their property during the war, and I am not in a position to finance my defense, so assets provided by ICTY will finance counselors from Republika Srpska. As far as your fee, I have statements of a large number of my friends an benefactors, who expressed their desire to gather assets so your work would be possible.

I am well aware of and greatly respect your commitment to defense of individual against state power. I believe that you will respect my commitment towards my people and to making peace at Dayton, Ohio talks on Bosnia that I attended throughout and where I played a constructive role. At that time I met President of USA, Prime Minister of GB, President of France, Prime Minister of Russian Federation, Prime Minister of Germany etc. This is one of a number of facts that are not logical, accusations against me were not even taken in consideration until 2000.

Tom Hanley, Nikola Koljevic, Momcilo Krajisnik and the Lawyer J. Lukic

This is why I believe that my case, which is likely to attract substantial and sustained international publicity, should be of interest to you.

I very much hope that you will consider this request. My associates in United States will contact your office in the next few days to discuss the matter with you. I will understand if your answer is not to be positive, because I am sure that can happen with extremely strong reason. No matter what you decide, I wish you all the best in your career, and to keep up good work.

Sincerely yours,

Momcilo Krajisnik
(signed)

Dershowitz became rather popular at the time, for he defended O. J. Simpson, the famous pro football star charged with murder of his wife. As a respectable professor of law and a renowned lawyer, Dershowitz was very expensive. His price for the defense of Momcilo Krajisnik was three million dollars. The attorney Deyan Ranko Brashich of New York City had been engaged in 2003, and he personally suggested that Alan Dershowitz takes the case and that an advance payment of one million dollars should be effected.

Having consulted Krajisnik, I entered negotiations with Alan Dershowitz. On principle, he was willing to take the job, but demanded a visit to Momcilo in The Hague so that he could talk to the defendant, get an authorization and take over the case-related material. As the Krajisnik dossier was extremely voluminous, Dershowitz requested $ 50,000 to cover his fee and travel costs, which he was paid. My role was to raise the funds for the rest of $ 2.950,000 – from the Serbian diaspora mostly.

I appealed on my American friends and respectable Serbs in the States to join in the funding of Krajisnik's defense. They were glad to respond, for Momcilo enjoyed good reputation as a Serb politician. He had been a member of the Serbian Democratic Party in Bosnia since 1990, and during 1992 participated in the creation of the Serbian Republic of Bosnia-Herzegovina, then became Speaker of its parliament, and then Speaker of the National Assembly of the Republic of Srpska. During the war in Bosnia, he earned the nickname of "Mister No" due to his unyielding attitude in the negotiations with the representatives of the international community. Radovan Karadzic had to search for a lawyer for the third time. These circumstances prolonged the stage of waiting for the trial to begin – with an ICTY record-beating period in this respect.

Krajisnik's new lawyers, an English-Australian team, immediately iled a protest to the Tribunal grounded on the fact that the defendant had been sitting in detention for four years without any trial procedures. So the trial commenced in that year, 2004.

At the moment of the 2006 verdict – by which he was acquitted of the charges for genocide and sentenced to 20-years' imprisonment for war crimes – Momcilo Krajisnik was the highest-ranking Serb politician/official and prisoner in custody at The Hague. Having served two thirds of conviction, he was released from the London prison in 2013 and returned to the Republic of Srpska.

RADOVAN'S WITNESS?

MY MISSION OF SAVING Radovan Karadzic, Ratko Mladic and the Serbs from the dooms of The Hague Tribunal judgment about the Serbian people being genocidal did not succeed. I guess that the efforts I and Jimmy Carter had invested into the option of Karadzic's surrender resulted in Washington giving up the imposition of sanctions on Serbia and Montenegro from January 20, 2005 on. Instead of punishment, the United States resorted to the praise of Serbia. The U.S. Ambassador-at-Large for War Crimes Pierre Richard Prosper made a statement which said that the U.S.A. expected the arrest of The Hague's most wanted indictees – Radovan Karadzic and Ratko Mladic – to take place in the fall of 2005. Upon his visit to Belgrade High Court's War Crime Chamber, Prosper said that the Serbian Prime Minister Vojislav Kostunica had assured him of the solution to the problem.

The ICTY repeatedly reported that there were information about Karadzic staying in Serbia from time to time at least, including Belgrade in 2004.

Ambassador Prosper's mission did not succeed either, because – as a pro-Russian man – Kostunica was protecting Karadzic and Mladic from the Americans.

It was only after Kostunica had stepped down and Boris Tadic was firmly in the driver's seat that Radovan Karadzic was arrested; thus, Tadic scored points with the Americans. This took place in Belgrade, late in July 2008. Three years later, at the end of May, 2011, Ratko Mladic was captured, too – in the village of Lazarevo near Zrenjanin. While Karadzic had been hiding disguised under the alias of Dragan Dabic, an energy healer, Mladic assumed the name of Milorad Komadic, a farmer.

The trial to Karadzic began in September 2009. Radovan decided to represent himself during the trial. He summoned many witnesses who would confirm his claims that he had not organized killings of Muslims and Croats, that he had not committed war crimes and that he had not ordered ethnic cleansing in Bosnia-Herzegovina. The witnesses included: Vladislav Jovanovic, former Minister of Foreign Affairs of the F.R. of Yugoslavia; Momir Bulatovic, President of Montenegro; Gen. Aleksandar Vasiljevic, head of counter-intelligence in the Ministry of Defence; Gen. Zdravko Tolimir, commander in the Army of the Republic of Srpska (intelligence and security); Bozidar Vucurovic, former leader of the Serbian Democratic Party at Trebinje, Herzegovina; Gen. Ratko Mladic; Momcilo Krajisnik, Speaker of the Serb parliament, myself etc.

Borko Djordjevic ge ing a star for humanitarism on Palm Springs Walk of Fame

Early in July 2012, I received the bidding of Karadzic's defense to be their witness in The Hague Tribunal. Peter Robinson, Legal Advisor, asked me in writing to testify at the trial through

Skype about the peace mission of Jimmy Carter and myself at Pale in 1994. And about the peace in Bosnia-Herzegovina which lasted until the spring of 1995. My testimony could improve the reputation of Radovan Karadzic and the Serbian people, for I carried out the said mission together with Bill Clinton and Jimmy Carter.

As I had not met Radovan since 1996, the bidding took me by surprise. I did not answer Radovan and his advisers in The Hague immediately, for I wanted to consult them first. I was curious about the particular issues Radovan wanted me to testify on. I supposed that the 1994 peace mission would be the subject matter, for the cease-fire had stopped bloodshed in Bosnia-Herzegovina. The Serbian side in the war sincerely wanted the fighting in Bosnia to end as soon as possible and in a peaceful manner. As to the other activities of the President of the Republic of Srpska, I did not take part in them and could not testify on those.

The last contacts between Radovan and me had taken place in 1996, at a moment when we were doing our best to get guarantees for his surrender. He authorized me in writing to negotiate on his behalf. We even made a concrete offer, the details of which I would here omit. But I can never forget the lengthy and difficult talk to Carl Bildt who was then the High Representative for Bosnia and Herzegovina. The man told me: "Karadzic's destiny has already been decided on." Jimmy Carter, the American missioner, sent me a similar message when I was trying to persuade Karadzic into surrender for a trial in Belgrade – before an afiliate court of the ICTY.

I was wondering: If the United States, as the political patron, refrained from testifying in favor of the Bosnian-Serb leader as a participant in the mission of its former President Jimmy Carter – how could my testimony contribute to the defense of Radovan Karadzic?

I gave up the idea, for it was only 16 years later that Karadzic and his lawyers thought of me and called me to be a witness of theirs. Too late.

– America wants Karadzic to be the new leader of the Serbs. We do not want Milosevic to be the Serb leader. If you can see to it that Karadzic becomes the top figure among the Serbs, you'll do the right thing for America – that is what the White House had once been telling me.

When Radovan turned to Slobodan Milosevic again, the man swept him away. As a loser, Karadzic had to run away from both Milosevic and the Americans.

For my humanitarian activities and the peace mission in Bosnia I got a recognition in the United States – a star on Palm Springs Walk of Fame; in the Republic of Srpska, I never got any official letter/certi icate of thanks.

So I declined the offer of the legal advisers at The Hague Tribunal to be the witness of defense in the Karadzic lawsuit; I had realized that the Tribunal was not a court of justice but a political penal institution intended for 'dangerous Serbs'.

*

The ICTY was established on May 25, 1993 by *Resolution 827* of the United Nations Security Council. As the story goes in the U.N. and U.S.A., it should be dissolved in 2016 after the verdicts to Radovan Karadzic and Ratko Mladic are pronounced.[40] In the meanwhile, Karadzic has been sentenced to 40 years imprisonment in the first instance, while the first-instance trial to Vojislav Seselj ended in his acquittal.

Over the two decades of its mandate, the ICTY indicted 161 individuals: as many as 110 Serbs, 34 Croats, 9 Bosniaks, 7 Albanians and one Macedonian. The Serbs make 76% of all sentenced indictees; in total, they 'collected' 11 centuries of imprisonment, while the others got much lower punishments. The 12 convicted Croats earned 166 years in jail, while 5 Bosniaks have to spend 43.5 years in prison. Among the convicted Serbs, two were presidents of their states (which did not happen to others). In mid-1999, during the NATO air-raids, the Tribunal launched its first indictment against a head of state currently in office. It was Slobodan Milosevic, charged of the crimes in Kosovo-Metohija. Milosevic died in the Tribunal's Detention Center on March 11, 2006.

The one and only female indicted and convicted by the ICTY has been Biljana Plavsic, former President of the Republic of Srpska. After a plea-bargain with the Prosecutor's Of ice, she was sentenced to 11 years in prison in 2003. Before getting to the Tribunal, nine indictees died, seven of whom were Serbs.

Following their transfer to Scheveningen, six individuals died – five of whom were Serbs; the deceased were: Djordje Djukic, Slavko Dokmanovic, Mehmed Alagic, Milan Kovacevic, Slobodan Milosevic and Momir Talic.[41] Four more men died while in captivity.

At the beginning of September 2015, Radovan Karadzic publicly protested against The Hague Tribunal and the Scheveningen Detention Centre because of ignoring his health condition.

– For seven years now I have not undergone a medical examination. I have high blood pressure, blood sugar, pains in my chest and bilious attack – Karadzic complained.

It was only after this cry for help that the Bosnian-Serb leader underwent surgery which saved him from dying in The Hague.

*

The western countries, spearheaded by the United States that supported The Hague Tribunal, i.e. the International Crime Tribunal for former Yugoslavia – ICTY, not only threw into prison and killed the indicted/convicted Serbs but also attempted to instrumentalize such judicial practise with the purpose to prove that the Serbs are a genocidal nation/people. The U.S.A. and E.U., that is, the creators of the New World Order, thus wanted to free the German Fascists from their collective guiltiness of genocide and transfer it to the Serbs.

The heaviest punishments, 20 years in prison, have been imposed on officers and commanders of the Army of the Republic of Srpska Krajina (in Croatia) and the Army of the Republic of Srpska (Bosnia-Herzegovina). The former President of RS Biljana Plavsic was sentenced to 11, and former Speaker of the National Assembly of RS Momcilo Krajisnik to 20 years in prison. Can Radovan Karadzic – as the former President and creator of the Republic of Srpska – hope for a less severe punishment? At this point, we should recall the remark of Florence Hartmann, spokesperson of the ICTY Prosecutor's Of ice, written down in her memoirs as a personal experience:

– The Tribunal is useful to major powers in their rule over the world!

Considering those circumstances, any testimony of mine in favor of Radovan Karadzic would have proved useless. Karadzic has been convicted in advance, there is only the period of imprisonment left to be declared.

END OF PART ONE

---

[40] Updating the U.N. Security Council on the ICTY's completion strategy in December 2014, the Tribunal's President Theodor Meron envisaged the closure of this institution in 2017. So far (mid-2017), this has not happened. – *Translator's note.*

[41] The list has been extended since the Author's count: in February 2016, Gen. Zdravko Tolimir died at Scheveningen of heart attack. – *Translator's note.*

PART TWO

SON OF A PARTISAN 1941 VETERAN

IF I HAD TO PRESENT my autobiography in just several outlines, I could say that I was an émigré in Bulgaria, a Communist in Yugoslavia, a physician and a bonvivand in America, an American doctor in Montenegro, a peacemaker in Bosnia and a 'body artist' in Serbia. Some of it was not a matter of my own will but one of the destiny.

I was born in Pirot, in the midst of war, in 1942, as a child of love between two people who were trying to escape Fascism. My parents –engineer Branko Djordjevic and an American girl, Mara Phillips Filipovic – fell in love with each other ignoring the second world war.

The Author's father Branko Djordjevic, delegate to the Municipal Assembly of Palilula, Belgrade

My father, Branko, was born in 1913. He came from the village of Gulijan near Svrljig. As a graduate of the Military Academy in Kragujevac, he moved to the capital of the Kingdom of Yugoslavia to work in the engineering corps of the Yugoslav Royal Army in Belgrade.

My father's parents, Grandpa Ljuba and Grandma Rusa, were landowners in the village of Gulijan. Grandfather Ljuba Djordjevic was killed at the beginning of the Great War, so my father and Uncle Dobri grew up with their mother, my Grandma Rusa. Both psychologically and physically, my father took after his mother; when she died after World War II, he was heavily stricken with grief.

Granma Rusa decidedly in luenced the formation of my father's and my uncle's characters. My father, Branko, grew into an intellectual with the manners of a true gentleman. He was a man who masterfully organized his own life and job, never getting involved in quarrels with anyone. He had an inborn tolerance for other people and their views. A 'diplomat', he would not take advantage from his position of power but rather resorted to the proverbial "sweet command" which has "great force hidden" in it. The same can now be said of my son Nikola who resembles his grandfather Branko Djordjevic very much.

Early in 1939, my mother Mara came from the United States to Belgrade to visit her illness-stricken grandmother Jelena. She had been born in Akron, Ohio, in 1922. She was only 17 years old when she appeared at the Royal Ball and caught sight of the statuesque officer Branko Djordjevic. Their love exploded with intensity. They got married in January 1941, but as soon as on April 6 Hitler sent the Nazi troops/air force to attack Belgrade and they had to run away. My mother's mom Dara stayed in the Kingdom's bomb-ruined capital to take care of her mother Jelena. It was a sacrifice entirely normal and customarily seen with the Serbs, for the priority was to save the young, in this case newlyweds, while the old would succumb to the windstorms of wartime.

My mother's family had come from Lika[42]. That is where her father and my grandfather Sava Filipovic hailed from; Grandpa developed a real estate business in Zagreb, where he lived at No. 9 Ilica Street while renting apartments. My mother's mother (my grandmother) Dara née Drenovac came from the town of Ruma (subregion of Srem/Syrmia, Vojvodina); she had persuaded her husband Sava to move to Belgrade due to her mother's grave illness. Granpa Sava and Grandma Dara emigrated together to the U.S.A. where my Mom was born. In America, my Grandpa changed his name and surname into Sam Phillips. They lived in Akron, Ohio and had four children: three daughters (Jelena, Marija and Ljubica) and one son, Nikola Filipovic. Jelena died young, of tuberculosis. Grandma Dara went back to Yugoslavia in 1939 with her children, including my Mom Marija-Mara, in order to take care of her ill mother, my greatgrandmother Jelena. And they all stayed to live in Belgrade.

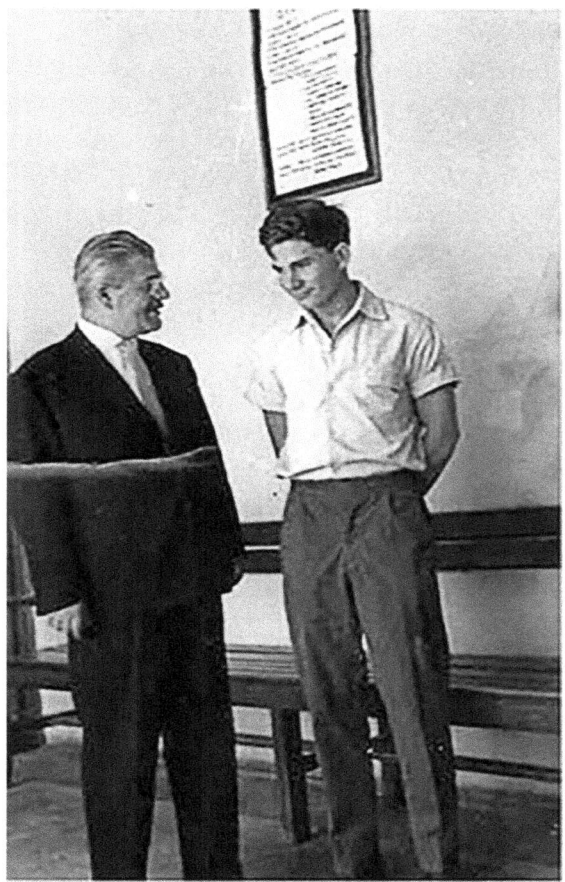

Father and son: Branko and Borko Djordjevic

My Grandma's brother (my granduncle) Nikola Drenovac was a respectable man in Belgrade. Writer, priest, translator, editor of some media (*Slobodna rec, Prosveta,* Radio Belgrade's Department of Literature), then director of Radio Belgrade. While living with his sister in America, in 1942, he was banished from the Serbian Orthodox Church and the U.S.A. – as a communist doctrinaire who spread his belief while serving as a clergyman. He published several collections of verse, including *Nezvani* gost and *Vetar i vlati* ('An Uninvited Guest', 'The Wind and the Grass'), long poem *Jevandjelje po meni* ('My Own Gospel') and the novel *Pukotina* ('A Crack'). A quite intriguing man to whom I, when we happened to meet, listened while talking about the rights of the masses and workers, about the Communist Party and discipline as the essence of life.

Running away from the Nazis, my parents went to Nish first, then to Dimitrovgrad near the Bulgarian border and to Pirot.[43] My mother was pregnant, so in Pirot, in the month of March, I was born into the world which was neither beautiful nor emboldening. Pirot was a small and poverty-stricken town. In such a milieu, my parents dared wish for their son to become a great man. They intended to give me the name of Boris, after the Russian Czar Boris Godunov, born – like me – in March (c. 1551). I am not sure what made them change their minds, but I was named Borko and I have stuck to it.

As a royal officer, my father thought that he had to defend his fatherland. However, the Yugoslav Royal Army was defeated and he joined the partisans, Tito-led guerrilla. They immediately registered him as a member of the Communist Party. His fellow-fighter and Party comrade was Lazar Kolisevski who in the postwar period became one of the leaders of the communist Macedonia and socialist Yugoslavia. Fortunately for myself, my father did not fight for long and was not killed, for the Bulgarians captured him and imprisoned at the Posabina Labor Camp where he stayed for the next four years.

Borko's class at the Jovan Popovic Primary School (Karaburma, Belgrade)

The Posabina Camp was situated in the south of Bulgaria by the Black Sea. The prisoners' families lived in the camp, too. We all lived there together. I never spotted my parents making love, yet I got two siblings soon: my sister Snezana was born in Posabina, and Angelina was born in So ia. I remember my childhood as one of modest and safe living. My mother used to say:

– All fortunes are in vain when the times come of being satisfied with a slice of bread and cheese, and peaceful sleep!

As a small boy, what I liked most was to spread lard on bread and powder it with red pepper. It has remained my favorite delicacy to this day.

Our lives were not in danger during the war. I adapted myself to the Bulgarian environment, quickly learned the language and even wailed in Bulgarian when I fell down and hurt my knee:

– Ole tatko, slomi si kračeto! ('Ouch, daddy, I've got my leg broken!') As it was the Church which took care of and protected us, my mother Marija began to eagerly practise religion and became a devout believer. My family used to celebrate St. Nicholas' Day in the home of Uncle Dobri, and I remember my mother helping Aunt in the preparations of this patron-saint's feast the Serbs refer to as the slava.

New Year's celebration at the club of the Fifth Belgrade High School (December 1958)

We were extremely happy when the Russians liberated us in 1944, but the joy was shortlived, for they proved to be ruthless investigators. The Russians interrogated my father, and we, the other members of the family, were also questioned and ill-treated, for they tried to force us to identify the Bulgarian spies in the camp. We came back from Bulgaria to Serbia in 1946 and found accomodation with my uncle Dobrivoje Todorovic, at No. 86 Gospodara Vucica Street; Uncle Dobri was a good friend of the leading partisan ideologist and propagandist Mosha Pijade.

Uncle Dobri was my father's brother, but had a different surname, for in the Kingdom of Yugoslavia two brothers could not both become university students. Therefore, my uncle took the last name of Todorovic so that he could continue his education.

In order to resume normal life, to work and provide for his family, my father had to report to the Communist Party and the secret police (UDB)[44] on his whereabouts and activities during the four war years. The interrogators concluded that he did not "betray the Party and the State" as had been suspected by the Communists. Due to his loyalty, he was proclaimed as a *prvoborac*, that is, the veteran of the first year of the war, and was awarded the Partisan 1941 Medal called *Spomenica* 1941. Thus, he became member of the Communist elite. Nevertheless, we still lived very modestly and most often ate *gersla* (barley porridge).

From Belgrade, we moved to Jabucki Rit near Pancevo[45] where my father worked at the Belgrade Agricultural Combine (*Poljoprivredni kombinat Beograd – PKB*). There, in Banat, I began to work – as a day laborer. I weeded corn fields and earned my first wage – one Dinar. Later, I worked at pig and horse farms.

In those postwar years I saw the Communist-run camps for the *Volksdeutscher* (German colonists from a few earlier centuries) and became familiar with Banat's 'Swabians'. I played with their children and within a short while learned how to quarrel with them. Also, taught by Guenther Schwarzmann, I learned the German language. I even mastered the Gothic alphabet, which roused some admiration by the Swabians. As to my education, I attended and completed Jovan Popovic Primary School in Belgrade's Karaburma quarter which at that time was a remote and scarcely populated suburb. We lived in an apartment in that quarter, at No. 46 Marijane Gregoran Street.

B. Djordjevic during the 1958 voluntary work drive at Ada Ciganlija, Belgrade

At school, I had wonderful teachers, some of whom I still remember. Osman Osmanovic taught biology. The bald man kept telling us that he had contracted baldness as an infectious disease due to wearing his friend's cap while serving in the army, which made him take the infective agent. He would also instruct us about moss indicating north.

Our teacher Milica taught mother tongue, so we referred to her as *Srpkinja* ('Serbian Woman'); she was married to the rather popular folk singer Nikola Kolakovic who sang with the orchestra of the famous

violinist Vlastimir Pavlovic Carevac[46]. My teacher Milica was hardly thirty at the time, an outstandingly beautiful brunette, very elegant and with admirably sculpted legs that she liked to expose. My classmate Milan Filipovic Fica and I would as early adolescents stare at our teacher's body and legs. Aware of our penetrating looks (the slang Serbian verb was *skrozirati*), she would grin, turning up the corners of her mouth. That I could not match her beauty and feminine qualities she let me know at the inal examination, when she gave me the mark 'B' instead of 'A' as I expected.

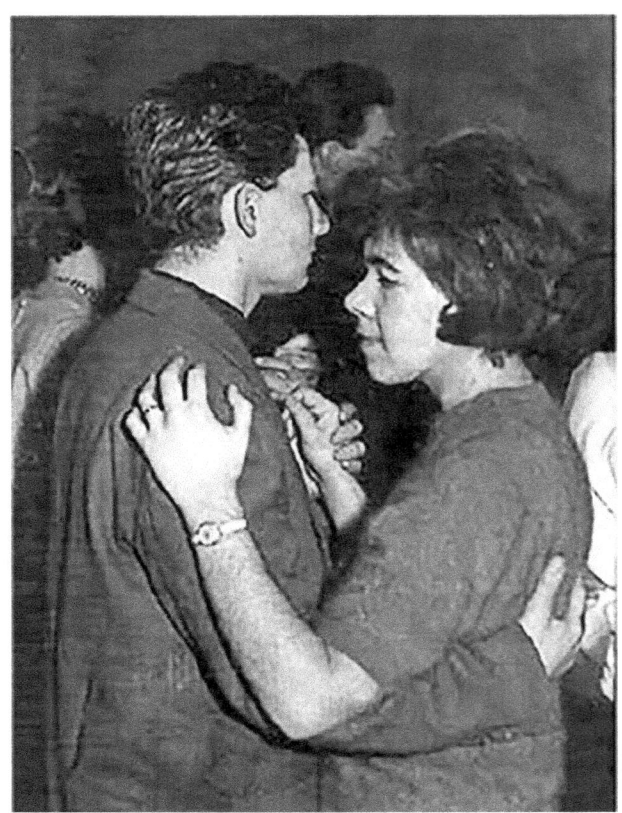

Borko Djordjevic and Gordana Najdanovic at the 1962 New year's party in the Medical students' Cluba

In the 8-year primary school I was a top student. Plus a 'model youth': the expression *uzoran omladinac* had an ideological connotation. Then I enrolled in the legendary Fifth Belgrade High School, where teachers made efforts at our character-training, and did so well. Mirko Sekularac, another student of the Fifth High School, described England as a country of beautiful parks which oppressed the peoples in its Asian colonies in order to obtain the famous English tea. Teacher Veljko was a blond, tall and smart man, whose wife was a teacher, too. Mirko Sekularac, brother of the great footballer/soccer player Dragoslav Sekularac, was at that time – in mid-1950's – only a young man who played soccer in the schoolyard. One of Gypsy-like dark complexion, short, bandy-legged and with pock-marked face. Later, his brother became the first-team player of the Red Star Football Club as an enchanting dribbler and scorer; he became a famous sportsman and extremely popular under the nickname of Sheki. As a genuine soccer star, he also starred in the movie Seki snima, pazi se! ('Beware, Sheki's Shooting!').

B. Djordjevic during the Skopje Youth Work Drive, 1963

Dragoslav Sekularac's first wife attended the Fifth Belgrade High School, too; that was the reason why Sheki frequented our schoolyard to play soccer with a rag-ball there.

In 1956, my father became director of the Belgrade construction company *Rad*, and I enrolled in the Fifth Belgrade High School. During the Belgrade Book Fair I would take a small student job in oder to earn some extra money and buy myself some clothes for school. The Fifth High School is one of the oldest of its kind in Serbia: instituted in 1863 as a 'Higher Girls' School', it grew into a *gymnasium*/grammar school in 1905, survived the Balkan Wars (1912-3), the Great War and World War II. During the latter, German military headquarters occupied the building, the Girls' High School was moved to another building and shared it with the male students of the bomb-ruined Second Young Men's High

School. When I became a high school student, the two grammar schools merged into the co-ed Fifth Belgrade High School located in the Tasmajdan Park area. It was attended by many renowned figures of Serbia's/Yugoslavia's public life, including Mira Aleckovic and Tanja Kragujevic (poetesses), Srdjan Karanovic and Goran Markovic (film directors), Goran Kicic, Jadranka Selec, Branko Cvejic (actors/actresses), Lenka Udovicki (stage director), Bora Djordjevic ('Bora Corba', influential author on the rock scene – singer, poet and songwriter), Suzana Mancic (TV presenter, singer), Lokica Stefanovic (ballet dancer, teacher and choreographer), Gaso Knezevic (jurist and politician) etc. And myself, Dr. Borko Djordjevic.

Duda Dragovic was a fellow-student at school and the Partyunit secretary who 'admitted' me into the membership of the Communist Party of Yugoslavia (he later became secretary of the University Committee of the CPY). Milan Milutinovic and Slobodan-Buca Prohaska, top officials in the Government of Serbia during the rule of Slobodan Milosevic, were my schoolmates. I was in the German-learning class, while they – as the children of the Serbian 'budding bourgeois' – were learning English. Somewhat later, they were joined by Vlada Stambuk, son of an ambassador, who happened to be my commander during the 1958 voluntary work drive at Ada Ciganlija[47].

There was also Gordana Najdanovic, daughter of the famed Dr. Najdanovic, cardiologist and personal physician of Marshal Tito. In high school days she had been Milan Milutinovic's girlfriend. They were dating for four years at high school, to break off during university studies. Later, Gordana became a gynecologist whose life road crossed with mine in an ugly way.

As a child of a partisan veteran, I was a model youth and participant in work drives. I joined in the young people's voluntary work drives in Nish, Trzic (Slovenia) and at Ada Ciganlija. In high school I was admitted into the Communist Party of Yugoslavia and became secretary of one of its 'basic organizations'; in early 1960's I banished comrade Milan Milutinovic out of the Party membership because he rejected to join in a work drive. Allegedly ill, he actually went on a trip to Dubrovnik with his girlfriend Gordana Najdanovic – for pleasure; thus, he subordinated a Party assignment to his private aspirations and, in consequence (after some consultation with the Fifth High School principal), the senior student Milan Milutinovic was banned from the Party. When and where he resumed the membership in the CPY is something I do not know.

My father noticed that, as a high school student, I took interest in the books on diseases and healthcare, so he advised me:

– Borko, my son, be a doctor, for people need doctors in every regime!

I trusted my father. When I enrolled in Belgrade University, Faculty of Medicine, I also became a political youth activist. During a work drive, I was elected Party secretary of the Faculty's 'Basic Organization of the Communist League'. My fellow-students Dusan Mitevic, Vlada Stambuk and Duda Dragovic were also my Party colleagues. Among the professors, I had an idol – Dr. Ivo Popovic Djani, a general surgeon working at Dragisa Misovic Hospital at Dedinje and also teaching surgery. He was the first to tell me something about education in America (he was born in Jerome, Arizona, in 1915).

During my fourth year at the University, I was elected Party secretary upon a recommendation by Ivan Ribaric, who monitored/supervised all that was going on at the Faculty of Medicine. When students' riots broke out in 1968, my colleague Ribaric gave me a piece of advice:

– Do not join in the rallies. This is an assault on the Communist Party!

In those years, 1960's, when I was a medical student at Belgrade University and also worked at the Medical Students' Club, Josip Broz Tito appeared to be a great friend of the Americans. Nobody knew – for nothing could be heard or read about it: in 1951, Tito had made the Federal People's Republic of Yugoslavia a member-country of NATO; also, the United States wrote off our state debts and covered Yugoslavia's budgetary gap. Ordinary people could feel that their living standard was growing better when American credits in dollar-currency began to low in. In July 1963 a disastrous earthquake took place in Skopje, capital of the Socialist Republic of Macedonia, killing some 1,100 people, injuring almost 4,000 and leaving more than 200,000 townspeople homeless. About 80 % of the city was destroyed. A largescale youth work drive was organized immediately. So it was in Skopje, in 1963, that I met Dusan Mitevic, a politician from the Milosevic clan who became Director-General of Radio-Television Belgrade. He was the commander of our work group, and I was an ordinary volunteer. Working side by side, we were clearing the ruins and pulling the injured and the dead out of a building by the Vardar river. In *Stara carsija* (Oriental-style business quarter) we ate *pljeskavice* (mince patties), and even today it seems to me that I can smell the charcoal they were grilled on. I still remember eating pork paste spread on bread as common food during the work drives, but – on the other hand – we used to smoke top-class cigarettes, 'Lucky Strike' and 'Chester field'. Tito was getting these from the Americans and sent them to "his youth". The (communist/socialist) youth organizations provided human resources for the ranks of the University Committee of the League of Communists of Belgrade; in 1964, the recruitment base was made up of the participants in voluntary work drives. I was admitted into the Committee as a member of the Party, for the number one of Yugoslav League of Communists, President Josip Broz Tito, would reward diligent people who sacrificed themselves, building a new, modern country. I understood Tito's message and the way in which the state operated. We were a poor country, yet a well-organized and disciplined one.

In late 1980's, on my way back from Italy, I noticed at Gorizia border crossing that only a simple rail track separated us from the West. It had been there for decades, and we – the poor Serbs from Yugoslavia – did not run away massively across it westbound. Those who did, and over the decades they counted mere few hundreds of thousands, came back during the 1990's to deliver lectures to Slobodan Milosevic and the Serbian people, lectures on democracy and western values. Incapable of understanding the system in Serbia, those returnee emigrants forcibly and without any rational plan ruined our lifestyle, human lives, and – moreover – Milosevic the 'Vozhd', because they persuaded us that the time had come for us to 'become the West'. What is worst of all, we are now neither in the East nor in the West; we have found ourselves in an abyss of purposeless living, deprived of our own system and way of life.

But let me go back to the sixties. As a manager in the construction company *Rad*, my father Branko and architect Branko Pesic, the

Mayor of Belgrade, began to design and build the largest bridge in the metropolis, one across the Sava river, named *Gazela* ('Gazelle'). My father thus took part in the establishment of a new city on the opposite bank, Novi Beograd. 'New Belgrade' sprang upon a onetime marsh after immense quantities of sand from the river had been poured thereon.

The time saw emergence of Yugoslavia's middle class, but also of the first wealthy people. One could get rich through some stategiven privileges, by taking larger amounts of foreign currency for travelling allowances and perdiem than prescribed, buying things on long-term (in lation-depreciated) credit, as well as corruption. Directors in export companies began to buy expensive fur-coats and cars and to take their gold-wearing wives to the theatre. For instance, my schoolmate Buca Prohaska belonged to higher class, so he wore fashionable clothes: light raincoat (plastic mac) called *suskavac* ('rustle-coat'), cardigan and espadrilles. I would go to the theatre in my father's coat with too long sleeves, which gave rise to my friends' mocking comments.

As a devoted Orthodox believer, my mother Mara secretly went to St. Mark's Church to pray for our wellbeing, taking precautions that the Communist Party or the secret police (UDBa) do not find out about it. Our family prospered when we got an apartment in the centre of the city; my father's company *Rad* allocated him an apartment at 16 Vojvode Dobrnjca Street. He aslo got a raise in salary, so he could send his three children to university studies – of medicine, ine arts and law respectively. My sister Snezana studied arts in Herceg Novi on the Montenegrin coast, so I used to visit her there; thus, I saw the Adriatic Sea for the first time in my life in 1960's. The seaside spa of Igalo, where I own a clinic now, was an extension of this coastal town.

Owing to Marshal Tito, who took care of socially balancing the classes and who was in held in high esteem by the United States, we were gradually growing into a modern country. Great worldfamous artists would come to Yugoslavia, including Duke Ellington and Sarah Vaughan. I served the army in Belgrade as an intern at the Medical Officers' School, attached to the headquarters of the Yugoslav National Army. I also attended a course in military intelligence at nearby Batajnica. Moreover,

I enjoyed the privilege to frequently leave the barracks and go around the city and – while dating General Siljegovic's daughter – raved it up with my girlfriend at the dancing parties held in the clubs of the Law School or the Faculty of Mechanical Engineering.

Upon graduation from the Faculty of Medicine, I got a job as a physician at the *Jasmin* company which advertised itself as a "house of beauty". The company was situated in Tasmajdan Park. Wives of cabinet ministers and ladies in ministerial posts frequented this beauty parlor.

One of them was spouse to Jovan Veselinov[48]; Belgrade's writers were crazy about her. I practised depilation and anti-acne treatment, applying the famed Dr. Lalosevic Cream in the latter.

In those years, the first spa pool was inaugurated; it was managed by Professor Lalosevic. I took part in some fashion shows of the Inex Company staged at Gradska kafana ('City Coffeehouse'). Belgrade's first discotheque was my favorite place of entertainment: it was opened in 1964 by Lazar Secerovic, alias Laza Secer in Ive Lole Ribara Street (now

Svetogorska), near *Atelje* 212[49].

In the *Jasmin* Company I was, once again, secretary of the Party unit. Croatian daily *Vecernji list* ('Evening Paper') wrote about me as a 'beauty doctor' in 1969. The make-up artist Lejla Mandzuka, who came from England to work in Belgrade, introduced me to the elite circles. Her make-up practice was frequented by ministerial wives and those of many Party and state officials, but also by the female singers of *Pesma leta* ('Summer Song'), the largest festival of popular music at the time. So I met some of those singers, like Radmila Karaklajic and Gabi Novak. Lola Novakovic was a lady of impressive beauty, while Tereza Kesovija was a Dalmatian diva. Tereza, who later appeared twice in Eurosong –once for Yugoslavia and once for Monaco – would reach for some perfumed deodorant, hitch up the skirt showing her sunburnt thighs and spray them with it. She talked loud so that everybody could hear:

– Oh, my dearies, I haven't had a bath, but I'll scent myself so I don't smell bad!

[42] **Lika**, an inland region in Croatia which used to be part of the Military Frontier of the Austrian Empire. About one half of its population were Serbs who prevailed in the eastern part of the region, while Croats prevailed in the western part. After the abolishment of the Military Frontier wherein most Serbian men served, in order to surpass poverty, the *Licani* used to emigrate to the United States in search of jobs and better future, many of them to stay there forever; they left their country in late 19th and over the first half of the 20th century. The next wave of emigrants from Lika arrived in America after World War II, and those were political opponents to Communism, persecuted in Tito's Yugoslavia. The third wave was made up of those (mostly young and educated) running away from the war of 1990's and part of the refugees from Croatia following the 1995 Operation Storm when the Croatian military and paramilitary drove out some 250,000 Serbs often killing the civilians, including children and very old people. The most famous emigrant from Lika to the U.S.A. was Nikola Tesla, one of the world's greatest scientists and inventors ever. – *Translator's note.*

[43] **Nish**, **Dimitrovgrad** and **Pirot** are towns in Southern Serbia; today, Nish is the third-big city in Serbia. – *Translator's note.*

[44] **UDB**(a), acronym of *Uprava Drzavne bezbednosti* (State Security Administration/Service); the secret police agency was a much-feared tool of state control which changed the focus of its activities in accordance to the current priorities in chasing 'the enemies of the state'. –*Translator's note.*

[45] **Pancevo** is a city on the opposite, left side of the Danube; part of its vicinity falls within the territory of Belgrade. It is situated in Banat, one of the three sub-regions in the Autonomous Province of Vojvodina. – *Translator's note.*

[46] **Vlastimir Pavlovic Carevac** (1895-1965) was a Belgrade lawyer but became a legendary figure in the world of authentic folk music heritage as a conductor, violinist and collector of traditional folk songs. – *Translator's note.*

[47] **Ada Ciganlija** – 'Gypsy Ait', commonly shortened to 'Ada' and nicknamed 'Belgrade Sea', the Sava river's island artificially turned into a peninsula. It falls within Belgrade's Municipality of Cukarica. – *Translator's note.*

[48] **Jovan Veselinov Zarko** (1906-1982) – national hero of World War II, later high Yugoslav and Serbian official. His offices included those of the President of Serbia's Government and Speaker of the Serbian Parliament. His wife Stanka Veselinov Seka (1820-1984) was herself a prominent participant in the People's Liberation Movement and later an influential politician, especially in journalism and publishing (e.g. editor-in-chief of *NIN*, the leading weekly). – *Translator's note.*

[49] **Atelje 212** is a prestigious playhouse of international reputation, founded in 1956. It staged some plays unthinkable to perform in other Communist countries (like Samuel Beckett's *Waiting for Godot*) and maintained an avant-garde repertory. The rock musical *Hair*, staged in 1969, was one of its breakthroughs. The name comes from the initial 212 seats in its auditorium. – *Translator's note.*

GRANDPA'S BOY

I USED TO FANTASIZE OF BECOMING A a renowned Belgrade-based gynecologist some day. So the job at the *Jasmin* Company (offering men's and women's beauty treatments) was something I only took as a point of departure toward my ultimate goal. I could never imagine that the inger of destiny would lead me in a different direction. When I was a university student, my mother Mara was trying – via Red Cross – to establish contact with her father in America. One day, my grandfather Sam Phillips Filipovic of New Jersey turned up in Belgrade. He immediately came to see me at the military barracks where I served at the Medical Officers' School. The greeting ceremony and formal exchange of kind sentences were followed by a determined utterance of Grandpa Sam:

– You're coming to America with me!

For the then high price of $ 300, he bought me a round trip air ticket to New York at Belgrade's *Pan American* office and handed it in to me. I kept the ticket for six months. I did not dare set out on the trip and visit my Grandpa, for my mother Mara threatened to kill herself if I leave the family. My father Branko told me one day in confidence:

– Borko, son, go to America and come back if you don't like it there!

Borko Djordjevic, YNA soldier, as an intern at the Medical Officers' School, 1969

That was in my line of thinking. I was also motivated by some events which had happened a couple of months earlier by a combination of various circumstances. The studies of medicine were rather easy to me, especially in the first years when general subjects made up the curriculum. However, owing to my waste of time on students' dancing parties, my student book, *indeks*, was full of sixes, the lowest passable marks. In the last years, when clinical subjects came into focus, I kept earning nines and tens, the highest marks. Due to my Party-related activism, there were good prospects for my professional progress and a career at the Faculty of Medicine.

Sava Filipovic/Sam Phillips – Dr. Borko Djordjevic's matrilineal grandfather

I aspired to specialize in gynecology at the *Narodni front* Maternity Hospital in Belgrade. The situation was working in my favor: a substitution of (doctors') generations was taking place in Yugoslavia in late 1960's. The partisans in high official and managerial posts were being replaced by well-educated Communists and intellectuals with whom I had a good communication. However, my abovesaid aspirations were blocked by the unsatisfactory average mark during the studies (7.5) and the daughter of President Tito's personal doctor.

Namely, only one graduate could be admitted to specialty training in gynecology. Two of us competed: Gordana Najdanovic and myself. Gordana, who was girlfriend and later wife of my friend, journalist Backo, enjoyed the privilege of being daughter to a professor of medicine and respectable Tito's doctor. Thus, she was admitted to specialize in gynecology with Professor Cemerikic. I was driven to despair by this defeat which was personal and professional alike.

Dr. Borko Djordjevic serving as *member of the Medical Corps*

In this state od desperation, a man turned up who gave me some hope that there existed a better future than the one Belgrade could offer. As a Party activist, I would stay up late at the meetings of the Faculty's 'basic organization of the Communist League'. The famed thoracic surgeon Mane Budisavljevic would usually give me a lift to my home at Palilula quarter. He was an easygoing man, open-minded and experienced, whose demeanor was humanistic rather than professorial. He was brother to Jovanka Broz nee Budisavljevic, wife of the Yugoslav President, which I was unaware of at the time. When I complained to him about being deprived of the gynecology specialization at the *Narodni front Clinic*, Dr. Budisavljevic told me that he had once left for France in order to specialize at the Sorbonne. For some time he had worked in Paris and 'learned the ropes', then came to Belgrade to show his skill and the professional 'way of the world' to his colleagues. He became Chief of Thoracic Surgery Department.

So Dr. Budisavljevic gave me this piece of advice:

– Dear Colleague Borko, go abroad to learn the ropes. Once back in Belgrade, you're gonna piss on them!

This manly advice turned into my vow to myself. Furious about the circumstances, I promised myself that night:

– I'll be back one day to show you who Doctor Borko is!

*

On April 13, 1970, angry with my Party, with my friend and his girlfriend Gordana, angry with my Belgrade – I took my Granpa's tickets bought six months before and lew to New York. It was only on my fourth attempt that I managed to get a visa to enter the United States. I had been declined one three times because I was a registered Communist. On departure, Mile Golosijan – then manager of Belgrade's *PanAm* office and husband of the singer Lola Novakovic – saw me off.(Lola had earlier been married to my teacher of physical education at the Fifth Belgrade High School, but got divorced to remarry Mile Golosijan.)

At the age of 28 and, strangely enough, as an activist of the Communist Party of Yugoslavia, I left for America. My grandfather Sam Phillips lived across the Hudson river, in Elizabeth, New Jersey. At an p y earlier time, Grandpa ran restaurants, a bookmaker's and a racecourse at Akron, Ohio. During the prohibition, together with Joseph Kennedy, he distilled spirits and sold them around Pennsylvania and the miners' colony at Woodbury. The Serbian miners would get their wages Fridays to spend them in bars on Saturdays and Sundays drinking Kennedy and Sam's liquors. That is how my grandfather earned his riches.

Grandpa was a tall and handsome man. He had one wife, Grandma Dara, five lovers, four children and two wills. One will was there to wave to various women, but it was empty. The other one was written out, and he kept it for his family. All of his properties were intended for his children. This will and other valuable papers were safeguarded in the spare tire bay of his car. When I came to live with Sam Phillips, he was an American retiree, a grumpy and harsh man.

He did not allow me to enter his house through the main door; I had to use the side door and the garage. Once, on the way home from Jersey City, I got on a wrong bus and was therefore one hour late for dinner. Grandpa said:

– No dinner for you, you're late! It's past six p.m. and the kitchen's closed!

To me, who grew up eating genuine healthy food of Serbian cuisine, deprivation of a meal was a severe punishment. Later, when I began to drive, Grandpa would not give me a guarantee and insurance. He was pushing me off in order to teach me to strive for my life-goals. He was seriously getting on my nerves, yet I did not hate him. I had respect for his willingness to take me to America and give me a chance to make my dream come true. So I resembled a tomcat that patiently waits for his prey.

I reached the United States as a highly trained person in a profession that was in demand. As a visitor, I was in "status limbo". I had my Belgrade diploma of graduation recognized, as well as the driving licence acquired while serving in the Yugoslav National Army; also, I got an ECFMG status. I learned English within half a year. The first thing I mastered were American swearwords: to a bus driver who unwillingly let me aboard I said "Shit!" and he got furious and threw me out because he thought that it was a referrence to a black man.

Professor John Terry who taught plastic surgery

Quite soon I obtained a PRC professional licence and started internship. At the City Hospital I learned to do all sorts of jobs: besides the tasks of a physician and specializing trainee, I was a doctor on call at nighttime, therapist, paramedic, patient transporter (gurney- and wheelchair pusher), as well as specialization student in Plastic Surgery Unit.

Americans, and my neighbors in Elizabeth and acquaintances from Jersey City in particular, thought me to be a doctor of the American poor people, black people and the Puerto Ricans. I invested some efforts in socializing with respectable individuals and making steps up on the American social ladder. A mocking response I happened to experience practically forced me to do so: During a donor's reception for the staff and patients of the hospital in New York, in 1972, the following dialogue took place:
- Who are you? – a gentleman asked me.
- A doctor! – I answered.
- What car do you drive?
- A Camaro.
- Aha! – he mocked me openly.

The very next day I sold my Chevrolet Camaro and bought a Mercedes.

As I had acquired excellent manners and got used to wearing elegant suits, my deportment in New Jersey and New York was one of a European gentleman. I went to the hospital in Italian suits and white shoes. Popular singers used to come there, and Frank Sinatra was something of a model to me.

My American girlfriend Lorraine Aklonis thought that I was a well-off guy. She was a teacher from Clark, New Jersey, daughter of a Polish immigrant. I was my Grandpa's boy, a Serb from Roselle Street in Elizabeth, NJ. Free from any suspicion, Lorraine introduced me to the elite circles of New York City. Her father, Mr. Aklonis – as is the custom in the States – would invite me for Thanksgiving feast in his home. Eating the feastday turkey, I learned from him that the best and most renowned hospital was Saint Barnabas Medical Center in the town of Livingston, New Jersey, owned by the Italian Scala family.

New York, 1971: Borko Djordjevic (right) with his first American girl iend Lorraine Aklonis, the famous TV anchor Branislav Surutka and Mrs. Surutka

---

– Elvis Presley and Jacqueline Kennedy were treated there – Mr. Aklonis told me.

To me, the information was something of a top professional secret of a physician. To treat successful and rich people, especially Americans, was a challenge of one's lifetime. So I applied for internship at that hospital in Livingston. One night, in the basement with the medical center's swimming pool, I saw through a misted glass wall some wealthy patients in their bathrobes – sitting at a table and gambling. It was my first lesson about the American wealthy class, which in just a few words read: work hard, make money and enjoy yourself.

Although I lived in Elzabeth, a town wherein many Serbs resided, I did not socialize with them. The most outstanding Serb there was a Tika Topalovic, owner of the bar named Europe; he was a chetnik from Trstenik, Serbia, and a benefactor to some ten thousand Serbian emigrants whom he had helped – by his personal guarantees – reach America. I never met this chetnik or any of his fellow- fighters in person. For, before I left for the

United States, my Communist Party forbade me to contact those people. Namely, before I departed on my trip to the U.S.A., I took a three-months' unpaid leave at the *Jasmin* Company. It was then, in the spring of 1970, that the Party officials close to me ordered:

– You must not socialize with any of Yugoslav emigrants in America.

There are a lot of *ustashe* and *chetniks*[50], traitors and spies, among them. They might recruit you to work against the Party and Yugoslavia. Report to our consul when you arrive in New York. Take care of what you're doing, for we're going to get all information about you from the consul!

I was so frightened by the warning that I still avoid socializing with American Serbs and Yugoslavia's political emigrants in the States. When I did meet a number of them, it was not in the the United States but in Yugoslavia upon their arrival in Belgrade in 1990's.

Frankly, I did not aspire to the medical career the way it turned to take course. I was resisting total Americanization and the 'melting pot' consequences. So I would often come back to Serbia: actually, I lived here in Belgrade and worked over there in the States.

A large number of Serbs studied or pursued postgraduate studies all over America. They would boast of that in Serbia, even when they did not have a working licence and only watched others perform. Many would come back to their homeland in order to assert themselves and score 'political points'; others returned to show off before their poor fellow-Serbs enacting the roles of American millionaires. I stayed a genuine Serb that I had always been: I never altered my Serbian name and surname, and I came back with the intention to support my people through my work and education.

Just as I was suspicious of the Serbian political emigrants to the States, the Americans had their suspicions regarding my status. My professional status in the United States implied hard work yet not some of the basic human rights. I was not allowed to leave the U.S.A. It took a long time to become a Green Card holder (implying permanent residence), and get American citizenship.

The Americans openly said to me:

– Do not hope to be granted permanent residence and American citizenship soon, for you are a Communist leader at Belgrade University.

– Never mind! – I encouraged myself. – I'll be waiting! The "never mind" response was not sincere. I felt wretched and humiliated. Even worse: I felt as if it had all been my fault. But I kept silent, for any conflict with the American authorities was out of the question. During my stay in the United States I perfected my afinity for careful listening to what other people said, absorbing the information which could prove useful to me. I interpreted this trait of mine as an inborn 'sense of survival' which urged me to get acquainted and socialize with the smartest, richest and best people I met.

Toward the end of 1973 I complained to a lady volunteering at the hospital that my father was dying and I was not permitted to leave the U.S.A. and go to Serbia to see him. It would be a great relief to see my father Branko, and I was extremely unhappy about his heart attack that happened after an explosion and fire at the Pancevo Refinery; as the director of the *Rad* Construction Company which had built the reinery he felt personally responsible for the accident. I felt very bad indeed about the impossibility to leave the States and visit him.

Mrs. Goldfarb (that was the name of the lady) was married to the head of New Jersey Immigration Ofice. I was not aware of the fact that she conveyed my complaint to her husband and asked him to help me. The Goldfarbs were a Jewish family, and when they invited me for a Friday dinner in their home, preceded by a visit to their synagogue, I met the American Jews for the first time.

It was also the first time I felt comfortable, for many elements of their habits reminded me of our Serbian tradition. Soon thereafter, I was summoned for an interview at the Immigration Ofice in Trenton, capital of the U.S. state of New Jersey. The interview resulted in Green Card issued to me, which enabled me to leave for Serbia and come back to the States to resume my job.

In 1974, my first return to Belgrade took place: after the four years of studies and training in America I had an opportunity to see my family, and also to appear before my colleagues,

Belgrade doctors. I took with me the prominent professor and cardiac surgeon Dr. Masterson with me, with an intention that he delivers a lecture at Cardiac Surgery Department of Dragisa Misovic Hospital. On that occasion, I dared tackle the role of an interpreter – although I had gone to the United States without speaking English at all. And here, I realized that I did not know the terminology of cardiac surgery in the Serbian language, for in the States I had learned the terms in English only. So at one point during the lecture I got stuck, speechless. Ashamed, I sank through the floor. Luckily enough, Professor Adamov, Chief of the Cardiac Surgery Department, reacted immediately and took over interpretation of Dr. Masterson's lecture, thus sparing me the shame.

---

[50] **Ustashe** – UHRO *Ustashe – Hrvatska revolucionarna organizacija* ('Ustashe – Croatian Revolutionary Organization'). For more, see: Misha Glenny: The Balkans: Nationalism, War, and the Great Powers, updated edition, Penguin Books, 2012. The Ustashe regime of the 'Independent State of Croatia' established the Jasenovac Concentration Camp (referred to as 'the Yugoslav Auschwitz') during WWII primarily aimed at extermination of the Serbs.

Chetnik – a member of the Chetnik Detachments of the Yugoslav Army, an anti-Axis movement led by Draza Mihailovic. The movement had long-range goals but engaged in only marginal resistance and for limited periods of time. It was by no means homogenous: some of its units often acted independently of the 'official leadership', occasionally committing war crimes. Basically, they were royalists who emphasized their Eastern Orthodox religion, and harsh anti-Communists.

After the war, a great many *ustashe* and *chetniks* emigrated to the West European countries and especially to the U.S.A. (Croats also massively left for Latin America).

The Communist regime tended to minorize the *Ustashi* crimes and augment those of the *chetniks* in order to balance the ethnic responsibility of the Croats and the Serbs, for the sake of "brotherhood and unity", one of the fundamental slogans in the postwar federated Yugoslavia. The old enmities were awakened in the 1990's, when the new military and paramilitary formations of the Croats and the Serbs called the opposite sides *chetniks* and *ustashe* respectively which in rude speech went as far as to label the whole nations of the Serbs and Croats. – *Translator's note.*

PLASTIC SURGEON

When I went back from Serbia to New York, in 1974, I still did not quite understand what America meant. I did not know the art of living and professional progress there. I did not know how to make further steps in my medical career. Professor Masterson seemed to feel this lack of awareness on my part, so he gave me a piece of fatherly advice:

– Dear Colleague, there's no American hospital in which you can make reputation or money. In America, if you're not a university doctor, you're not a rich man! But if you want to succeed as a doctor in private practice and be in high esteem as an expert in the States, you have to pass specialization at one of the top ten universities.

He started to name these: Harvard, Yale, Princeton, Stanford, Johns Hopkins, Pennsylvania University, Ohio University...

I followed Dr. Masterson's advice and enrolled in the third year of specialization studies in general surgery at the University of Pennsylvania in Philadelphia. The specialty was my choice due to a great event: Dr. C. Everett Koop had just separated the Siamese twins from Argentina. I had the honor of meeting this famous physician who was the Surgeon General of the United States under President Ronal Reagan, and of working for him. After separation, both twins had skinless body surfaces left behind, which required coverage of the skin defect. It was then that I eyewitnessed plastic surgery and watched the delicate work of the surgeons performing it. At that moment I made up my mind: that was to be my specialization. As a university employee, I was earning a 10,000-dollar salary per year. As soon as I received the first payment, I sent one hundred dollars to each of my parents –mother Mara and father Branko.

Internship in New Jersey: second year of surgery specialization at the Mountain Sight Hospital

I was progressing fast in my job in Philadelphia, for I was 'captured' by an aspiration to perfect my skill, go back to Serbia and present my success. In the United States, the university system of promotion is pyramidal, which means that only the best climb up steadily. The others 'fall off' and proceed at minor universities. At one moment in 1975, just two of us were left in the 'race' toward the top of the pyramid: Dr. Larry Reed, a small competition-spirited Jew, and myself, a small competitionspirited Serb. We were both busy as beavers, working days and nights. Daytime was for studying and internship, and night-time would be spent on duty.

Borko Djordjevic with John Masterson, Professor of General surgery

In the 1970's, Philadelphia saw a war between police force and drug cartels; this implied a dozen casualties each night taken to our hospital. As a duty doctor I had to diagnose the patients, treat their wounds, operate when necessary, take care of their therapy and further cure. In the morning, reporting followed to the board of the university clinic doctors chaired by Dr. Neymar.

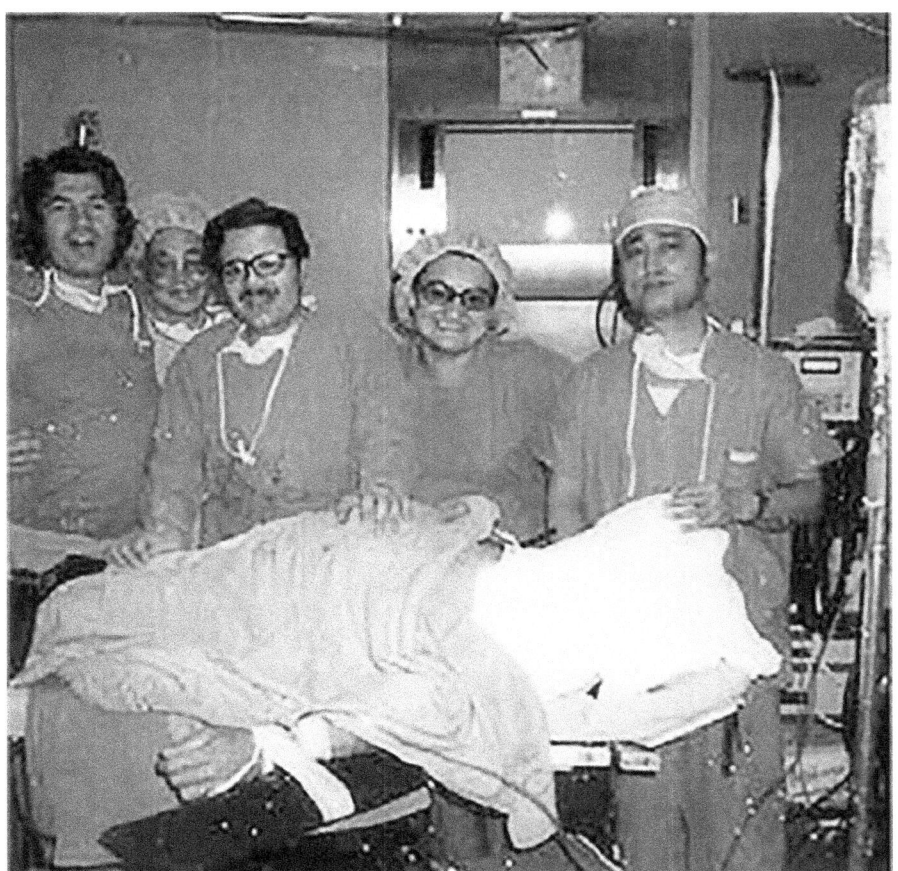
Borko Djordjevic (left) in an American operating room

When not on duty, I would watch experiments on live human beings, the homeless taken from the streets of Philly and other cities; on these, American doctors were gaining experience in emergency cases and unpredictable situations. These patients underwent testing of painkillers or new anti-diabetic medicines, induction of coma and recovery from it. I did not think about the ethical and legal aspects of such experiments, but the fact is – the Americans did practise them. They would sacrifice people one night in order to learn how to strive to keep them alive the next.

As an assistant-on-duty to my colleague Reed, I had to obey his orders and work in accordance with these. The roles were inverse when I was on duty. One night, when Dr. Reed was in the theatre on duty, a patient arrived with a kidney shot through; Dr. Reed extracted the kidney and threw it into the waste bin. In the morning, Dr. Neymar listened to his report. Hearsay had been passed around about his uncaring attitude and dormant behaviour during this kind of meetings. But in the said situation, he took my colleague Reed by surprise:

– Tell me, what did you do with the extracted kidney? And what was the uninjured one like?

The question was essential and principled. The protocol order said: before you extract the injured kidney you have to perform intravenous pyelography (IVP) on the healthy one in order to see if it functions. If not, you must save the injured kidney and keep its function at minimum.

Reed was dodging the straight answer, for he had not undertaken the IVP of the healthy kidney. He earned low evaluation for not honoring the medical principle and procedure. That was the moment when I was unofficially proclaimed as the best surgeon in Philadelphia, my competitor out of the race. And that is how I climbed to the top of the pyramid at the University of Pennsylvania.

*

As an American doctor and a citizen of the United States I went to the Ohio University for the next two years in order to pursue advanced plastic surgery. I chose Ohio despite the invitations I had received from New York and San Francisco because my mother Marija-Mara had been born in Akron and had relatives in that state. My knowledge was evaluated as matching the requirements of the Ohio University which boasted one of the supreme specialization programs in plastic surgery.

At the Methodist Hospital, the teaching base for the Ohio University, surgeons used to perform dozens of aesthetic/plastic surgeries a day. When I appeared there for an admission interview with the chief of the department, I asked to see the operation protocol for the past six months. From this document I learned that three to four esthetic surgeries had been scheduled and performed daily. To me, the fact sufficed for the decision to accept their specialization program, for it obviously offered a broad 'repertory' of surgical procedures in which I took interest.

Columbus, Ohio was a city of white population, owing to the domination of the Ku Klux Klan and the elite Rednecks brethren. This hospital was also for the white people. Of the ten plastic surgeons employed therein, nine taught me the lessons of how not to work, and only one taught me the proper performance. The experience was invaluable.

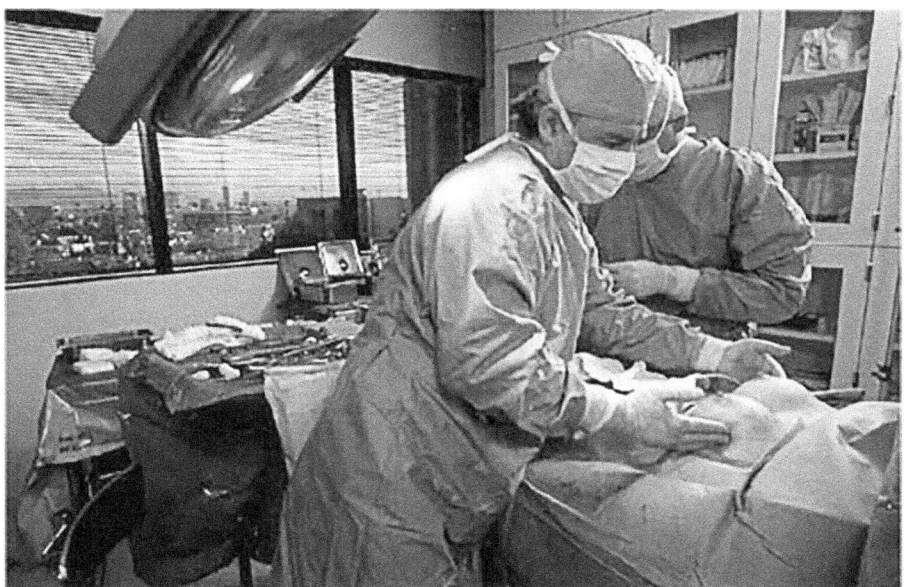

Borko Djordjevic performing a plastic-surgical procedure

There, in Columbus, the famed doctor John Terry worked. The man was an artist of the scalpel and a ballet dancer in the theatre. He had graduated from the University of Pittsburgh School of Medicine (UPSOM), the best place to study surgery in the States, to become a supreme master of plastic surgery. Rows of patients could be seen in the anteroom of his office, people from all over the region – from New York, via Chicago and Columbus, to San Francisco.

He admitted me as the best intern from the University of Pennsylvania, but had some difficulty with my European background.

My English had a strong accent, disliked by Dr. Terry. Yet he appreciated my knowledge and my attitude to patients. For seven months I used to assist at operations every day, take care of his patients, their therapy, the regularity of their checkups; I was smiling while bringing them potties or seeing them off on their departure. In return, the patients (and elderly American ladies especially) praised me in their letters to Dr. Terry as a good doctor and a good person. Gradually, Dr. Terry completely accepted me as an associate of his. After a morning report, when I had given a survey of the duty shift and said "We've done three nose surgeries, two on breasts and one on the belly", Dr. Terry reproached me:

– Dr. Djordjevic, we're working with human beings. Kindly call our patients by their full name and surname!

Soon thereafter, he appointed me Chief of his Plastic Surgery Unit.

I entered the circles of great surgeons. Obviously, I satisied their social taste. White, good-looking and on specialization in their Plastic Surgery Department. Each of them interviewed me. Moreover, they would assign me to operations of their private patients. Dr. John Terry was the last to do so.

He invited me to a party held on his yacht. Fortunately, I had enough money for fancy clothes. So I put on a blue blazer and grey trousers, to arrive there in my red sports car, a Corvette. When I got aboard the boat, anchored in Sandusky Bay, there were only Dr. Terry, his lover and a black cat stretched on the deck.

– Sorry, the engine won't start, so all the guests have left as we haven't been able to sail off. Will you help me see what's wrong with the engine? – said Dr. Terry.

I went down below the deck in my clean white shirt, wondering: "I didn't really need *this*." In his white gloves, Professor pointed out to the dirty screws I had to drive out and passed me an oilsmeared wrench, looking at me as if I'd been a wonderworker.

I had to work quickly, as it was getting dark. He passed me all sorts of tools: wrenches, screwdrivers, a hammer... And I was trying to do something about it.

– That'll be enough. Let's go home – Dr. John Terry said all of a sudden.

Over the next two years I kept wondering about what happened on the boat. Did he test my obedience or determinedness to get things done? Why did he make me get dirty? Only two years later, after I got my degree, during the ceremony attended by my parents, Professor Terry admitted:

– I had to test him, to see how resourceful he is, whether he obeys me and – most importantly – whether his hand works quickly enough. Also, if he's got taste in dressing, if he can look like a real gentleman.

AMERICAN FIRST LADIES

As to Professor Terry's lesson on good manners befitting doctors, I immediately applied it in the daily routines of my 'American life'. I wanted the American public and the American patients of mine to know and remember my name. Yet the method I resorted to in order to reach the goal was bad: I decided to work little and earn much. I started up a plastic surgery office at Palm Springs, in the sunny and expensive California. The full name read: "Plastic Surgery Clinic Borko Djordjevic, M.D." I doubled up the prices for procedures, for I thought it would lead to well-chosen clientelle and less work. However, what happened was exactly the opposite: a large number of patients kept pouring in, and I had to work hard.

U.S. First Ladies

In California, I had a reputation as a young, good plastic surgeon, but a bit too expensive. In response to such a recommendation, Betty Ford, spouse of the former President Gerald Ford, wished to meet me.

– I'm going to Palm Springs to see Doctor Borko Djordjevic! – Betty Ford said to some journalists in 1979.

Owing to some photos where we appeared together, the American media were guessing about me being her plastic surgeon. They wrote and talked about me as "the golden boy" of the former First Lady.

Betty Ford was born in 1918. She married Gerald Ford who became President of the United States after Richard Nixon's resignation. As the First Lady, during her life in the White House (1974-7) and thereafter, Betty Ford earned great respect due to her frankness and courage in battling with breast cancer, painful arthritis and dual addiction – to drugs and alcohol. She was also an outspoken champion of women's rights who advocated the right to abortion. She had five children.

Former U.S. Presidents and First Ladies received by Ronald Reagan (1991)

Her fame rose with the establishment of Betty Ford Center for the treatment of chemical dependency. The Center's clientele included many famous persons, such as Elizabeth Taylor, Johnny Cash and Lindsey Lohan. She never forgot me. I would occasionaly hear from her – she would call or write toward Christmas and New Year's Eve. To express my appreciation, I would send letters of thanks with lowers to the First Lady. She was a loyal friend. Unfortunately, she passed away in a Californian hospital on July 12, 2011. A minor media spotlight I owe to Betty Ford helped me appear on the list of American celebrities.

In 1980, Los Angeles Times wrote about me as a celebrity for whom the prominent artist Sascha Lautman painted a portrait. The same artist portrayed Pope Paul at the Vatican. Prior to assuming the presidential duties, Ronald Reagan visited my clinic at Palm Springs –on September 14, 1981. The media all over the States reported on this event, mentioning the fact that Dr. Djordjevic had performed dozens of extremely successful esthetic and related medical surgeries.

– Dr. Djordjevic has won fame by the surgery on the mutilated face of Jane Byrne, Mayor of Chicago and friend to John F. Kennedy, recovering its original beauty and function – the media wrote emphasizing the admiration of the U.S. President to the surgical achievement.

The renowned Regina M. Blume of Los Angeles said in public, in 1985:

– Dr. Borko Djordjevic is the God of Beauty for Hollywood divas! As soon as in late 1980's I was the most popular plastic surgeon in the United States. I resided in Palm Springs where I had a clinic and a 10-million worth house on a hillside. Californian illustrated magazines published features on my home. My first and only neighbor was Bob Hope, American actor, singer, dancer, athlete and comedian. The Americans still claim that my "artistic scalpel embroidery" brought happiness to at least 16,000 women.

Bob Hope and Borko Djordjevic

*

It was the world-famous Gabor sisters that made me stay on the celebrity top list for the next ten or so years. These Hungarianborn ladies of Jewish background enjoyed the reputation of European ladies and beauties welcomed as guests of the wealthiest Americans. Their mother, Jolie Gabor, took care of her girls – Zsa Zsa, Eva and Magda –and some two hundred more 'Gabor Girls' that 'embellished' high-class parties.

Jolie and her husband Vilmos Gabor were members of a wealthy family in the line of jewellery trade. After her parents got killed in a Budapest bombing, they emigrated to the United States in 1941. The most famous of her daughters was Sari Gabor, broadly known as Zsa Zsa Gabor, Miss Hungary in 1936, who became an American movie, theatre and TV actress. Zsa Zsa had nine marriages and only one child –Francesca Hilton – who died. As a true friend of theirs, I often accompanied Jolie and Zsa Zsa. Jolie passed away in 1997. Zsa Zsa Gabor survived a horri ic automobile crash which left her partially paralyzed and later necessitated leg amputation; she now lives in California. I have not seen her for quite a while.[51]

Prince Andrew and Princess Eva Marija Karadjordjevic with Borko Djordjevic in his Palm Springs home

Eva Gabor was the youngest of the three sisters; her mother said that she was not a desired child. But she was a most talented actress who featured in Vincente Minnelli's 1958 musical *Gigi*. Upon the family's arrival in the U.S.A., she made a career in Hollywood: her fame was based on starring in the TV sitcom *Green Acres* about life on a traditional farm. Eva got married five times, and all of her spouses were affluent men. She had no children. In the year 1986, when she was in her late sixties, I helped Eva Gabor shoot five more movies. That is, I performed a facelift and body sculpture for her. She fell in love with me and I was appearing with her around Beverly Hills dressed up in white tuxedo and white shoes. In 1997, the newspaper Desert Scene wrote that I "almost married Eva Gabor". Unfortunately, she died of pneumonia in 1995.

The ever-beautiful and ever-successful Gabor sisters kept me by their side and presented me to the American society. I was a guest of honor in the residences of numerous senators, congressmen and their wives, as well as politicians and Hollywood artists. I hosted a ball in my own Palm Springs home where my special guests were Prince Andrew Karadjordjevic[52] and his spouse Princess Eva Maria Karadjordjevic. By the way, I was a Serb who taught the Americans how to faultlessly pronounce and spell my name and surname.

*

Now I have to reveal the secret of my surgical practice and art of beauty: it does not lie in my skillful hands and ingers that do intricate needlework on one's face and body; it rather lies in my mind, oriented to accurately assess the patient's ability to bear his operation and take pride in the result. When my patients tell me that they think of me each time they look in the mirror, I know that I have done a good piece of work. In America, it takes three major qualities to undergo this kind of surgery: first, to find the best surgeon; second, to have a lot of money; and, third, to have balls. American women have all of these qualities.

On the other hand, Serbian and Montenegrin women are not predisposed for such operations, for they lack the courage needed to go and see a plastic surgeon in the first place, and, in the second place, to face the effects of the surgery done.

I have described my medical experience in the five-volume university text-book on plastic surgery. Today, I am an associate professor of Belgrade University and the University of Nish respectively. I have received an appeal on the part of Professor Ljubisa Rakic, Member of the Serbian Academy of Sciences and Arts, to undertake lecturing at the English-language Department of Belgrade's Faculty of Medicine, but I still want to maintain the practice.

In early 1980's, I had 40 employees working in two operating rooms. My clinic offered nine apartments, and I used to receive eleven patients weekly. I would put them together in the dining room during the midday meal so that they could share their fears and discuss the risks of their operations. Thus, they could exchange experiences and encourage one another. Lastly, they would often accept the suggestion to undergo another surgery and embetter some other parts of their body.

There were two kinds of patients. Some were naturally beautiful, others could not stand aging that 'stole' their beauty. One of the latter kind was a brilliant actress, a true embodiment of film beauty and my acquaintance, who withdrew from her artistic carrer and public life due to her advanced age. Another actress, a corpulent girl from New York and a heavy smoker, could not stand her age and therefore came to me for help. I had so many clients that I could pick up those whom I wanted to operate on and those whom I did not want to see on my operating table. So I made up my mind: I was going to work beautiful persons only – in order to recover their beauty, slow down their aging or remedy the illness or shortcomings of their skin.

My 'oeuvre' includes facial corrections for an American king of entertainment, the wife of a British pop star, and a famous actress from TV serials about the moneyed classes. The *Globe* magazine published a photo of my bandaged patient on the front page, with the title "Plastic Surgery Shocker: GUESS WHO". Inside, on pages 27-28, an illustrated feature spread about me and my patient who paid $ 30,000 for rejuvenation of his face.

In California, I had the reputation of an 'exclusive surgeon'. My results were exclusive indeed, and so were my patients. Personally, I reckoned that I was as good as my last patient.

In keeping with the rules of the American elite, the person who makes you happy deserves your full appreciation. And the one who protects your dignity and remains discreet deserves a reward from you.

The plan of the destiny was that my new and affluent patient Gene Washburn should not leave Palm Springs – she became my first wife. In the year 1981, I was nearing the end of my thirties. Invariably preoccupied with work and fame, I found no time for marriage. I made$ 10,000 per surgery, and my weekly income amounted to $ 100,000. The heiress of the Washburn family that ran the *7 Up* Company came as a patient to my Palm Springs clinic for some facial corrections. Yet she changed her mind and decided to put her whole body to surgical procedures. She stayed at my clinic for 30 days.

Upon the operation, she brought an extremely big diamond necklace, put it round her neck and started to dance. Pleased with her new look, she rashly accepted my invitation to have a drink at my hillside villa above Palm Springs. In that residence of mine which had provided set for a James Bond movie we drank pure whiskey and then dined at the *Le Vallauris* Restaurant in Palm Springs. What followed was Gene's rather eccentric proposal:

– People talk about us. We should get married!

She was two years my senior, and terribly jealous. She would not allow beautiful patients approaching me, and that was fatal to my job.

We had no children. Gene died prematurely of pancreatic cancer.

---

[51] After the appearance of the Serbian edition of this book, Zsa Zsa Gabor passed away; the fatal cardiac arrest happened on December 18, 2016, less than two months before she would have celebrated her 100th birthday.
– *Translator's note.*

[52] **Prince Andrew of Yugoslavia** (b. Bled, Kingdom of Serbs, Croats and Slovenes, 1929 – d. Irvine, Ca. 1990) was the youngest child of King Alexander I of Yugoslavia. After the fall of monarchy in Yugoslavia during World War II, Prince Andrew lived in exile in England and the United States. – *Translator's note.*

ROSALYNN CARTER'S FRIEND

As my job of a doctor was public in character, and I was a public figure, the circle of my friends and acquaintances kept increasing. One of the peculiar men was Fred Mannix, the greatest magnate of Canada in the eighties who owned an oil company and a construction company that built roads, railways, airports etc. His wife Lynn Mannix introduced me to her friend Rosalynn Carter, spouse of President Jimmy Carter. The First Lady was born in Plains, Ga., in 1927, into the family of Edgar Smith. She married Jimmy Carter in 1946; it was nowhere near her
mind that this peanut farmer could be elected the 39th President of the United States of America. The couple had four children. She was the First Lady from 1977 to 1981. Her activities included work for the Carter Center as Chairperson of its Mental Health Task Force; in addition, she established the Rosalynn Carter Institute for Caregiving at the Georgia Southwestern State University.

Borko Djordjevic with Rosalynn Carter

The Carters were on close friendly terms with Gerald Ford and his wife. That is why I guess that it was Betty Ford who told Rosalynn Carter about me. Mrs. Carter was herself a well-informed lady. I got the impression that – as the First Lady of Georgia and, later, America – she was not happy about statesmen's servants and political advisers. She never behaved as a spouse to the number one statesman or a powerful 'swayer' of the United States. She took me as a friend and enabled my introduction to President Jimmy Carter.

Here is what Rosalynn Carter told me about her husband:

Jimmy is an extremely diligent and modest man. He is a descendant of a French-Irish family that settled in Georgia in 1830 and pursued cotton and peanut farming. He was born in 1924, in the little town of Plains where I happened to be the best friend of his sister Ruth Carter. It was owing to this friendship that we met, fell in love, got married, had children and stayed to live in the little Plains that counts merely 637 inhabitants.

It was on the basis of Mrs. Carter's accounts and my own American experiences that I sketched a portrait of this quiet and unpretentious peanut producer, carpenter and amateur painter, not quite popular American president yet one of the world's most prominent peacemakers. He grew up under the influence of his mother Lillian, a nurse and a liberal-oriented woman with a strong Baptist trait in her character. James Earl Carter Jr. graduated from the Naval Academy in Annapolis and specialized in nuclear submarines. He was a great humanist, a very educated person with a B.Sc. degree in nuclear physics and – simultaneously – a master's degree in management.

Carter was highly dedicated to the human rights issues and the implementation of the U.N. Declaration on Human Rights. His work was based on frankness and honesty. As a member of the Democratic Party, he became the Governor of Georgia in 1970 and Rosalynn was thus the First Lady of that state. Jimmy employed a large number of black staffers. As early as toward the end of 1975, he started preparations for the presidential campaign and ran for the White House as a comparably unknown and minor candidate with a reputation of a conservativist and a peasant from a peanut farm.

*

That's the way of America: Rich individuals like Jimmy Carter enter politics and continue to work hard. Whereas in Serbia, penniless fellows go into politics to rob the country and the nation in order to get rich.

Carter enjoyed the support of the American media, charming them with his mild smile, beautiful blue and weepy eyes and also his commonsense farmers' logics demonstrated during his governorship in Georgia. He put an end on racial segregation and stayed untouched by corruption. His rival whom he had beaten with narrow majority, Gerald Ford, was his family friend.

As the 39th President of the United States of America, the peanut farmer moved into the White House on January 20, 1977. He immediately launched the foreign policy which greatly differed from that of his predecessors. The Americans claim that he was a mediocre president, and even bad in interior politics. In diplomacy, he proved to be a seasoned negotiator and peacemaker with sincere intent. That was the quality which drew me to this man.

Carter substituted Richard Nixon's aggressive politics with a policy of respecting human rights as the prime standard in international relations. The objective of this new course in the American policy was to redeem the position of the United States which had been shaken by the defeat in Vietnam and by the compromising support to some bloodthirsty dictators in the Third World. Carter continued the process of nuclear disarmament, for his goal was to weaken the Soviet diplomatic stance, especially in the strategically significant Middle East. For that purpose he initiated the negotiations between Egypt and Israel resulting in the Camp David Accords of September 1978 and the retreat of the Israeli troops from the occupied Sinai. He was mistaken in his support – for reasons of confronting the Soviets – to Reza Pahlavi, Crown Prince and dictator of Iran, which led to the Iranian Revolution of 1979 and dethronement of the Shah. Carter allowed the Shah to come to the United States for medical treatment, and the revolutionaries of Iran occupied the U.S. Embassy at Tehran in response; that was the beginning of the hostage crisis in which Carter, as the leader of a global super power, failed to act determinedly enough. The Soviets took advantage of the situation and poured into Afghanistan; Carter's answer to that was the refusal of the United States to take part in the 1980 Olympic Games held in Moscow.

Carter's national security adviser Zbigniew Brzezinski, however, had designed a quiet 'winning over' of Poland and crash of Communism through the Solidarity Movement, which implied Carter's persistence in the Cold War between the U.S.A. and the U.S.S.R. The story goes among Americans that Carter was paranoid about the Soviet President Leonid Brezhnev who ruled until 1982. In reality, Carter maintained 'business' with Brezhnev through Yugoslavia's President Tito.

Jimmy Carter did not wish to run for the second presidential term. He was succeeded by Ronald Reagan, who solved the hostage crisis in Iran and managed to dissolve the Soviet-led bloc together with the Polish electrician Lech Walesa and the Vatican. Upon expiry of his presidential term, Carter went back to his birthplace in Georgia to resume peanut farming, carpentry and painting art, and to write books and memoirs. It is noteworthy that Carter as a carpenter is credited with providing shelters to many a homeless in his native Georgia.

In the year 1982, the Carter Center was founded as one of the world's most reputable institutions of international diplomacy;

among other pursuits, the Center tends to monitor elections in young democracies. Jimmy Carter was persuading President George Bush to apply a more tolerant policy in Iraq. His diplomatic capability was relied on by President Bill Clinton, too: in 1994, Clinton asked him to tackle the issue of North Korea's nuclear armament. Carter also visited Fidel Castro, America's great enemy from Cuba.

*

It was early in 1992 that my cooperation with Jimmy Carter gained in intensity. My mother-in-law Betty Stevens recommended me to him, and I became an unofficial associate of the Carter Center. In that capacity and with Carter's knowledge I contacted the leadership of the Federal Republic of Yugoslavia, President Dobrica Cosic and Prime Minister Milan Panic. However, they turned a deaf ear to me. For instance, I wrote to Milan Panic on August 19, 1992 suggesting that I would gladly organize a meeting for him with Jimmy Carter in Geneva to discuss a peaceful solution to the crisis in Yugoslavia; the meeting would be held without much publicity. Panic never even answered the letter.

What drove me into politics was a great fear from new massive killings remindful of Jasenovac[53] and Kragujevac[54] during World War Two and repeated large-scale sufferings of the Serbian people. So I left my Palm Springs paradise and set out on a journey to the Balkans. But I faced a major brain-teaser there: Who was actually the real enemy of my people? The protagonists of the sanguinary war were those who had 'until yesterday' been proclaiming Yugoslav brotherhood. It was only when they turned into murderers that I could identify them. All I wanted was an end to the general frenzy.

Jimmy Carter was *the* man who came to Pale and Belgrade to meet the Serbs during the wartime and the dissolution of Yugoslavia, in 1994. I was the discreet arranger of the encounter. My connection with Carter was mediated by his associates from the Carter Center – the scholar Joyce Neu and Ambassador Harry Barnes – and my lawyer Tom Hanley. (The whole mission is described in Part One of this book.) When we had met, the former U.S. President talked about me, Borko Djordjevic, as an honorable man. That was the most appealing compliment any American has ever payed me.

[53] The **Jasenovac Concentration Camp**, often referred to as 'the Auschwitz of the Balkans' or 'the Yugoslav Auschwitz' was an extermination camp established by the governing Ustashe regime of the 'Independent State of Croatia' (Fascist puppet-state) and not operated by Nazi Germany. The victims were mostly Serbs; others included Jews, Roma and some political dissidents. The figures of victims are controversial: immediately after the war the authorities claimed between 600,000 and 700,000. Croatian leaders have always tended to diminish them to as 'low' as 30,000 or less. Current estimates operate with the numbers around 100,000. It is the methods of execution which cause greatest abhorrence. – *Translator's note.*

[54] **Kragujevac Massacre** took place on October 21, 1941 in German-occupied Serbia. The troops of *Wehrmacht* shot some 2,800 men, including a large number of high-school students, from the city of Kragujevac (central Serbia) and the surrounding area. The mass murder came in reprisal for 10 German soldiers killed and 26 wounded, following the official rule that one dead German 'cost' 100 Serbian lives, while each wounded German was 50 lives worth; the basic number of victims in this case grew by additional hostages, Jews and communists. The whole punitive operation included burning of several villages near Kragujevac. – *Translator's note.*

MARSHAL TITO – CARTER'S SPY

My homeland, Yugolavia, was not an unknown country to Jimmy Carter. Those who followed the pre-electoral campaign in the United States in 1976 and the TV debates between the Republican Gerald Ford and his Democrat challenger Jimmy Carter, Governor of Georgia, could deduce that Yugoslavia was unusually important to both of them. It was mentioned in two out of their three TV encounters and referred to the health condition of President Josip Broz Tito and the threats to the state once the aged leader is gone. In his first reference to the country, President Ford said that the states he had visited – Poland, Romania and Yugoslavia – were not under the Soviet domination. The statement caused waves of criticism in the U.S.A. and also gave Carter an unexpected chance to score political points: in between two debates he said that he had no intention to send the U.S. Army Force to help Yugoslavia in case of Soviet invasion.

Rosalynn and Jimmy Carter with President Tito at the White House (1978)

In response, Gerald Ford criticised Carter, his opponent, accusing him of practically inspiring Moscow to attack Belgrade. When Carter moved into the White House, his adviser Brzezinski wrote in an analysis that Tito's death could increase the instability of the Socialist Federal Republic of Yugoslavia and that the Yugoslavs would resist any attempt on the part of the Soviets – led by Leonid Brezhnev at the time – to occupy their country. Therefore, Zbigniew Brzezinski advised Carter to 'send messages' to the Yugoslav people which should be in correspondence with the American interests: *To maintain independence and territorial integrity is of essential importance to the U.S.A. so that Yugoslavia could act as a non-aligned nation.*

In 1978, intent on confirming his support to Tito and Yugoslavia, and on rubbing the Soviets' nose, President Carter invited Josip Broz to be his guest. In many ways, the visit was a triumph. As a White House guest of Jimmy Carter, the First Lady Rosalynn and President's mother Lillian, Tito delivered a toast-speech which took as long as 35 minutes! And he managed to impress the Carter family.

Broz's 1978 visit to America roused expectable reactions, but also met with admiration, even among the Yugoslav dissidents. In his diary, Tito's opponent and Croatian nationalist, Gen. Franjo Tudjman, wrote: "Carter has welcomed him as a great statesman of the world ..."

One should remember that the scholars of Canberra-based Australian National University have ascertained that the year 1978 was the peak of the global wellbeing. In support of the claim, they enumerated some facts: the U.S.A. was led by Jimmy Carter, the U.S.S.R. by Secretary General Leonid Brezhnev, Yugoslavia by Marshal Tito; the first baby conceived *in vitro* was born; for the first time since the 16th century, the Roman Catholic Church got a non-Italian Pope – Polish Cardinal Karol Wojtyla; Sony released the first walkman onto the market.

However, what nobody knew and I found out from the confidential sources in the Carter Center, those were the years when the U.S. President Jimmy Carter relied on Yugoslav President who secretly conveyed American messages to the Soviet leader Brezhnev. Tito was Jimmy Carter's secret courier at Moscow through whom the American President and Leonid

Ilyich continued the policy of détente, i.e. of the control of military arsenals and nuclear weapons in the possession of the two super powers. To Jimmy Carter, Tito's death was a substantial loss.

When Yugoslavia's lifelong president passed away (May 4, 1980), the State Department delivered an analysis of Yugoslavia's situation to the White House: The Soviet invasion of Afghanistan has intensified Yugoslav fears from a possible Soviet action against their country; they will expect encouragement from us and our allies, but they will not thrust themselves into our embrace. That was the conclusion of the American experts in foreign policy. None of the Yugoslav politicians appeared to be a 'world statesman' of Tito's calibre, so the collective leadership of the S.F.R.Y. was expected to proceed with the transition process.

The State Department immediately suggested to Jimmy Carter that –bearing in mind Tito's greatness on the global scale, the significance of Yugoslavia for the West, and the situation created by the Soviet intervention in Afghanistan – "we strongly recommend" that President heads the American delegation to the funeral in Belgrade. President grappled with a dilemma. The U.S. Government and the European allies were rushing him into the attendance. Their viewpoint said: You have to decide who is going to attend the funeral of Josip Broz. Under normal circumstances, to go personally would be a good message, better than sending the Vice-President. Under the present circumstances, the decision is much harder to make.

However, Carter feared meeting Leonid Brezhnev, for he was afraid of the U.S.S.R. attacking Yugoslavia. It was possible that Leonid Brezhnev appeared personally in Belgrade to attend Tito's funeral ceremony. Meeting him while the Soviets were in Afghanistan would have been extremely delicate politically. Yet to avoid the possible Carter-Brezhnev encounter at the funeral in Belgrade could be criticized as an irresponsible decision within the context of the global peace. To meet and insist on the American standpoints would have implied new straining of their relations. Any modification of policy on the part of the United States would have intensified the accusations of inconsistency. The presidential elections were nearing, so Zbigniew Brzezinski advised President Carter to delegate Vice-President Walter Mondale as his envoy. (Mentions were also made about Kirk Douglas, old friend of

Yugoslavia from the world of motion picture, attending the event, too.) Jimmy Carter decided that the last tribute to Yugoslavia's leader Josip Broz Tito should be payed by Vice-President Walter Mondale and Ambassador Averell Harriman on behalf of the United States, as well as by his mother Lillian Carter on behalf of the President's family. In Yugoslavia and in the world's public, Lillian Carter was held as a sincere friend in mourning on the occasion of Marshal Tito's death.

In his memoirs, Jimmy Carter wrote about Josip Broz: Tito "resisted the Nazis during World War II and later defied Stalin and the Soviets". At the time when "multiple ethnic and political groups constituted Yugoslavia", "Tito was holding them together". He was one of the founders of the Non-Aligned Movement and a man who sought practical and sustainable solutions…

Less than two months after Tito's funeral, the U.S. President Jimmy Carter and his wife Rosalynn came from Venice to Belgrade. In June 1980, the Carters had a dinner at the *Milosev konak* restaurant. The head waiter Milonja Misko Lekic fulfilled their wish to talk to a group of school students from Bosnia who were on an excursion to Belgrade and stopped at the same restaurant; in good Serbian tradition, the man saw his guests off presenting a bouquet of lowers to the First Lady.

Fourteen years later, when Jimmy Carter and his spouse Rosalynn came to Belgrade again in order to meet President of Serbia Slobodan Milosevic, it did not occur to anyone to present the former First Lady of the United States with lowers.

Reagan's Man

PALM SPRINGS, as my place of residence, chosen for its warm climate and exemplary silence, offered more advantages than disadvantages. One of the former implied the fact that this town on the California-Nevada border was a stopover to many outstanding people, American and world-famous alike. My acquaintances included Elvis Presley (with whom I shared a girlfriend), Elizabeth Taylor, Tony Curtis, Cary Grant, Joan Collins, Larry King, Elton John and many others. I was lucky enough to befriend some of those celebrities. One of those was Leonore Lee Annenberg.

Five U.S. Presidents, acquaintances of Dr. Djordjevic

Her husband Walter Annenberg was Ambassador to the United Kingdom in the time of President Richard Nixon, who had a vast estate, *Rancho Mirage*, at Palm Springs. On the Independence Day and New Year's Eve they used to host grand-scale banquets. It was at that ranch that I heard an unbelievable story: in 1979, Yugoslavia's President Josip Broz Tito had been a secret guest of Ambassador Annenberg and the industrialist Ferguson.

During the preparations for the Sixth Summit Conference of the Non-Aligned, scheduled for Havana in September 1979, Tito went to Cuba for a secret encounter with Fidel Castro. On that occasion, Tito was waging his last battle for the defense of the original principles of non-alignment. He was accompanied by Budimir Loncar, Minister of Foreign Affairs. Some believe that the Cuban Summit was nothing but roleplaying on the part of Tito and Castro, two politicians who shared some similar experiences in common and were pretty close personally; the 'theatre' was to gain support – Washington's to Yugoslavia and Moscow's to Cuba.

In those years, the Third World provided arenas to numerous conflicts: Afghanistan – Pakistan, Algeria – Morocco, Angola – Zaire, Kampuchea – Vietnam, Chad – Libya, Central African Empire – Senegal, Ethiopia – Sudan, Ethiopia – Somalia, India – Pakistan, India –Bangladesh, Iran – Iraq, Iraq – Syria, Jordan – Syria, Libija – Tunisia, Libya – Egypt, Libya – Sudan, South Yemen – North Yemen, Ghana –Togo, Kenya – Somalia, Tanzania – Uganda etc. All those conflicts turned into a growing burden for the Non-Aligned Movement which often had to side with a party in conflict. On the other hand, the conflicts were pushing those countries closer toward either of the superpowers/blocs, facilitating foreign interferences to the extent of arrival of foreign troops.

– On the way back from Cuba, Broz took a two-days' rest at *Rancho Mirage* in Palm Springs before he resumed the journey to Yugoslavia – I was told by Ferguson's wife.

Owing to this lady and Mrs. Lee Annenberg, I was introduced to Ronald Reagan's family. Nancy and Ronald Reagan were guests at the New Year's celebration and banquet. America's former First Lady was born in 1921; she succeeded Rosalynn Carter for the period 1981–9. Just as Rosalynn Carter had been the First Lady of Georgia in early 1970's, Nancy Reagan had been the First Lady of California, since Ronald was Governor of that state from 1967 to 1975. She was an actress who became active on the political scene as a member of the Republican Party where I belonged, too. Mother of two children and a truly refined lady, she was a witty person and always ready for pleasant talks.

Ronald and Nancy Reagan leaving Palm Springs after New Years' party (1982)

My readers in ex-Yugoslavia should know that the Americans – and Californians especially – never use strong words or foul language. Their dialogs are imbued with optimism, full of praise, kind remarks and compliments. Nancy Reagan recommended to me a number of other ladies from the White House and helped me cooperate with her husband more closely.

I became a member of the Republican Party in 1980, but knew Ronald Reagan from the time of his governorship. We became closer at *Rancho Mirage* in Palm Springs, and I joined in his team. Presidential elections required candidates' good look and glamor, which Reagan as an actor could certainly boast. During his race for the U.S. President, broad public treated him jokingly, referring to him as an 'easy guy' due to his Hollywood career. He would take the comments as folk jesting. A man at the age of 70, with dark and thick hair, Reagan had an excellent look of a tall and wellfavored American.

Djordjevic holding the medal awarded him by Ronald Reagan

Having won the presidential race in 1981, he composed a 'kitchen cabinet' of his best friends and businessmen. They were delegated to rule while he lived on his Santa Barbara ranch. He would ride horses, trim tree-branches, cut the logs for ire and tend to fruit trees. While Jimmy Carter was a land-farmer, Ronald Reagan was a rancher, which he stayed after leaving the presidential post. Some ten years later, he resumed political activism. I was a Republican activist, too, one who acted as the Party's sponsor and Reagan's confidant during the senatorial campaigns. That is, I participated in Reagan's/Republican political games played in California.

I was entrusted with organization of donors' parties and fundraising for Ronald Reagan. In that way, I 'made' quite big money for the future U.S. senator, gaining a political and public reputation for myself, yet no riches. For, in the United States, politics is not coupled with money. In this country you cannot draw wealth from politics; what you can earn is respectability. Once you honestly complete your job in the service of the American nation, you – as a former president – may rightfully make money for yourself. In other words, in the U.S.A., politics may become a source of moneymaking only when you have quit it. That is how the American system works, with the purpose to prevent a U.S. president from compromising himself and corruption while in power. Accordingly, it was only after Ronald Reagan had retired from presidentship that he could – as a guest of honor – throw out the ceremonial first pitch at a baseball tournament in Japan and earn a million-dollar honorarium therefor.

Raising solid funds, I proved to be a successful promoter of the Republicans. 'My' candidate from the territory of Southern California was Richard Goldwater, son of the famed Senator Barry Goldwater who had once suggested use of atomic bombs to counteract the Russians. 'My' candidate reached an excellent rating very soon, getting an opportunity to be elected congressman from Southern California; however, when the electoral campaign was at its peak, someone accused him of snorting cocaine in his room and a public scandal broke. Richard Goldwater thus disqualified himself from the further campaign, and the case confirmed my conviction that nobody is perfect.

My political route led me from a Yugoslav youth activist and leader of the Party's budding professionals to a senior American partisan and reputable organizer of political campaigns. In early 1990's, I became an official promoter of the Republican Party and Ronald Reagan. Moreover, I was awarded lifelong membership in the Republican Party Inner Senatorial Circle. In other words, I held a position of trust with Ronald Reagan and the Republican Party of the U.S.A.. Ronald Reagan personally awarded me a medal of merit on the behalf of the Republican Party.

Owing to my political activities, I had an opportunity to meet yet another American president – George H.W. Bush. Prescott Bush Jr., elder brother to President George Bush, visited the town of Igalo in Montenegro, whereafter we became good friends. Representing *Pan American* in Latin America, President's brother was a successful businessman. In 1988, Prescott and his wife visited the Gulf of Kotor in Montenegro with an idea to buy the Jaz Beach (now a very popular vacation place among the young) and erect a large American-style hotel thereon.

PRESCOTT BUSH & COMPANY, INCORPORATED
441 LEXINGTON AVENUE, SUITE 1100
NEW YORK, N. Y. 10017

PRESCOTT S. BUSH, JR.
PRESIDENT

Tel: 212 490-7710
Fax: 212 557-0145

December 23, 1988

Borko B. Djordjevic, M.D., Inc.
Cosmetic Surgery Center
Yugoslavia 85347 IGALO

Dear Dr. Djordjevic:

I am authorizing you with this letter to request, on my behalf, information concerning the hospital and hotel at Igalo. In order to determine what role I can play in helping to develop the business of the complex, I will need detailed information concerning income, operating expenses and any development plans that may exist for expansion and promotion of the business.

It would also help to know the number of people employed in the management and operating departments. Any other information that you think would assist in our appraisal of this complex as an investment opportunity would be appreciated.

Please convey my best wishes to your associates at the hospital.

Yours sincerely,

Prescott P. Bush Jr.

122388IG.ALO

Prescott Bush's letter to Borko Djordjevic

In 1989, when George H. W. Bush was inaugurated the President of the United States of America, I attended the New York celebration with his brother and met the newly-elected president there. George H.W. Bush had been a millionaire from oil business, congressman, ambassador to the United Nations, CIA director, and the 41st U.S. President. The world remembers him for sending the American troops to Iraq, into the First Gulf War, for waging political battles against Saddam Hussein and Slobodan Milosevic and for his contribution to the sanguinary disintegration of my fatherland, the Socialist Federal Republic of Yugoslavia.

Toward the end of the 1980's, the Republican George Bush awarded me a medal of special merit for the U.S.A. and a golden watch with engraved inscription *George Bush*. Of all the encounters with Bush Senior, I remember best the one of 1990 when he uttered an interesting remark. Namely, when we met at Palm Springs in the said year, he divulged that, as the CIA Director, he had held my secret dossier in his hand which he had read out. During our conversation at *Rancho Mirage*, he friendly told me:

– I know you, Mr. Djordjevic, from the year 1988. At the time, you demanded that we the Americans save Yugoslavia?

Save Yugoslavia!

WHEN GEORGE BUSH told me that he was aware of my hidden urge and subdued love for my native country, I was not surprised. I was not angry with him, for his words were true. He knew that I was loyal to the Republican Party and the United States, so he did not take me as a case for intelligence. On the contrary: he appreciated my invariable care about my fatherland and its people. During the first decade of my life in America, while I was pursuing studies, professional work and raving it up, I was constantly planning and delaying a trip to Yugoslavia/Serbia. It was easier to bring my family to the States than rush to Belgrade and back in order to see them. So I arranged for them to come to California: for my father and mother first, then sisters and their husbands. My father Branko, who spent seven years in the United States, liked feeling important and introducing himself to the Americans:

– I am Dr. Djordjevic's father!

On the other hand, one of my brothers-in-law was disappointed by America and went back to Belgrade with my sister.

– What kind of country is this America? They don't even have the *Niksic Beer*. We're going back to Serbia – said my brother-in-law who now lives at Slavija Traffic Circle, in the heart of Belgrade's downtown.

In 1983, my father Branko returned to Serbia, too. He was seriously ill and wanted to die in Belgrade. That is when my second visit to Serbia's capital took place. I was stricken with grief, for my father was my hero and my idol.

Before that, I had rarely visited Yugoslavia. Much too preoccupied with my job in the States, I had concentrated my thoughts on surgery-related matters and duties to my patients.

Dr. Djordjevic accompanied by beautiful ladies

Leaving Yugoslavia, I left behind a happy nation and a happy country. Coming back in 1986, I found the country in a nascent phase of chaos. The leaderships of the six republics were quarreling, the Albanian lobby kept attacking Serbia, to be joined by Slovenia's and Croatia's politicians. And I was showing off before my fellow-countrymen: I arrived in Montenegro in a brand new BMW car, appeared on their television and started business. I offered the Montenegrins to sell Serbia's crops to the Americans and buy American slot machines, so that they could turn the coastal town of Budva into a paradise. Such a deal with the *Univerzal* Company failed.

I hugger-muggered with the Yugoslav-Italian actress Marija Baksa/Maria Baxa around Budva and Rome. Also, I was squandering money in Belgrade's Skadarlija (bohemian quarter) and boasted with my expensive, tailor-made suits. At the same time, I was examining the opportunity to come back to Serbia with my family. It was in such a mood that Dr. Milan Obradovic found me. He was Director of Dr. Simo Milosevic Institute from Igalo, Montenegro[55]. In 1987, he summoned me to help in a problem with some patients who had got a dangerous habit of self-harming.

A new range of the Institute's building had been inaugurated in 1986 as a joint venture of the Montenegrins and Norwegians, intended for treatment of rheumatic disorders which Scandinavians often suffered from. The state of Norway invested 30 million Deutsche Mark into the construction of a hospital building and spa center where mud baths would be applied, using the hot and healing mud from the Adriatic Sea; the therapies were intended for Norwegian invalids, for medical services cost way too much in their country's health and insurance system.

With the Norwegian support, the founder of the hospital and rheumatologist of high reputation Professor Dr. Zivkovic turned the small seashore spa (in which President Tito was treated in 1975) into a modern European-style medical center. He ensured conduit of sea mud from the shore to the hospital bathrooms and bedrooms. The 'repertory' of the diseases/disorders he treated included all kinds of gout, rheumatism, arthritis and fatigue of bones caused by aging. Due to the therapies with sea water and mud, along with sunbathing, the Norwegians would not only get better and replenish their energy, but also feel rejuvenated. In late 1980's, the Igalo Institute – as the largest health and medical-science center Balkanwide – became symbol of Yugoslavia's construction industry and medical achievement.

The state of Norway was very satisfied with the results of the treatments in Igalo and significantly lowered costs of healthcare provided for their invalids, so the number of the Norwegian patients kept increasing. This worked very well for more than two years – by the moment the patients discovered the 'Montenegrin panacea' – loza. Accustomed to the sour and strong vodka in their homeland, they began to excessively drink the 'throat-friendly' Montenegrin vine-brandy and get drunk much too often.

Dr. Milan Obradovic complained to me:

After doctoral degree award ceremony: with Deputy Dean Simeunovic and Vice Rector Kuburic (1994)

– Completely drunk, our patients fall down head first. There was a Norwegian woman whom we could not treat here at Igalo or Herceg Novi, but as far as in Risan[56]. It was a risky, remote and extremely expensive treatment. Norway's Government was worried about the health and lives of their citizens. They even notified the Montenegrin authorities about their readiness to terminate the related agreement if such cases repeated. You see, my dear Borko, all of this could come to grief – just because of a drunken Norwegian woman who got her head broken and skull fractured...

I suggested to Dr. Obradovic that they should establish a surgery unit at the Institute in Igalo which could prove more efficient and less expensive than the hospital at Risan. The management accepted my idea, but summoned some physicians from Sarajevo to work plastic surgery, for the injuries of the Norwegian patients required delicate stitching up on their heads/faces. The Sarajevo doctors wanted to know who I was and what I knew about plastic surgery. So I told them I had come from America:

– Two greatest plastic surgeons live in the United States. And I am the third one – I said, unburdened by modesty.

They went back to Sarajevo, leaving to the Institute their operation programs and a list of expensive and too sizeable equipment. I calculated that their engagement would cost dearly, for their come and-go practice would include excessive travel costs, perdiem, fees and the expensive equipment. At the same time, the famous Yugoslav-born cardiac surgeon Dr. Ninoslav Radovanovic from Switzerland was inquiring about the possibility to build a surgical center of his own atop the building of Simo Milosevic Institute. I said that I could make a better and less expensive arrangement.

– I will operate on the Norwegians alone! The hard work will pay off to me when I set out to work their breasts, bellies and bottoms – I was joking.

But it was sincerity speaking out of me. It was a time when I was considering a final homecoming. I believed I had fully obeyed the advice given me by Dr. Mane Budisavljevic – to get education and build reputation in America, then come back to Yugoslavia and show my colleagues new styles of work. My plan had been to establish a plastic surgery center in Belgrade, applying American knowhow and equipment. The management of the Igalo Institute were sincere, too, in their acceptance of my proposal, accompanying it by a silly-sounding remark:

– Now we have an American immigrant here in Igalo! In the new surgical unit at Igalo I used to operate on four injured Norwegians per month, but also on a dozen of Scandinavian ladies who wanted some cosmetic procedures. I advertised my new clinic with the slogan "California at Igalo!".

A lot of work awaited me there. One of my patients was Selim Numic, once associate and friend of Aleksandar Leka Rankovic, former minister of Yugoslavia's police and number two figure in the postwar period, next to Marshal Tito.[57] Having suffered persecution by Tito and his Belgrade clique, Numic moved to Igalo. Rumor was passed around about his skin cancer, but it turned out that he had been given wrong medical treatment: There was a 'hole' in his head which was so deep (4.5 cm) that one could see the skull bone. I inserted live tissue therein which mended, and the hole disappeared.

Numic was a man of good conscience. Politically ruined in 1966, at the time of the Brioni Plenum and dictatorship of the Miskovic brothers (Ivan and Milan, Chief of Counter-Intelligence and Minister of Interior respectively) who contrived the whole scandal about Rankovic's bugging of Tito and Jovanka Broz, he was not defeated spiritually.

– Leka did not install the bugging devices to Tito and Jovanka! –Selim Numic told me in confidence. – The whole scandal was framed. It was a political revenge of Tito, that is, of Kardelj and Krajacic[58], who had heard some rumor about Leka Rankovic saying that he was going to succeed Josip Broz.

Personally, I did believe this story of his, for I knew that Rankovic was betrayed by both Krste Crvenkovski and Petar Stambolic[59]. I knew Leka's son, Mica Rankovic, and his wife Merima. They were truly nice people who confirmed my assumptions.

*

At Igalo, my earnings were quite large in comparison to normal Montenegrin salaries. The doctors working at the Institute were disturbed by this and they threatened to start a strike; 120 members of staff, physicians and nurses, rose up against "Dr. Djordjevic's pro it-making", which did not surprise me. I told the management that my purpose was not to get rich on their patients, but to expand the Institute's business involving other doctors/surgeons, so that they could earn foreign currency, too; yet time was needed for the project to progress and the business to develop. My idea was to make the Igalo Institute become a large regional center for plastic and reconstructive surgery. The idea was a subject of my talk to Ljubomir Djukic, a Montenegrin, and Consul-General in the United States.

I wrote an exhaustive Development Report on Simo Milosevic Institute for Physical Therapy, and Consul Djukic despatched it to the Institute's director and to the Republic's International Relations Committee of Montenegro. Personally, Djukic told me that the plan provided an excellent opportunity for the development of Yugoslavia's health tourism, and especially for the tourism in the subregion of Kotor Gulf.

However, the Montenegrins proved to be rather distrustful; their jealousy concerning my earnings in Deutsche Mark currency surpassed their understanding for my long-term plans. As I was later told by Consul Ljubomir Djukic, the Institute's director, a Mihajlovic, never cared to read it, while the International Relations Committee had misplaced it.

Borko B. Djordjevic, M.D., Inc.
PLASTIC AND RECONSTRUCTIVE SURGERY

BEVERLY HILLS MEDICAL TOWER
1125 S. BEVERLY DR., SUITE 720
LOS ANGELES, CA 90035, U.S.A.
TEL. (213) 556-8404

COSMETIC SURGERY CENTER
1091 N. PALM CANYON DR.
PALM SPRINGS, CA 92262, U.S.A.
TEL: (619) 320-9732

September 14, 1987

Senator John McCain
Chairman Republican Presidential Task Force

Dear Senator McCain:

    As a charter member of the Republican Presidential Task Force I'am writing this letter in order to seek your advice, which relates to foreign policy in relation to Yugoslavia.

    Being a native Yugoslavian and citizen of the USA and vitaly interested in events taking place in Yugoslavia over the last year and a half. I've been to Yugoslavia four times, as a private citizen as well as a businessman.

    There are some dramatic changes taking place in Yugoslavia which ought to be of concern to the USA. I had a long talk with Ambassador Scanlon he agrees with me. Because of poor economic conditions Yugoslavia is on the verge of a Civil War. I think that most of the leaders of the present Yugoslavian goverment recognize that, in talking to them I believe they are ready to accept "The American Way", if properly approached. I still believe that America still has vital interest in this part of the world and considering how much was invested in Yugoslavia. I think this is the time to collect.

    Please advise how we go about it.

Sincerely,

Borko Djordjevic, M.D.

Djordjevic's 1987 letter to Senator John McCain

The strike of the staff might have developed into a political problem of Montenegro, but in 1988 the authorities in the republic's capital (Titograd, renamed as Podgorica) decided to allow sale of fuel for foreign currencies. As soon as the Deutsche Mark began to pour into the wallets of all Montenegrins, their interest in the foreign-currency pro it of Dr. Djordjevic waned.

*

In those years, late 1980's, an abrupt national awakening took place. The Serbs, led by the new 'Vozhd' Slobodan Milosevic, were rallying in the major cities around Serbia, intent on 'winning over' Montenegro, too. The Albanians rose against Serbia and the Serbs. The Slovenes and the Croats supported the Albanians, advocating independence – not only of the Autonomous Province of Kosovo-Metohija (constitutionally within Serbia) but also of their own federal republics. I could see that something big and ugly was going to happen in my fatherland.

For instance, during the 1987 Zagreb Fair, I noticed that the Croats 'promoted' their republic into an independent country, yet (still) within the Socialist Federal Republic of Yugoslavia. Red-and white checkerboard-patterned lags were lying at the Dubrovnik Airport. In Croatian towns, one could buy souvenirs and torches with the symbols and signs of the second-world-war (Fascist) 'Independent State of Croatia'.

I said to the U.S. Ambassador to Belgrade John Douglas Scanlan:
– Disintegration of the S.F.R.Y. is being prepared. The United States should interfere in order to save Yugoslavia and turn it into Europe's economic paradise!

The wording of his answer made me freeze:
– The United States takes no interest in the S.F.R.Y. After Tito, the country has lost significance to America. There's nothing to do in it!

Ambassador Scanlan was totally right. Until 1980, there was Tito who had been working for the United States. He had been Jimmy Carter's friend who negotiated with the Soviets on his behalf. Josip Broz was persuading the U.S.S.R. President Leonid Brezhnev into signing an agreement on limitation of nuclear weapons. When Tito died in 1980, the new (annually rotating) presidents of Yugoslavia had no idea how to deal with either

Americans or the Soviets. Yugoslavia's international reputation was on a downswing, and the country was sinking to the status of an insignificant Balkan state.

Borko Djordjevic with his schoolmates at the 30th reunion (1991)

Confronted by a strong resistance on the part of Communists, Prime Minister Ante Markovic[60] did not manage to carry out reforms and introduce capitalism into Yugoslavia's system of 'worker's self-management'. His greatest achievement was the establishment of an internationally free market in Yugoslavia and opening of credit lines for the citizens. Concerned about the situation burdened with the nationalist sentiments which generated quarrels among Yugoslavia's peoples/nations to the extent of a political war waged between Belgrade, Zagreb, Ljubljana and Prishtina, I sent an appeal to Senator John McCain, member of Reagan's political elite: *Save Yugoslavia! It's time the U.S.A. came to the S.F.R.Y. and helped the country!* That was the message underlying my letter, written in September 1987.

The person speaking through my words was a onetime communist who wished all the best to Yugoslavia and the Serb people who in this country lived united and within one state. The person speaking through my words was also an American who believed that – if the U.S. had supported Tito's Yugoslavia turning it into a bridge toward the U.S.S.R. and a leader of the Non-Aligned Movement – my country could do without Broz and, under the American influence, carry out a *'Perestroika'* of its own.

In the said letter to Senator John McCain, who in 1987 chaired the Republican Presidential Task Force, I asked for advice concerning the American policy for the S.F.R.Y.:

"There are some dramatic changes taking place in Yugoslavia which ought to be of concern to the USA. I had a long talk with Ambassador Scanlan, he agrees with me. Because of poor economic conditions Yugoslavia is on the verge of a Civil War. I think that most of the leaders of the present Yugoslavian government recognize that, in talking to them I believe they are ready to accept "The American Way", if properly approached. I still believe that America still has vital interest in this part of the world and considering how much was invested in Yugoslavia. I think this is the time to collect.
Please advise me how we go about it."

Yugoslavia was a country of industrious and good-natured people. Life was good, due to the American economic support and crediting. That money was the key to President Tito's rule. The most important issue on the agenda of the Central Committee of the Yugoslav League of Communists was the situation in the economy, including in low of foreign currencies from abroad, owing to the large Yugoslav companies that carried out projects in other, mostly Third World, countries. Yugoslavia was earning billions of dollars abroad, ensuring social harmony in the country. Tito's Yugoslavia was actually a multinational corporation making high foreign-currency revenues and pro it. For that reason, it could be very attractive to the American business and in terms of comfortable life. In late 1980's, I tried to confirm the belief by personal experience.

Namely, in 1987 I got married for the second time. My second wife, Joy Stephens, was born in a well-off family in 1957. Her father John and mother Betty were proven successful business people who owned two companies. Our daughter Aleksandra was born in 1989. We lived in Palm Springs, but the quarrels we had with my mother in-law Betty who interfered in our private lives made us decide to 'escape across the ocean', to Austria first, then to Switzerland.

My preoccupations with surgery were lessening, and those with business were growing. In Vienna and Geneva I started a foreign trade firm named *Atalanta* which supplied diverse commodities to Yugoslav duty-free shops. The partner-company in this business was *Srbija turist,* with its director Jovan Djosic.

In Lausanne, Switzerland, I met Armand Aeberhardt, representative of *Philip Morris* Company for the Balkans and talked him into marrying a Serb girl. In sign of gratitude, he appointed me an exclusive representative of the company for Yugoslavia. In that capacity, I reached an agreement between *Philip Morris* and the Industrija duvana Nis (Nish Tobacco Industry) about privatization of this factory which should –after modernization – produce as much as 12 billion cigarettes per year. The agreement was signed by my friend Armand Aeberhard.

Working for *Philip Morris,* I met Yugoslav businessman Mirko Vucurovic and Ambassador Nebojsa Dimitrijevic, Yugoslavia's representative at the country's Permanent Mission to U.N. Of ice in Geneva. As an expert in biological weapons, the latter was in high esteem with the Americans, but Slobodan Milosevic hated him because the man was a friend of Zoran Djindjic[61]. So he substituted this representative. It was then that I realized that the spirit of Tito's system was dead and that a new Serbian leader came into power. Milosevic the Vozhd never cared for the 'old' Yugoslavia.

Sensing the nearing collapse of the sole country in which all Balkan Serbs lived together, I wrote the above-cited letter to Senator John McCain, asking him for American action. However, there was no response to my appeal/warning on the part of the American senator and friend. He either did not know what was going to happen with Yugoslavia, or he did know yet did not wish to tell me. He once only mentioned that he knew about Yugoslav Prime Minister Ante Markovic, assigned with the introduction of capitalism in the country, having visited the United States repeatedly.

Ante Markovic submitted to the IMF all the data about the economic power of the S.F.R.Y., emphasizing the fact that the country had 10 billion dollars cash in its Treasury and an economy worth more than $ 100 billion.

I found myself facing a dilemma: To stay in Montenegro was not possible, for a major confrontation had been sparked in Serbia against the Albanians, Slovenians and Croats. My native Serbia needed me. I closed up my medical office in Igalo and – in 1990 – moved to Belgrade. I hired a part of the premises in the residential & business building of *Genex apartmani* in New Belgrade, and, unaware of what this implied, 'landed' into the political nest of the Socialist Party, their political elite, police and tycoons. The green-glass building near the bank of the Sava river housed the operative headquarters of the circle in power.

As soon as I arrived in Belgrade in 1990, I refreshed my acquaintances with Vlada Stambuk and Slobodan-Buca Prohaska; the latter became Vice-Premier of Serbia's Government and Deputy Minister of Foreign Economic Relations. They accepted me as one of their own and a sympathizer of the SPS, Socialist Party of Serbia. I voted in the 1990 elections in December, favoring Slobodan Milosevic against Vuk Draskovic, his rival presidential candidate. Following the SPS victory in the elections, Prohaska introduced me to PM Dr. Dragutin Zelenovic and his successor in the office Dr. Radoman Bozovic.

I founded the firm *Atalanta International* in Belgrade in 1991, at the time when I tried to introduce the hire-purchase (leasing) system. Such a deal was supposed to be applied on the supply of 200 buses and automobiles for the Yugoslav market, but the project failed. One year later, I established the *Mak Morris* Company in Skopje, F.Y.R. of Macedonia.

All along, I kept warning people of the upcoming collapse of the S.F.R.Y. which could pull us, i.e. Serbia, into the abyss. For nearly five decades Josip Broz Tito and his Communists had been building their 'self-management' empire which was now threatened by implosion due to the interior political conflicts and failing transition. I kept talking about it – both to Americans and to my friends and acquaintances in Belgrade. But on both sides I was perceived as an ordinary 'twister' from America, a know-it-all incapable of *doing* anything.

[55] See the footnote in the (4th) chapter of Part One, "I Treated Children". – *Translator's note.*

[56] **Risan** is a coastal town in the Municipality of Kotor, at the far end of the jord Boka kotorska (Kotor Gulf), known for its ancient monuments, as a city which existed in the 4th century BC. Its infirmary – Vaso Cukovic Special Hospital for Orthopedics, Neurosurgery and Neurology, founded on the eve of World War II – was famed for surgical breakthroughs and physical therapy. – Translator's note.

[57] **Aleksandar Rankovic** (1909-1983) was a Yugoslav communist leader of Serb origin who opposed decentralization of the country. He was a National Hero of World War II (Colonel General), Vice-President of the People's Assembly of Serbia (1944-6), Chief of OZNA and, later, UDBa (secret police, state security agency), Minister of Interior (1946-53), the first Vice-President of Yugoslavia (the office established in 1963). He was forced to step down and even expelled from the Communist Party in 1966, at the so-called 'Brioni Plenum' of the Central Committee of the CPY, owing to the allegations of bugging President Tito's bed chambers. Rankovic, often referred to as Comrade Marko (partisan/wartime nick-name) or Leka, retreated to Dubrovnik for the rest of his life, but his funeral in Belgrade attracted thousands of people who believed that he had been set up as a defender of Serbian/Serb interests by the Croatian and Slovenian leaders. – *Translator's note.*

[58] *Edvard Kardelj* (1910-1979) was Slovenian/Yugoslav political leader, creator of the Yugoslav system of worker's self-management. A pre-war Communist and wartime leader of the Liberation Movement of the Slovenian People, he was the first Chairman of Slovenia's Communist Party (1937-43), second Foreign Minister of Yugoslavia (1948-53) and seventh President of Yugoslavia's Federal Assembly (1963-7). He is most often referred to as one of the authors of the 1974 Constitution of the country which decentralized decision-making shifting it to the level of federal republics and their respective leaderships.

Ivan Krajacic Stevo (1906-1986) was a prominent Yugoslav Communist from Croatia, participant in the Spanish Civil War, World-War-Two National Hero of Yugoslavia and, from 1963 to 1967 (during the scandal and Brioni Plenum), President of Croatia's Assembly. –*Translator's note.*

[59] At the time, **Krste Crvenkovski** was President of the Communist Party of Macedonia who chaired the committee investigating the 'Rankovic Case', while Serbia's **Petar Stambolic** was the President of the Federal Executive Council (i.e. Government) of Yugoslavia. – *Translator's note.*

[60] Ante Markovic (1924-2011) was the last Prime Minister of Yugoslavia (1989-91), formerly (19868) the 15th President of the Presidency of the Socialist Republic of Croatia and (1980-85) the 10th President of the Executive Council (i.e. government) of the SR of Croatia. His ambitious program of

economic reforms, launched when he took the office of Yugoslav PM, proved successful yet failed to satisfy the political programs of the leaderships federal republics. When the League of Communists of Yugoslavia (LCY) broke up in January 1990, he took advantage of his broad popularity and established a new party, Union of Reform Forces (Savez reformskih snaga). In the last months of his tenure (by December 1991), Markovic tried to find a compromise between the secessionist forces (Slovenia and Croatia) and those who wanted the federation to survive, but did not get the support of the Army. Slovenia proclaimed independence on June 25, 1991; on the same day, Croatia decided to secede from Yugoslavia, too, which came in effect in October. Both Slovenia and Croatia gained diplomatic recognition by the European Economic Community on January 15, 1992. Following the breakup of Yugoslavia, Ante Markovic dedicated himself to a business career. – *Translator's note.*

[61] **Zoran Djindjic** (1952-2003) was a Serbian politicians, one of the original restorers of Serbia's Democratic Party and its President from 1994 on. A major opposition leader during the 1990's, this Doctor of Philosophy and university professor was in 1999 described by Time magazine as one of the most important politicians at the beginning of the 21st century. He played one of the key roles in the 2000 presidential elections followed by an overthrow of Slobodan Milosevic. In 2001, Djindjic became Prime Minister of Serbia. On March 12, 2003, he was assassinated in the courtyard of the Government Building. – *Translator's note.*

COMMUNIST-WAY TRANSITION

IN BELGRADE, my friend Mihajlo Misko Jeremic, director of *Jugopetrol* and father of Vuk Jeremic (Serbia's foreign minister 2007-2012, President of U.N. General Assembly 2012-3) told me about the great test awaiting Yugoslavia: A fundamental reform of the state system had to commence aimed to transform – as painlessly as possible – the country from communism/socialism to capitalism. The transition of the S.F.R.Y. was opened and increasingly advocated by Yugoslavia's Prime Minister Ante Markovic. Jeremic asked me to help about it, that is, to involve my American fellow-members of the Republican Party, friends from the U.S. Congress and Senate, acquaintances from the world of business. We were considering the offer made by *Texaco* Inc. and *Shell Oil* Co. for the privatization of the state-owned company *Jugopetrol*. Some other privatization related offers arrived for *Energopetrol*, *Nish Electrical Industry* and many other large state-run companies of Yugoslavia/Serbia.

On an occasion I met Slobodan Milosevic and repeated to him the story about Yugoslav enterprises being privatized by American companies. I brought *Motorola's* Mr. Goldstein to support Milosevic and his reform of the Serbian economy. We appeared on CNN together.

With the Slovenian Janez Drnovsek I met at the Davos World Economic Forum; there, he talked about the necessity that Yugoslavia's communists should gradually transform into democrats. In 1990, when Drnovsek was President of Yugoslavia, I tried to talk him into enabling Motorola to come into the country and privatize *Nish Electrical Industry, Serbian Broadcasting Corporation (RTS) and PTT.*

My friend Buca Prohaska engaged me as an adviser of his in privatization-related matters; in that capacity, I had talks with Serbia's PM Dragutin Zelenovic and Belgrade's Mayor Milorad

Unkovic. Also, I payed a visit to Milorad Miki Savicevic, Director-General of *Genex*. Moreover, I organized the presence of a Serbian delegation at the World Economic Forum in Davos gathering the world's leaders and economists/businessmen. In addition, my efforts threw Prohaska and the Americans together.

New York businessmen in Belgrade toward 1990 elections

Privatization was supposed to trigger the reconstruction of the communist-style economy and ownership transformation, i.e. establishment of capitalist proprietary relations and the way onto, as well as exposure to, the free global market. The recipe was feasible within a short time and painless in terms of social peace and administrative system.

John D. Scanlan, the U.S. Ambassador in the period 1985-8 spoke fluent Serbian and attended domestic patron-saints' feasts (*slave*) out of his personal liking for socializing with the Serbs. He supported Slobodan Milosevic, in the belief that – as a modern-time politician –the man had grasped the necessity of large-scale transition in Serbia. Therefore, his reports on Sloba (as was the popular nick name of Slobodan Milosevic) to the White House and Department of State were favourable. Scanlan wrote that Milosevic was a modern man, a banker inclined to changes, as well as a democrat, for he organized the first multi-party elections.

Ambassador Scanlan opened the door for the American capital in the *Galenika* Pharmaceutical Company, thus enabling its privatization. The new American ambassador, Warren Zimmermann, who came to Belgrade in 1988 (to be the last U.S. ambassador to Yugoslavia), continued to invest efforts in a fast-implemented privatization in Yugoslavia/Serbia.

Unfortunately, it seems that this American, who had earlier served in Croatia, never penetrated the core of the Serbian mentality. We, the Serbs, are deep inside people from the forest, *hajduci*, our ancestors who preferred snatching things to hard work. Even today, we, the Serbs, act like the haiduks from the time of Prince Milos[62]. We work from May to November, then enjoy ourselves and undertake *hajduk*-style reaching for what belongs to the state in order to endure the wintertime. This kind of conduct saved us from the Ottoman oppression but became part of our genes and has meanwhile turned into our most serious law.

As *hajduci*, we the Serbs do not tolerate leaders. As soon as a new 'vozhd' appears, we tend to remove him. Only one leader can be put up with, the one whom we expect to work instead of us and lead us into the future.

At that point, in 1990-1991, there was no awareness of, understanding for, or readiness to start transition in the American way. As usual, the Serbs chose a sanguinary road to change.

What happened, actually?

On March 9, 1991, the Serbian opposition led by Vuk Draskovic, struck against Milosevic state system and 'his' Serbia. The opposition and the aggressive rallying crowd on the Republic Square in downtown Belgrade were counterattacked by the Minister of Interior Radmilo Bogdanovic whose police used water cannons; in the evening, upon Milosevic's instruction, Borisav Jovic[63] deployed military tanks and armored vehicles. The event opened the eyes of the Americans and the West to the real option of Slobodan Milosevic – against the changes and for the safeguarding of communism. In order to safeguard Yugoslavia as a political structure and all of her properties, Milosevic impinged the state budget of the S.F.R.Y. and took seven billion dollars, then put all of Serbia's money under his own control.

At Davos Forum: Djordjevic, Prohaska, Zivanovic and Drnovsek

*

In early 1990's I practiced plastic surgery in a rented operation room within Belgrade's Dragisa Misovic Hospital and its Gynaecology and Obstretics Institute. At that time I collaborated with Dr. Stanoje Glisic. My patients belonged to the Serbian elite circles. Enthusiastic about expanding my business in Yugoslavia, I had sold everything in the United States, but – unfortunately – there was no serious business for me as a doctor there. 'Seated' in the *Genex apartmani* Building and paying a DM 3,000 rent per month, I observed the 'physiology' of the Serbian economy run by the banker Slobodan Milosevic.

The firm/building *Genex apartmani,* situated in Novi Beograd/

New Belgrade, accomodated the 'headquarters' of high-profile smuggling business and deception of the Serbian people. For, that was the place where Milosevic's 'shadow-staff' operated: owners and traders from the black market, organizers of international smuggling of goods from Greece, F.Y.R. of Macedonia, Bulgaria, Turkey and Hungary. And – two 'legendary' false bankers known under the names of Dafina and Jezda respectively. They lived like gods.

The man who supervised Dafina Milanovic and ran her *Dafiment* pyramid-scheme bank was Mihalj Kertes (Mihály Kertész), the number one of the Federal Customs Bureau. The real boss of Jezdimir Vasiljevic, the famed *gazda-Jezda* ('Master' Jezda), and of his pyramid-scheme bank *Jugoskandik* was Jovica Stanisic, head of the Serbian secret police.

When Dafina Milanovic moved into the building, crowds began to queue for money transactions. Dafina was frequently visited by Zeljko Raznatovic Arkan, referred to as an "O.K. guy" in her milieu and by the state's top staff. I did not quite understand what I saw and heard, but one thing appeared clear: it was the country's top ranks that were plundering the masses via Dafina and Jezda. For, the pyramid-scheme banks which offered high interest rates were actually a large-scale deception at the cost of the people – carried out by Slobodan Milosevic and his clique.

In the *Genex apartmani* Building, the opposite-door neighbors of my medical practice were two clerks in an office of the company Delta banka. The owner was Miroslav Miskovic. This first Serbian tycoon was 'given birth' there, in the luxurious *Genex apartmani*, under the wings of the authorities. It was at *Genex* that I got acquainted to Zoran Kojic, Director of the nearby *Intercontinental* Hotel which was part of the *Genex* company. The circle included some individuals that looked rather strange to me: a Marcetic who wanted to buy the casino of the *Intercontinental* Hotel, a Mr. George Jablan, French citizen later killed in Czech Republic, a Mr. Bosko Radonjic, policeman who worked with General Radovan Badza Stojicic, later Acting Minister of the Interior.

*

Milosevic wished to rule as a dictator. He was fighting for Serbia like a lioness fighting for her litter. In the beginning, the

Americans supported his conduct, for they believed he could change his mind and – as a banker of western like manners – commence transition process. Personally, I thought likewise: that Slobodan Milosevic was going to open toward the West and carry out transition. Therefore, I was – as a kind of grey eminence from the United States – helping my friends in Milosevic's government replace communism with democracy.

From the Socialist Party's glass nest, most of those Milosevic men were looking upon me as an American 'sheep' they could 'shear' repeatedly.

– Doctor, you're a millionaire! Give a couple of dollars for Serbia!Help us endure this unjust embargo imposed by the Americans and the Europeans! – Those were the words uttered by the men from *Genex apartmani.*

Some of them spoke with sincerity and good intentions, others with insidious thoughts and a wish to provoke and humiliate me. Having gained power through their state-related jobs and money, they liked presenting themselves as the overlords of Yugoslavia and Serbia. My answer would be:

– Of course I'll help. Serbia is my homeland, too, not yours only!Despite extensive professional obligations, I wanted – as a Serbian patriot – to take advantage of the good cooperation between Serbia (and Yugoslavia especially) and the U.S.A., and to persuade my former Party comrades that they should commence transition – in an American way. I reminded them of the situation when, in 1988, Zivorad Kovacevic, Yugoslavia's Ambassador to Washington D.C., conveyed the American offer to the S.F.R.Y. to – via the KPMG multinational company – purchase military equipment and weapons for the Air Force of the Yugoslav National Army. The offer, worth $ 3.000,000, reached General Jovan Matovic. I also reminded them of another American offer: In 1989, the Yugoslav Union of PTT could make a 200 million deal for privatization and modernization. I was personally involved in the negotiations, and Mr. Vucic Cagorovic was Director General of the state-run PTT Union.

[62] **Prince Milos Obrenovic** (1780-1860) was Prince of Serbia from 1815 to 1839, and again from 1858 to 1860. He participated in the First Serbian Uprising (1804-1813), led the Second Serbian Uprising (1815) and founded the Princely/Royal House of Obrenovic. – *Translator's note.*

[63] **Borisav Jovic** (b. 1928) was the President of the Presidency of Yugoslavia and Serbian member thereof at the time described. – *Translator's note.*

KPMG and Sloba

During my first visit to Milosevic, early in 1991, I was accompanied by Guido Schmidt-Chiari, CEO of the Austrian bank *Kreditanstalt* which at that moment planned to open an affiliate bank in Serbia. It was part of a set of opportunities for the speeded development of this Yugoslav republic. Earlier, during the 1990 elections, I had brought a group of Americans to Serbia: two senators, Deputy Mayor of New York City and some twenty businessmen. On the very eve of the election day, they were received by President Slobodan Milosevic, and that convinced me of his honest will to establish cooperation with the Americans.

During the year 1991, I maintained correspondence with Selimir Savic, a director at *Genex*, over cooperation with the Brussels-based company *Federal Express Europlex* and its foundation of an affiliate office in Belgrade. Materials and a conference at Brussels in late January 1991 were being prepared, related to the entry of *Fed Express* into Yugoslavia. I also represented the telephone company *Nynex* in Serbia.

KPMG representatives visiting Radovan Karadzic

In addition, I created conditions for the inclusion of the American millionaire Rose Mihata in the Serbian business; the lady was close to the British royal family and fairly influential in the business and political circles of the United States. Mrs. Mihata was also a well-known humanitarian and representative of a foundation which took care of handicapped children worldwide.

Additionally, I was associated with the KPMG Company (one of the Big Four auditors) and its representative for Serbia Peat Marwick.

To Americans, in early 1990's, Serbia was the most important business partner on the Balkans. According to an analysis made by KPMG, the free market in Yugoslavia (dominated by Serbia's economy) was rather poorly developed. Two kinds of property prevailed there: state property and the so-called social property; private property made a minor portion on the overall economic scene. From 1988 onwards and owing to Yugoslavia's Prime Minister Ante Markovic, some newly-passed legislation opened way to the development of the market economy and privatization processes. This provided good reasons to the KPMG for direct participation – on behalf of the U.S.A. – in the economic reforms which concerned the state-owned enterprises.

The Americans wanted to carry out proprietorial transition in Yugoslavia and at the same time to accomplish favorable business deals on a large scale. They were willing to pay full prices for healthy Serbian state-owned firms and minor enterprises. The multinational company KPMG was supposed to take the role of the leading investor into the privatization process. This American consortium is held by the Masons and Jews, as an instrument of their rule over the United States.

Luckily enough, my onetime Party comrades and members of the ruling Socialist Party of Serbia reasoned well and accepted cooperation with the KPMG trust in the issues of economic reforms and privatization in Serbia. I possess a letter sent from KPMG toward the end of 1991 in which the corporation offered to the Government of Serbia to invest 40 billion dollars in the privatization of major Serbian companies during the first stage of the process, plus 30 billion for the medium-size enterprises in the next stage. The highest-ranking officials of the Socialist Party and the Government were directly informed about the planned American investments in Serbia of 70 billion dollars; they included Vladimir Stambuk, Radoman Bozovic and Nebojsa Maljkovic.

The central headquarters of KPMG was next to the White House in Washington D.C. in terms of power. It was there that the crucial assessments were made and guarantees issued for any big business deal around the globe. The KPMG trust determined which business was secure in terms of money and pro it, and which was not. For instance, the KPMG consortium assessed the *Nish Tobacco Industry* as one of the best Balkanwide, recommending it for 'obligatory' purchase and privatization. Why? Because this factory in Nish possessed enormous reserves of high quality tobacco from the region of Vranje and the F.Y.R. of Macedonia, good enough to produce Marlboro Lights branded as American. The sources of pro it laid in low-cost labor, low production price in Nish and high selling price in the United States and worldwide. The envisaged deal could have pulled Serbia out of the economic quagmire.

In 1992, Dr. Daniel Schein of Vienna, Va. mediated the opening of the direct business cooperation between Peat Marwick as the U.S. representative of KPMG and the members of Serbia's government officials aimed at reforming the Serbian economy and privatization process. The Government of Serbia accepted the initiative and the talks with the representatives of KPMG, one of the world's major corporations that embosied the economic and political power of the United States of America.

I still have in my possession documents about the cooperation between KPMG and the Government of Serbia aimed at reforming the Serbian economy and society which implied privatization process; these papers clearly testify to the transition plan offered to Serbia by the United States.

On March 24, 1992, following the meetings in Belgrade which had lasted from March 17 to March 19 and the discussions about the Program of Economic Reform and Privatization, KPMG with their representative Peat Marwick and the representatives of the Government of the Republic of Serbia led by Vice-President Dr. Nebojsa Maljkovic set a special *Agenda* to be carried out by the Serbian Government; the *Agenda* consisted of five projects:

- Public debt management and macroeconomic policy;
- Negotiations with international development institutions;
- Privatization, commercialization and restructuring of large state enterprises;
- Reforming financial institutions and acquisition of investments; and
- Establishment of an Export Development Bank.

The *Agenda* was composed on March 31, 1992; its objective was to promote sustainable growth of the Republic of Serbia and help the Government gain trust of the international financial circles. Peat Marwick's team was supposed to assist the Government of Serbia in creating sustainable state budget, policy of public debt management and setting up of efficient state administration. The team was to work on a new agreement with the IMF and World Bank regarding loans for the structural adjustments in economy, economic stabilization, support to privatization and implementation of new financial mechanisms that should have promoted Serbia's export and import capacities.

The whole process included the American offer to acquire the support by the European Economic Community (EEC) and World Bank.

The Americans proposed establishment of a local/Serbian affiliate office of KPMG LLP with Lior Samuelson, their managing partner, as their representative and partner to the Serbian Government.

The Program of Economic Reform and Privatization, made by KPMG, was handed in to the Government of the Republic of Serbia on April 1, 1992. It provided a detailed description of the Program implementation process in Serbia that was to be superintended by six experts from Washington. As proposed, the most interesting part of the Program concerned privatization which had been centered around the following goals:
- Enhancement of efficiency and competences of medium-size and large state and social enterprises by way of restructuring, ownership transfer and control of private sector;
- Attraction of foreign investments for reasons of financial capital, technology transfer, management staff and new markets; Mobilization of public support to the Government of Serbia and its privatization program through communication with interest groups and the media;
- Continuing analysis-related education for the members of the Government of Serbia and for private advisors to work on the KPMG privatization program;
- Establishment of non-beaurocratic organizations for privatization on the ground, entrusted with assessment of companies and their proprietorial transformation.

According to the proposal by KPMG, the Government of Serbia was to establish a team of professionals assigned to co-work with Peat Marwick's team; as an adviser of the Serbian Government, Marwick would claim two per cent of the worth of the transitions/privatizations done. For the first year of work, the estimated costs of the two teams amounted to $ 2.4 million. Their financing was to be ensured by the United States, European Commission, IMF, World Bank and some European banks.

Unfortunately for Serbia, Slobodan Milosevic and the Serbian Government rejected this Program of Economic Reform and Privatization offered by KPMG, i.e. by official Washington. On May 1st, 1992 – due to the rejection of transformation and modernization with American support – the United Stated punished the Serbs/Serbia by imposition of international sanctions. Being responsible for the embargo, Slobodan Milosevic threw his Serbian fellow countrymen and the Serbian state into an abyss.

Today, it is clear to me that Milosevic did not know that the essential message sent from the U.S.A. read: Let us administer the F.R. of Yugoslavia and organize it as a modern capitalist country. Milosevic thought that the United States was going to depose him and take over his power if he relinquished to the American experts the Serbian/Yugoslav economy, public and state-owned capital. At the same time, he thought he was indestructible owing to the backup of his rebelliously anti-American people, police and, finally, the Yugoslav National Army. He kept lying in the face of American politics, thus defeating both himself and the state and the people. Today, my conclusion is rather simple: Slobodan Milosevic was incapable of practising politics with competence. Sloba was preoccupied with his own power only.

Selfish Rulers

WHEN SLOBODAN MILOSEVIC decided to decline the American offer, which actually meant a provocation to the imposition of sanctions, I tried to seek help for the salvation of Yugoslavia/Serbia addressing the new prime minister, Milan Panic, who had arrived from the United States. On August 19th, 1992 I wrote a letter to the Yugoslav PM Panic, suggesting that we should act as a bridge between Washington and Belgrade, between the business people of the two countries – for the benefit of both:

I've been here [in Belgrade] for the last two years trying to identify major problems in which I can help with some of my friends from Washington and Europe. I think the problems are right here and some of the steps that have been suggested to me is one process of privatisation which I have worked out with KPMG-Washington office, and made some inroads here, but, as you know, it is very hard to work outside the Government channels. If Yugoslavia would sign the KPMG agreement, I can activate very powerful PR machinne that they have, including some serious possibility of canceling the embargo. We can talk about it.

Slobodan Milosevic and his spouse Mira Markovic

I am sending you in the separate envelope the contract that KPMG signed pre embargo and the Letter of Intent that Mr. Maljkovic, Deputy Prime Minister, signed prior to that. Mr. Milosevic is aware of this. I do not see any reason why this program cannot be implemented in whole Yugoslavia and give you a powerful argument against the foreign press. There are many more programs that I started here and in which I was using American businessmen and politicians who spoke in our favour, but as I said, I need official channels.

I proposed to Panic that we meet and carry out the agreement with KPMG. He never answered. Milan Panic, a U.S. citizen with a *Partisan* episode in his biography who established himself as a politician (and an even wealthier man) in Belgrade, set out to carry out *one* privatization –in his private interest. That is, he personally owned a pharmaceutical company, selling enormous quantity of medicines to the Russians and Chinese. At the same time, he held the ruling throne of a premier, although neither the Americans nor the Serbs were giving him full support.

As the relationship between the President of Serbia Milosevic and the Prime Minister of Yugoslavia Panic were bad to a considerable extent, the situation was one of stalemate. I persuaded President of the F.R. of Yugoslavia Dobrica Cosic to try to handle the situation relying on the Constitution of the F.R.Y., but also the Army of the F.R.Y. Cosic failed to reconcile Milosevic and Panic, for he was a soft touch who could not get on with his presidential job with executive authority. In between the two confronted men, the President of Serbia and the Premier of Yugoslavia, he appeared to be just a buttinsky.

There was another letter, the content of which was similar to what I wrote to Panic, addressed to the Government of the Republic of Serbia. I sent it in the hope that somebody there would respond and prevent the disastrous effects of the embargo imposed on the country. The Government did not answer my appeal either.

When I realized that the sanctions were going to endanger both Yugoslavia and my business in Belgrade, I made another attempt at starting the transition process in Serbia – through George Bush Senior. Living in two mutually remote places on the globe, I was in a position –like an onlooker watching a chess game – to see and anticipate the moves each of the two players, the U.S.A. and the F.R.Y., were going to make. However, I did not succeed in doing so, for one player – Slobodan Milosevic in Belgrade – was helplessly bad.

*

At that time I failed to realize that the Serbian leaders in Belgrade –both Milosevic and Panic and Cosic – did not care about the wellbeing of the Serbian citizens; what they did care about was their personal wellbeing, which they successfully accomplished. The Serbian people did not protest too much, for there was no alternative to choose; worse than that: it seems that the Serbs like living with inflictions and sufferings.

Unlike Franjo Tudjman[64] who, with the assistance of the United States, managed to attract the Croat diaspora to help him privatize state-owned firms and fight for an independent Croatia, Milosevic was turning away the Serb diaspora. Instead, he and his wife created a new communist-profiled political party – JUL (*Jugoslovenska udruzena levica* – Yugoslav Left).[65] He wanted to fulfill the dream of his spouse Mirjana Markovic and enable her to become an official 'heiress' to Josip Broz Tito. Together, they would be the rulers of the reduced Yugoslavia, thus resembling the 'legendary' couple – Tito and Jovanka.

Milosevic took advantage of nationalism, using the sentiments for taking power in Serbia. Using the misfortunes of the Serbs in Kosovo-Metohija, he abolished the autonomy to Serbia's two provinces (Kosovo-Metohija and Vojvodina), took control over the Presidency of Yugoslavia and over the Yugoslav National Army, which implied inauguration of Serbia as the prevailing power within Yugoslavia.

It was a mixture of communism and nationalisms that defined the roles played by some individuals in power: Slobodan Milosevic in Serbia, Franjo Tudjman in Croatia and Alija Izetbegovic in Bosnia-Herzegovina.

Partly in response to Milosevic's moves toward centralization of Serbia and its domination in Yugoslavia, and partly of their own will, nationalists rose to power in other republics, too.

Franjo Tudjman, once a general of the Yugoslav National Army and the leader of the newly-established Croatian Democratic Union (Croat abbr. HDZ), relied on nationalists in Croatia and became the first president of the republic/country. He had also written a revisory version of the history of *Ustashe*-led actions during World War II in which he downplayed the magnitude of the crimes committed by the authorities of the Independent State of Croatia[66]; this only stirred up the nationalist feelings of the Serbs.

In Bosnia-Herzegovina, Alija Izetbegovic[67] came into power as the leader of the Party of Democratic Action (local abbr. SDA). He had been imprisoned in 1980's for Muslim nationalism; earlier, in 1970, Izetbegovic had published a manifesto entitled *Islamic Declaration*, which was broadly interpreted as a call for establishment of a Muslim theocratic state in Bosnia.

The Bosnian Serbs relied on Izetbegovic's biography in order to present themselves as the first frontline of Europe's defense against penetration of Islam into the Old Continent. They were also demonstrating the importance of living in a separate Serb state and not together with the Bosnian Muslims.

To varying degree, each of the three leaders (Milosevic, Tudjman, Izetbegovic) manipulated the masses by way of nationalism, all in order to gain financial capital and political power, and remain in their respective power-granting offices.

---

[64] **Franjo Tudjman** (1922-1999) was a Croatian politician and historian who rose to power as the 1st President of the Croatian Democratic Union (1989-99), a conservative political party which fought for the secession from Yugoslavia and was in power throughout the 1990's; Tudjman was elected the President of the Presidency of Croatia elected in 1990 while Croatia was still one of Yugoslavia's six republics, to be reelected President in 1992, after Croatia had obtained recognition of a number of foreign countries, then again in 1997. During the war in the former Yugoslavia, he led the operations against the Yugoslav National Army and the Serbs in Croatia and Bosnia-Herzegovina, as well as the Muslims/Bosniaks in Bosnia-Herzegovina. The latter armed conflict jeopardized the international support to Croatia, so Tudjman and Izetbegovic signed the Washington Agreement in March 1994 to end it and re-ally the two sides against the Serbs in both ex-Yugoslav republics. In 1995, Franjo Tudjman authorized the Operation Storm (Aug.4-14) and brought the so-called Croatian War of Independence to an end – through massive expulsion (over 200,000) and killings of the Serbs. He was one of the signatories of Dayton Accords later that year. – *Translator's note*.

[65] For more on this, see footnote in the Chapter "Sloba's Bird", Part One of this book. –*Translator's note*.

[66] For more, see footnotes in the chapters "Grandpa's Boy" (Ustashe) and "Rosalynn Carter's Friend" (Jasenovac Concentration Camp). – *Translator's note*.

[67] *Alija Izetbegovic* (1925-2003) was a Muslim/Bosniak politician who in post-Dayton years held the offices of the 1st Bosniak Member of the Presidency of Bosnia-Herzegovina (1996-2000) and Chairman of the Presidency of BH (February-October 2000). Himself a Sunni Islamist, he joined the organization "Young Muslims" during World War II and favored the regional largely Muslim *Waffen SS Handschar Division* over the Yugoslav *Partisan* movement. In 1970 he published the *Islamic Declaration* and got a sentence to imprisonment in 1980's. His book *Islam between East and West* was published in the U.S.A. in 1984. In 1992, on the eve of the war in BH, he withdrew his signature to the Lisbon Agreement (Cutilheiro Plan, which envisaged Bosnia-Herzegovina as a three-ethnic cantonal state) and called an independence referendum. When the Parliament of BH (without the Serbs) proclaimed independence, he took over the government, from which the Croats pulled out to establish their own Croatian Republic of Herzeg-Bosnia. In addition, the so-called Autonomous Province of Western Bosnia (with it center in Velika Kladusa), led by Muslim

Fikret Abdic (see the related footnote in the chaper "A Secret Trip to Georgia", Part One of this book) was also beyond Izetbegovic's control. Alija Izetbegovic was one of the signatories to the Dayton Accords. – *Translator's note.*

Saddam Hussein's Man

It was in Iraq I celebrated my fifty-fourth birthday. Never before could I imagine that I would find myself in Baghdad on March 3, 1996. Or that I could celebrate a birthday of mine with the Iraqi President Saddam Hussein. At dinner hosted by him that day, fish baked in mud was served, one of his favorite meals, and the occasion was embellished with birthday fireworks. I must admit that for a moment I felt to be a happy man. Everything else in Iraq made one feel dispirited and unhappy.

I arrived in Iraq as an emissary of Jimmy Carter and the Carter Center, at a moment when they engaged in a mission of saving Saddam Hussein's family, that is, his sons and their children. Carter had been summoned by Tariq Aziz, Deputy Prime Minister of Iraq; the Carter Center accepted the mission but transferred it to me in the hope I could carry it out efficiently.

Tariq Aziz and Borko Djordjevic

– Go there and see what it is about, and help if you can – Jimmy Carter asked me.

In order to disguise my mission trip to Iraq partly at least, I set out on the journey accompanied by my girlfriend (now my wife) Sandra Lucic. We pretended to be tourists and flew from Belgrade, via Athens and Beirut to Amman. In Jordan's capital we were accomodated in the Intercontinental Hotel. One whole floor of the hotel was reserved for the two of us and our company, that is, bodyguards who were there for us in those two days we spent in Amman.

From there, we continued the trip to Baghdad in a Chevrolet jeep. Our 'guide' was Dr. Mahmoud H. Al-Modafar, a military official of high rank whose burnt face and hands I had treated earlier. That spring, in 1996, Iraq was set as a target for a large-scale operation. The Americans had ended the Gulf War years before, but a military operation codenamed *Operation Desert Fox* was in preparation; its goal was deposition of Saddam Hussein and his family.

Iraq's conflict with Kuwait and Kurdistan Region effected Baghdad being declared – by the U.S.A. and the U.N. – responsible for occupation and ethnic cleansing. Due to previous bombing, the road to Baghdad was empty of vehicles. While getting fuel at a gas station in the desert, I was watching oil jetting freely out of the soil. In that year, the price of crude oil in Iraq was 50 cent per 100 liters.

In Baghdad, my girlfriend and I were accomodated at Hotel *Rasheed*. We were looking forward to the audience with Prime Minister Tariq Aziz, a legendary figure and official in Saddam's government. Reading his biography, I found out the following facts: Born in 1936 as Mikhail Yuhanna, this Christian became a member of the top leadership of the Ba'ath Party. He was Minister of Foreign Affairs (1983-91) and Deputy Prime Minister (1979-2003). He was personally credited for the renewal of diplomatic relations between Baghdad and Washington D.C. in 1984. During the Iraqi occupation of Kuwait, Aziz was in charge of the contacts with the Western countries and the United States.

Toward the American 1991 intervention – the story goes – Aziz wanted to lee Iraq. His wealthy home had already been sacked, and the hearsay around Baghdad said that he had been killed while en route to the Kurdish part of the country. Tariq Aziz denied it all then. Five years later, however, that is, in 1996, when my mission took place, Aziz wrote to Jimmy Carter asking him to enable his light from Iraq and help spare that country of war.

When my girlfriend and I headed for a meeting with Tariq Aziz, our escorts harshly remarked:

– No women, please!

At the very beginning of the dialog, Tariq Aziz openly said that he needed my advice and help of Jimy Carter in order to enable the family of Saddam Hussein to leave Iraq and thus escape the American bombing. I asked for a recess of a couple of hours in order to consult Carter. On the phone, the former U.S. President told me:

– Do that, but under the aegis of the United Nations. The United States should not interfere with Saddam Hussein's private problems!

The family of Saddam Hussein was under the control of American forces and the United Nations. Iraq was under an international embargo and air traffic ban. One could hear about Uday, Saddam's elder son, trying to secretly contact the Americans and offer to become a renegade in the United States. My idea, which I conveyed to the Deputy Premier, was that Tariq Aziz, accompanied by two Saddam's sons and their families (wives and children), which made ten persons in the group, come to New York City and the U.N. seat where they should seek protection and shelter.

A channel was worked out for the departure of Saddam's 10-member family via Jordan to the United States. Jimmy Carter was prepared to back up such an action and personally get involved if necessary. But the message I got from the United Nations said that Saddam Hussein's family could be saved only if he stepped down.

– Mr. President is ready to step down and relinquish his authority to his sons. In return, he demands lifting of the Iraq blockade and embargo, and reestablishment of air traffic to and from foreign countries. – That was Tariq Aziz's proposal.

Through a mediator, President Bill Clinton let me know that such a scenario for the developments in Iraq and the Presidential Palace in Baghdad did not suit him.

REPUBLIC OF IRAQ
Council of Ministers
Deputy Prime Minister

March 1, 1997

To: Dr. Borko B. Djordjevic.

I have read the letter of Mr. Harry G. Barnes Jr. addressed to you dated February 20, 1997.

I want to assure you that I am ready to receive Mr. Barnes here in Baghdad and to discuss with him at length all the matters he raised in his letter to you. I will, also, be ready to provide him with any sort of relevant first hand information and data, he wants, regarding these matters.

Sincerely,

Tariq Aziz
Deputy Prime Minister
Republic of Iraq

A 1997 letter to Dr. Djordjevic by Tariq Aziz

Like their father, Saddam's sons Uday and Qusay were targeted by Washington and the U.S. military. The middle son Raghad and the daughters Rana and Hala Hussein were of no interest to the Americans. Officially, the elder son Uday was chairman of the Iraqi Olympic Committee, Iraq Football Association and Iraqi Journalists' Association, owner of the most influential newspaper *Babel*, an anchorman at the popular TV broadcaster *Shabab*, and – most importantly – the heir to his father's presidential throne.

Saddam's younger son Qusai was the supervisor of the elite Republican Guard of Iraq and the secret police which guarded his father. When the Iranians attacked Uday Hussein and wounded him early in 1996, Saddam named his younger son as his heir to presidency.

The French President Jacques Chirac, Saddam's friend, organized the medical treatment for Uday Hussein. He sent an MRI scanner to Baghdad so that the bullets could be located in Uday's body, and also commissioned a surgeon from London to operate on Saddam's son. I sutured Uday's wound and was rewarded with decorative elephant tusks and a couple if Iraqi gold coins. My friend was presented with silken ladies' Muslim-style pantaloons by Mahmoud Al-Modafar.

I stayed in Baghdad for eight days. The city was ravaged, but clean and full of birds lying around freely. A traditional Iraqi bazaar was organized at Hotel *Rasheed* which put on display paintings and items of arts and crafts, along with a sale of the items of Kuwait's cultural heritage taken as plunder from that country. I was told that President Saddam Hussein thought of me as a trustworthy person whom he wanted to receive and thank for his son's (Udai's) salvation.

Before I met Saddam Hussein, his guards had advised me to kiss the hand of their President. Which I did, giving a bow. The audience took place in the presidential palace. Saddam Hussein was accompanied by his nephew, a niece of Tariq Aziz and Dr. Sami Sadoun, Iraqi Ambassador to Belgrade. The President of Iraq was wearing a Versace suit with a bow tie. Dressed as a civilian, he had an unreal and strange look.

I was seated next to Saddam Hussein, at a table amply covered with various dainties. Tariq Aziz was standing beside me, translating into English the words of the Iraqi ruler. It was actually a monolog, while I was listening, nodding and putting in a word or two of agreement.

– You used to be a pioneer[68] of Tito's. You must be a good man! – Saddam Hussein said, confirming that he knew everything about me. –Tito was a great man. He helped the reconstruction and modernization of Iraq. I feel so proud of him!

He also mentioned Serbia's interest in cooperation with Iraq and the fact that a pharmaceutical plant of our Hemofarm Industry operated in his country:

– Hemofarm is curing our people!

George Bush Jr.

I tried to remind Saddam Hussein of our encounter in mid-1980's, when he was buying fifty fighter aircraft in the United States. Aziz translated this briefly, but he did not respond. He served me the fish baked in mud and uttered, seemingly off-handed:

– Happy birthday to you, Mr. Djordjevic!

My rescue mission for the two sons of Saddam Hussein and their families failed. George Bush Jr. started the war against Iraq in order to 'revenge' his father, the former President George W.H. Bush whom Saddam wanted assassinated. Also, Bush Jr. needed that war in order to establish the New World Order, so my peace/rescue mission did not it in his plans. That was the political backdrop of my Baghdad mission's failure.

A new attempt at the rescue of Saddam Hussein's family was made in 2003. The Carter Center acted as mediator again, and I appeared as a missioner along Harry Barnes. The plan was to bring Saddam Hussein (with his family) to New York City and enable him to speak before the U.N. General Assembly. Actually, he was supposed to surrender and thus stop the war in Iraq. However, the White House refused to grant him the U.S. entry visa, for – according to the information of the CIA – he was in possession of nuclear weapons and weapons of massive destruction. The reason, which later proved false, served as America's excuse for manhunt after Saddam Hussein.

This was by no means unusual. For, the United States had repeatedly demonstrated its manhunt-marked style of turning some foreign countries into its colonies after their leaders got removed. By secret operations of the CIA the Americans had similarly entrapped Chile's President Allende, Iran's Shah Reza Pahlavi, Slobodan Milosevic in Serbia and, of late, Lybian head of state Muammar Gaddafi.

Gerald Ford and Jimmy Carter were the only U.S. Presidents who did not apply this kind of secret operations. But it has recently been resorted to by George Bush, Bill Clinton and Barack Obama.

The political context accounts for the supremacy of the U.S. military over the peace mission undertaken by Jimmy Carter and myself, Borko Djordjevic. Uday and Qusai Hussein were killed in a 2003 American military operation. Saddam Hussein was captured and liquidated in 2006. Tariq Aziz died as prisoner in 2015.

[68] **Pionir**: The word designates a member of the Union of Pioneers of Yugoslavia (*Savez pionira Jugoslavije*), an organization founded in 1942, the membership of which practically encompassed all children age seven and above. The children would ceremonially wear red scarves (sometimes the so-called *titovka* cap, navy blue with a red star), white shirts and recite the "Yugoslav Pioneer Pledge" at a solemn ceremony of admission held on the occasion of the Republic Day, November 29th. The last generation to go through this kind of initiation was born in 1982. – *Translator's note.*

MY PRIVATE WAR

I HAD SENSED BEING under surveillance by the FBI and CIA, but did not take the matter seriously until I was back home to the States. Because of my peace mission at Pale during the war in Bosnia (see Part One of this book) and the one in Baghdad (described in the previous chapter), as well as my attempt to return to Belgrade, I sacrificed my private/family life. My second wife, Joy Stephens Djordjevic, gave birth to our daughter Aleksandra in 1989. I failed to dedicate myself appropriately to my wife and child during the war in Yugoslavia and my frequent travels abroad. Aware of that, I believed my care and love would make up for the absence from home. However, my wife Joy did not share my conviction.

She declared a private war of hers on me and filed for divorce. In order to misrepresent my personality to the American court and depict me at my worst, she accused me before the police and the prosecutor's office of hiding properties, tax evasion and collaboration with state enemies. In other words, I was portrayed as an embezzler and foreign spy.

But what was it all about?

Before coming from the United States to Belgrade, in early 1990's, I had lived in Switzerland and France for a while. In Geneva, I socialized with Dragan Zivanovic, alias Daniel Boyer, a business partner of the Parisian banker Philipp von Liechtenstein. As a friend and protégé of the First Lady Eleanor Roosevelt, Zivanovic was in high esteem with the Americans.

The man was a Serb and my confidant. Leaving for Serbia, I 'deposited' some of my most important documentation, business- and profession-related, in his New York apartment. He was the number four man in the Democratic Party of the U.S.A. and an influential figure in the circles of the Kennedy family. As a successful publisher, he worked on a number of books for the Holy See and Pope Paul. He boasted a passport issued by the State of the Vatican City and a Merzedes car with the Vatican plates.

Since life in Geneva proved fairly expensive, I bought a house in France. In choosing and securing my new home I was helped by

Raymond Ray Carter, high-profile French security expert.[69] My choice was a house in Divonne-les-Bains, a spa town by the Swiss border, seven-minute drive far from Geneva. World's politicians held their conferences there. At this residence in Divonne, I used to receive my associates and guests for debates and agreements related to the current situation in Yugoslavia.

My wife Joy occasionally came to stay with me in Vienna, Geneva and Divonne. She allowed me to take our daughter Aleksandra to Igalo and Belgrade. In 1996, however, she discovered that I had a girlfriend in Belgrade. Enraged, she denounced my discreet political activities to the U.S. authorities, interpreting these as anti-American and spy business.

Her accusations referred to the house in Divonne as my hidden property – hidden from the American institutions and tax administration. She said that I intentionally evaded paying tax on property. Before the Californian court I had to prove my lawful behavior and counter the allegations of being an enemy of the United States of America and a spy delegated by the Bosnian Serbs.

Throughout the lawsuit, I referred to the Carter Center and my cooperation with the former President Jimmy Carter, yet my wife persisted in spreading the rumors about my alleged anti-American activities in conspiracy with Radovan Karadzic, a war crime indictee by The Hague Tribunal.

– My husband took his mistress to the war criminal Saddam Hussein – my wife Joy Djordjevic claimed publicly, at the time when the United States waged its second sanguinary war against Iraq.

In support of the charges for being "an Iraqi spy", Joy presented my photo with Tariq Aziz taken in Baghdad in March 1996. She also availed of my documentation, the correspondence with Radovan Karadzic and a number of photos from Pale. Having "unmasked a traitor", she won over her influential family to side with her. Which was not difficult at all.

My mother-in-law Betty Stephens was a very successful businesswoman. She owned a company which produced and distributed special cat litter "Johnny Cat" intended for cats' feces and urine collection which was made of scented clay; the firm was full 43 million dollars worth. I became my mother-in-law's partner when I added some antibiotics to prolong the expiration date and increase health-related quality. My daughter Aleksandra was involved in the business, too. She was a model in the sale campaign for the products launched by her grandmother's company. In return, I came into possession of 50% company shares.

Admittedly, I did love money very much, but not as much as I hated my mother-in-law Betty Stephens. She had an ugly habit of interfering with my private life, influencing her daughter and instructing her how to 'wage' the quarrels. At one point, in order to escape her pressures, Joy and I moved to Vienna. She arrived there soon. We moved to Geneva, and she joined us again.

The reason why she kept interfering in my life was rather simple: As Joy had inherited her father's properties, Betty started to impose her presence in her daughter's life in the hope that she could grab part of the inheritance.

Additionally, my mother-in-law Betty was a member of the Democratic Party, while I was a Republican. I was member of the Republican Party and of the Republican Congress Committee in Washington D.C. Most of the American Serbs are Republicans, for that is a party of workers which respects hard work and creativity rather than riches.

The Democratic Party mostly gathers wealthy class, those who have inherited money and power, that is, members of the 'dynasties'. My mother-in-law belonged to those circles. Betty Stephens was an evil and powerful woman. A member of Philip Morris Company, she was also a friend of Milan Panic and invitee to his inauguration ceremony as Yugoslav prime minister.

*

While I was building my career of a plastic surgeon, in 1980's, I was a Hollywood-style celebrity; in late 1990's, during the divorce from my second wife, I was a creature in disgrace in California. In the earlier period of my life in America I had been known as a 'golden boy' of an American First Lady; in the later period I became an 'Iraqi spy' and a 'traitor'.

It was a close thing that my divorce could lead me to imprisonment as if I had really been an enemy of the state. Fortunately, the FBI had a survey of my whereabouts all over Europe, Montenegro, Republic of Srpska and Serbia, as well as copies of my correspondence with the Carter Center during the peace missions with Radovan Karadzic and Saddam Hussein; this enabled me to stay undetained during the lawsuit.

I was not fully confident about the power of my defense, for everybody I knew in the States turned against me. I was scared by the possibility of being sentenced to ten-year imprisonment. It occurred to me that I might take to light to Yugoslavia and live with my friend Sandra Lucic. She lived in Belgrade, and I had met her at the clinic of Dr. Ninoslav Radovanovic. She was young, beautiful, vivacious and full of understanding for my restless spirit. I genuinely fell in love with this most charming girl.

In the United States, if you fail to defend yourself, you fall victim to the circumstances very soon and get ruined. I made up my mind: I should counter every single charge to which my second wife exposed me. So I hired eight lawyers, people specializing in divorce matters, taxes, political lobbying, crimes against national security...

I decided to be disputatious to the utmost. To the American public, I was already a 'roast hare'. The United States District Judge from the 9th Circuit, Honorable Manuel Real, was a Democrat, like my friend Jimmy Carter. I asked Carter:

– What shall I do now?

He did not say a straightforward word. However, Jimmy Carter discreetly wrote a letter to the judge who – following his information –made the following decision:

– As a judge of this district court, I have no jurisdiction to hear and determine the lawsuit pertaining to the divorce and other charges pressed by Mrs. Joy Djordjevic against Mr. Borko Djordjevic. Hence I transfer the whole case to the local court!

This formulation meant that – according to the district court/judge – I did not perpetrate any criminal acts I was charged with, and that the prosecution and accusations made against me by my wife and the Californian D.A. Of ice was but an ordinary case of family law. The jurisdiction over the said legal proceedings was now in the power of the Municipal Court in Los Angeles.

The lawsuits and divorce took full two years. My defense cost me $ 1.2 million. The Municipal Court in LA cleared me of all the charges pertaining to tax evasion, property hiding and collaboration with the national enemy. However, the CIA and FBI maintained their suspicions and secret surveillance. A couple of FBI inspectors interrogated me for three days in connection with my ties to Karadzic and Hussein.

I had made it clear to the court that I was no Iraqi spy and that, in 1996, the former U.S. President Jimmy Carter had personally summoned me in writing to visit Saddam Hussein. Harry Barnes had coordinated the journey. Politically, for Carter, the mission had justification in complieance with the U.N. Security Council Resolution 687 and the silent approval by the White House.

*

In spite of me being acquitted of her grave charges, my ex-wife Joy Stephens did not free me from her paranoia. She hired private investigators to follow me, and her net – launched in order to ruin me both psychologically and financially – was getting tighter. She falsely accused me of domestic violence, for a court verdict in such a case would ensure custody over our daughter, which she would further have used to change Aleksandra's Serbian name and surname. She also wanted to present our daughter as a victim to such domestic violence, which could have provided basis for depriving me of all possessions of mine.

Somewhat later, and due to the ugly divorce, our daughter Aleksandra left home at the age of 16 and adopted some really bad habits, which was actually her 'distress call', for she wanted her father to spend time with her and not with other women.

Both the Court and the FBI investigated the origins of my properties. In the property-related lawsuit, the items of interest included the Palm Springs house and clinic, an apartment in Palm Springs, a house on the Balboa Peninsula, a house in France, an apartment in Belgrade, and two cars – a Bentley and a Mercedes.

I am a born fighter who does not succumb to any defeat. Once attacked, I launch a counterattack. It was a habit since my boyhood, when I collected small pictures of the footballers (Serbian soccerplayers) Mitic and Bobek, ready to fight for them. It was awakened when Milosevic threatened to pay $ 400,000 for my killing. It also happened when my people was threatened by destruction. And once again when my wife Joy accused me of being an Iraqi spy, traitor of America and a domestic bully.

I was lucky enough to have a child who defied her capricious mother. Fed up with her mother's lies, Aleksandra testified against her.

Since the charges concerned family violence, the Medical Board of California got involved. Bearing in mind that my daughter was only 12 years old, and unwilling to involve her in the dispute as a witness before the court, I admitted that Joy and I were once qaurreling, that she spat at me and I slapped her in response. That was the truth.

Borko Djordjevic with his wife Sandra in Paris

The incident sufficed for the Medical Board to find me guilty of domestic violence and suspend my physician's license for three months plus seven years' probation. As I was holder of five licences for five states (New York, New Jersey, Ohio, Pennsylvania and Nevada), the Medical Boards of New York and New Jersey responded immediately, transferring the suspension within their authority.

 The Medical Board of California
2005 Evergreen Street, Suite 1200
Sacramento, CA 95815-5401

PHYSICIAN AND SURGEON
CERTIFICATE NO   A31228   EXPIRATION   03/31/2012

BORKO DJORDJEVIC
123 KAVENISH DR
RANCHO MIRAGE CA 92270

ORIGINAL
ISSUANCE DATE
06/20/1977

RECEIPT NO
04800126

Californian Physician and Surgeon Licence valid until 2012

The accusations against me before the Boards of California, New York and New Jersey never pertained to my professional work with patients or any other activity of mine in the capacity of a physician. Indeed, my wife tried to put some blame on me in that respect, too: she sent three of her friends to me and staged their accusations of careless treatment of the patients. The charges were dismissed. In other words, my Californian licence was valid from 1977 to 2012. During the long period, I was never deprived of it.

That is to say, my licence has never been cancelled; it was valid until 2012. The said case with the Medical Board took place in 2006-7, whereafter I had it renewed biennially, for the years 2008-2010 and 2010-12 (according to the rules on renewal, the licence is valid for two years). After 2012, I decided to stop payments and corresponding renewals (unless paid for, the licence expires automatically).

The court acquitted me of the charges for domestic violence, and my ex-wife Joy Stephens Djordjevic appeared to be an immoral person. This enabled me to register all the properties she wanted for herself as the inheritance of my daughter Aleksandra Djordjevic.

This private family war waged against my former wife Joy exhausted me completely and I was verging on devastation. Anything may have happened to me. If Joy had grabbed all of my properties, I would have ended as a moneyless American. Fortunately, I managed to annull the premarital/prenuptial agreement which envisaged shared property, so that Joy could use it only jointly with our daughter Aleksandra. The divorce was 20 million dollar worth, with Aleksandra as the beneficiary.

At the same time, I found happiness with Sandra Lucic. We had met in 1991. In 1998, I brought her to Palm Springs, to live with me and my mother. Since then, Sandra gave birth to two children of ours: in 2003, Nikola was born (his American name being Nico Bossi Djordjevic), and Nina Ricci Djordjevic came in 2005. Our wedding took place at Laguna Beach in 2006. We live in a house at Rancho Mirage. Meanwhile, Sandra graduated from a teachers' college, completed aesthetics and nutrition schools, plus the Law School. As she herself puts it, her main job is to keep our family happy.

My eldest child, Aleksandra, has forgiven me my earlier parental inadequacy. She completed her studies in art in California and has come to live with me and my family at Rancho Mirage and Belgrade.

---

[69] A detailed biography of Raymond Ray Carter is provided in the chapter titled "Ray Carter Protecting Radovan", Part One of this book. – *Translator's note.*

A PLOT: LIBEL AND BADMOUTHING

OWING TO THE HELL on earth staged by my second wife, some serious problems ensued for me in Montenegro where I was expanding my professional business. Namely, I had first built and equipped a surgical outpatient clinic at Igalo, within Simo Milosevic Institute, which grew into the Mediterranean Surgery Center and, finally, the American Hospital for Plastic Surgery. It took me more than two decades, from 1987 to 2015, to establish and maintain these institutions, yet some of the Montenegrin media found me worth spitting at. All the allegations my former wife Joy Stephens Djordjevic used to throw against me in California, supplemented with additional fabrications and lies, appeared in some Montenegrin weeklies. It was a pure media-launched libel.

The articles were headlined "Montenegro, Impostors' Paradise", "The Suspicious Biography of Dr. Djordjevic" (original: „Crna Gora raj za prevarante", „Sumnjiva biogra ija dr Đorđevića"), and the like. The article "In Impostors' Paradise", published in the weekly *Monitor* in 2010, contained multiple libeling. Yet it is noteworthy that just one year earlier the same newspaper had written about me as a successful physician and surgeon who enjoyed worldwide renown:

"The British BBC enlisted him among the ten most famous and most successful plastic surgeons worldwide, while the Americans, in addition to numerous signs of recognition, awarded him a Hollywood star on a sidewalk in Palm Springs for his professional endeavors and humanitarian work during the war in Bosnia.

It is not only knowledge but also money that Dr. Djordjevic has brought to his homeland, and with his 'signature' and references it has a better investment weight. A clinic of his has been in operation for years now at Igalo, within the well-known Mediterranean Surgery Center which attracts patients from all over Europe, as well as prominent figures of the Montengrin business and public life." – This is what Monitor wrote –earlier.

The weekly also wrote about my name on the list "The World's Most Powerful Hundred Serbs" composed by the Belgrade newspaper Blic.

The change of Monitor's editorial policy and attitude was due to the political wrangling in Montenegro. Some opposition leaders got the idea that "Dr. Borko Djordjevic is a man of Milo Djukanovic"[70], and therefore had to be "torn apart like a greasy sack gets torn by a pig".

The whole campaign against me was orchestrated so efficiently that *Monitor* and other media publishing this sort of 'reports' never gave me any chance to deny the untruths, libels and lies. I did write a disaffirmation, but only small excerpts thereof were made available to the readership; in the denial, I explained that what *Monitor* had published were allegations made by my exwife in a lawsuit filed 14 years before and discarded by the court.

It also turned out that the editorial team of *Monitor* did not grasp the American institution/system of physicians' licencing: such licence is only issued to a person during his/her work in the United States; it has to be renewed biyearly and is issued after you submit evidence of not being sentenced by court, of paying tax regularly and of possessing all school-related qualifications for the job. My letter to *Monitor* had attachments: copies of working licence, agreement for the clinic in Igalo/Montenegro and the Certificate by the American Board of Plastic and Reconstructive Surgery.

My specialist qualifications cover general plastic surgery and aesthetic/reconstructive surgery, including facelifting (rhytidectomy), rhinoplasty, blepharoplasty, chemical peels; augmentation and reduction of body parts (breasts, hands, feet), hip and abdomen reduction and sculpting, liposuction, genital repair and reconstruction. In a BBC special program titled *Hollywood Knives,* I was presented as one of the world's ten most renowned and most successful plastic surgeons.

In that year, 2010, I was one of the awardees of the Ellis Island Medal of Honor, founded in 1986 by the National Ethnic Coalition of Organizations (NECO). The list of medalists includes Muhammad Ali, Bill Clinton, Henry Kissinger, Frank Sinatra,

Donald Trump and Vlade Divac[71]. I became one of them owing to my accomplishments in professional and humanitarian work.

All of those information/evidence did not matter to the editors and reporters of *Monitor*, for their objective followed the one of the opposition party leaders: to present me as an impostor and a criminal. Hence the title of the follow-up article published in *Monitor* – "Dr. Djordjevic's Deception" ("Prevara doktora Djordjevica").

And what was the background to the plotted scandal, that is, to my second private war? I was 'guilty' of starting to advertise myself in public, endangering the plastic-surgery 'territory' of the local colleagues, especially the self-proclaimed plastic surgeon Borovic who was employed by the Montenegrin Clinical Center where he worked for state-payed salary in the morning, while working in private sector in the afternoon; this man would size up the financial profile of his morning patients and choose whom to send to the private *Kodra* Hospital for treatment. This doctor confronted the threatening draft bill which envisaged strict division between state-controlled and private medical sector, for that could deprive him of enormous extra incomes. For, the patients were coming to see him in the private hospital not because of his professional excellence but because he channeled them out of the public clinic. It was that same man who launched the campaign against me through the weekly *Monitor* and his sister working in that newspaper company. His allegations also touched on the treatments with stem cells: he claimed that in plastic surgery stem cells did not provide any genuine therapy. To ensure 'passableness' to the article, someone had to effect an adequate payment to the editor-in-chief who at that time happened to be Milka Tadic, cousin to Boris Tadic, President of Serbia at the time. As I heard, the price for the article was 30,000 Euro. Tadic's cousin was surfing the internet, collecting whatever had been written about me, but mostly newspaper headlines, as far back as to the early 1990's; she did not care about checking on the truthfulness of what she found. In spite of my claims, supported by evidence, that the allegations in the article had been false, she was forced to publish it.

*

Ms. Tadic proved to be corrupted no less than her cousin Boris Tadic who, while in power, practically ruined Serbia's economy, squandering all the money earned by the country through the false privatization of some 25 large enterprises. Slobodan Milosevic had refused privatization, and Tadic accepted it, with the intention to spend all the money invested by the European Union and other donors – some $ 70 billion; the money was shared by his associates, and the Serbian nation has been driven to the edge of an economic abyss. The process had been part of the 'philosophy' imposed by Zoran Djindjic[72] and his adherents. To my mind, those guys were 'white-collar thieves', as they are called in America. A mafia system and group thievery.

*

I had met Djindjic in Geneva, in the home of his friend Nebojsa Dimitrijevic whom he promised the post of foreign mister once he came into power. In return for the promise, Dimitrijevic set out to raise funds from the Serbian diaspora in Europe intended for the Democratic Party in Serbia. Expectedly enough, when Djindjic became prime minister, he booted the man out, although he had been a career diplomat, and a good one. But Djindjic began to distribute important posts to those who shared his attitude to administration, managerial matters and working style. At this point I cannot help thinking of a conversation I had with Misko Jeremic, Director of *Jugopetrol* after the Democrats had taken over the rule: Djindjic had rushed into *Jugopetrol* Oil Company, intending to arrest the Director-General Dragan Tomic and other top managers, for they had allegedly lived much too comfortably at the company's cost, and demanding that the hard cash of Jugopetrol Bank be taken out of its treasury in Belgrade's *Hyatt* Hotel.

My encounter with Zoran Djindjic as the Premier concerned the possible arrival of the largest American bank, the City National Bank, in Serbia. Among other business deals, the Americans wanted to buy off the four-storeyed bank premises of an affiliate office of JIK Banka (now in the possession of *Banca Intesa*) in Knez-Mihajlova Street; the building housed treasury safes and store-rooms for mink furcoats. The gentleman's will to receive the chief of the CNB was 'estimated' to cost 50,000 Euro, reportedly intended for the Democratic Party. The same mentality was spread within the circle of the Democratic Party surrounding Djindjic as their leader, including Mr. Tadic. Misko's son Vuk Jeremic, Minister of Foreign Affairs 2007-12, once complained to his father about the corruption in the cabinet of PM Mirko Cvetkovic which, as he claimed, reached some 90%; they deserved being behind the bars, for everybody had been involved in shady deals in their personal interest. This Democratic gang in power ' finished off' the Serbian people. When I told Pierre Prosper that Kostunica and Tadic would help me about amicable surrender of Karadzic and Tadic to the ICTY, Prosper answered that he would not reckon with it, for the two men were not trustworthy; his perception proved true.

*

Now let me be back to the Montenegrin weekly newspaper, *Monitor*, and its executive director, Tadic's cousin. It has been for years that she has sunken into corruption, taking big money for defamatory articles. Her chief target is the Djukanovic family and the party in power, DPS. These articles are full of crap, untrue 'facts' and endless prevarication. The newspaper has nothing to do with actual activities of the opposition parties but serves to launder money for a number of suspicious individuals – through Ms. Tadic.

As for Milo Djukanovic and his accomplishments that include the establishment of the Montenegrin state as it is today, it was a long, long way to go. As long as Serbia and Montenegro shared the same country, he was exposed to the offensive conduct of Slobodan Milosevic and Mira Markovic on personal level. I am illustrating the situation:

In 1998, I was back in the States, and a South California representative of CIA came to my office asking about possible partners of theirs in the Federal Republic of Yugoslavia. Milosevic had imposed a total blockade on information and nobody could see through his upcoming political moves. I put forward two names: Milo Djukanovic and Vukasin Maras. I had known Maras from an earlier period as a man of trust within his party who also enjoyed my confidence. The proposal turned out to be the right one to the Americans, for Maras was later invited to Washington

D.C. and introduced to all of the national institutions there, while Milo got the support in his intention to leave the State Union of Serbia and Montenegro (which happened in 2006). The American politicians/statesmen, including Presidents Clinton and Obama, consider Djukanovic to be one of the most competent and talented politicians over the post-Titoist period. He saved Montenegro from the Serbian 'pro-chetnik' abyss, that is, the passionate propaganda disseminated by Vuk Draskovic and Vojislav Seselj throughout Serbia and Montenegro.

1992: Signing of joint venture agreement with Bato Djurovic, Director of Dr. Simo Milosevic Institute at Igalo

One part of this chetnik lobby, which rules in the city of Herceg Novi, has practically ruined the town in terms of tourist industry and financial prosperity on the whole. Milo had hard time confronting the interest group which is probably made up of many Serbs from Serbia who own their second homes there.

As a Serb by birth, and owing to living in the West for thirty plus years, I have realized that the Montenegrin nation (in ethnic sense) does exist, and that it differs from the Serb one. The Montenegrins do not lie or send one to a wild goose chase. This proved helpful in my efforts to stand on my two feet there and reckon with predictable future conditions. That is why the people in Montenegro will be grateful one day to Milo Djukanovic for his leadership on their way to independence, freedom and capitalist transition. Which implies that – provided you are an industrious person who really wants to work – you can find a job and earn your living, and more. This has led to Montenegro's rising international reputation. But there were difficulties on that road, bearing in mind that the Serb chetnik lobby keeps attempting to depose the legally elected authorities from the DPS and their leader.

My message to the opposition parties in Montenegro reads: You cannot get anything by force. Sour grapes! If Serbia had chosen the same road, it could have licked the world. However, the Democratic Party in Serbia proved to be a worse thief than the parties led by Sloba and Mira.

*

Despite my unquestionable success and distinguished humanitarian work, I fell victim to the malicious policy of the Montenegrin Ministry of Healthcare headed by Miomir Mugosa. At a point, the Ministry banned my Mediterranean Surgery Center because of, as the decision read, "lack of doctors on duty". What happened? When the related inspection visited the clinic, there were no patients there at all, so the doctors on duty were not needed either. I filed a complaint to the Supreme Court of Montenegro and won the lawsuit.

I used to work under extremely difficult conditions. Due to the international sanctions, the Institute would often be left without fuel needed for heating. I refrained from complaints and provided heating at my own cost. Instead of expanding business in the field of healthcare, the state found it necessary to close my clinic, grounded on the formal assessment of healthcare inspection. It may have happened because of my exagarated activities and fight for justice.

Moreover, some powerful locals were trying to impose a racketfee on me, that is, to make me pay a bribe for "living and doing business on my (their) territory". I was required to pay 10,000 Deutsche Mark per month to a local 'boss' if I wanted to keep my business in Igalo, the town which falls within the Municipality of Herceg Novi. When I refused to obey the corrupt municipal politicians of Herceg Novi, the libeling through the weekly *Monitor* began. The newspaper had its headquarters in Podgorica, the capital of Montenegro.

*

I introduced a new, uninvasive method of plastic surgery, and lectured on it, promoting work with adult stem cells taken from the patient's fat (adipose tissue). Their injection provokes formation of the cells which are capable of generating new tissue and thus – in a revolutionary way – rejuvenate the old tissue, without using knife.

At the time when Yugoslavia was disintegrating, I – as Chairman and Director of the Department of Plastic and Reconstructive Surgery at Igalo – managed to buy one part of Simo Milosevic Institute. The Institute's shareholders are the state of Montenegro (56%), the state of Serbia (26%), while I own 1,400 square meters in Block A of the giant hospital complex in Igalo.

Some Montenegrins claim that my range is the most impressive one, for it stands next to a beautifully wooded hill where the villa of late President Josip Broz Tito stands. The villa, named *Galeb* ('Seagull') is also part of Simo Milosevic Institute. Built four decades ago, it was the place where three historic events took place. First, the Presidency of Yugoslavia was in session therein while Tito was still alive. Second,

Veselin Djuranovic[73] was elected President of the Federal Executive Council (i.e. Prime Minister in Yugoslavia's Government) there in 1977. Third, Lord Peter Carrington held a conference there with the presidents of Yugoslavia's republics, trying to persuade them not to opt for a war.

*

Early in September 1991, The Hague saw the International Peace Conference on Yugoslavia presided by Lord Carrington. He scheduled sessions of this Conference to be held alternately in Igalo, Montenegro, and the nearby coastal town of Cavtat in Croatia. The first one took place in Tito's villa at Igalo, on

September 16, 1991. The participants included President of Croatia Franjo Tudjman, President of Serbia Slobodan Milosevic, Minister of Defence Gen. Veljko Kadijevic and Chief of the YNA General Staff Col. Gen. Blagoje Adzic.

The war had already been under way, but Montenegro did not take part in it. Battles were fought between the Yugoslav National Army and the newly-founded army of Croatia; the combats were taking place around Vukovar, in the subregion of Banija, over some YNA garrisons in Croatia and (minor) confrontations in the areas of Dubrovnik and the Neretva River.

The objective of the Igalo meeting was to stop the war operations and resort to negotiations about the further destiny of Yugoslavia. The negotiations were held in the Grand Hall of Tito's villa, at a small table, where coffee used to be served. I was not there, of course, but some witnesses told me about the five-hour argument during which Lord Carrington was trying to calm down the antagonizing interlocutors, Tudjman and Milosevic. Both generals, Kadijevic and Adzic, were only nodding in support of what Slobodan Milosevic was saying.

The quarrel dragged on during the dinner in the *Galeb* Villa, hosted by the Presidency of Montenegro. According to the account of my Montenegrin acquaintances, Milosevic was so angry with the Croats, Lord Carrington and the hosts that he refused to shake hands with the Montenegrins on his departure from Igalo. As soon as on October 1, 1991, the Montenegrin leadership stated that "30,000 Ustashe were advancing from the direction of Dubrovnik in order to take hold of the (Kotor) Gulf" and that "we are attacked and must therefore defend ourselves". Decisions were made that "the entire Montenegro shall make a war effort".

That is how Montenegro entered the war during the process of Yugoslavia's disintegration. It even occurred to some Montenegrins that they could re-establish a Republic of Dubrovnik of their own.

The above-described events worried me a lot, for they heralded untoward conditions for my professional and private plans related to Igalo. Whatever had been going on around me in Igalo and Montenegro absorbed me, and the historic events inspired my nascent thoughts about politics as my occupation. For, my personal experience made me deduce that in this region only politics endures for ever. The rest is ephemeral and pointless.

The revelation ripened in my mind during the media-launched assault on me in Montenegro in 2010. That was yet another cruel lesson I had to learn. As an immigrant in the United States I felt to be an alien. Having been through all sorts of agonies in America and having passed all sorts of American-style 'training', I have not changed as a person; I took the whole process as one of education and not character-shaping. When I came to Montenegro, I brought with me all my mental and professional 'luggage', but none of that knowledge fell on fertile soil.

Whatever I attempted to do in the fields of healthcare, politics or humanitarian work met with misunderstanding and wondering on the part of Serbs and Montenegrins. Therefore, I decided to take my doctoral degree in Belgrade, so that I would not remain an outsider boasting just American diplomas, certificates and degrees.

My endeavors aimed at conveying my knowledge and experience for the benefit of healthcare and economy in my homeland resulted in failures outnumbering successful outcomes. For, the Serbs – whether they live in Belgrade, Podgorica or Herceg Novi – lack the sense of successfulness. Incapable of adopting novelty and modern ways, they stick to outdated patterns of behavior and incomplete accomplishments. It was with great resistance that they accepted me –in Serbia, in Montenegro, in the Republic of Srpska... The war made them have me. I have proved to be a successful surgeon, humanitarian, businessman and peacemaker. In Serbia, Montenegro or the Republic of Srpska nobody has shown thankfulness.

However, all of those adversities have not sufficed to kill my idealism. I continued my struggle with my fellow-countrymen of the former Yugoslavia, those who are in power, be it politics or healthcare system. Despite the fact that I am a shareholder in Simo Milosevic Institute at Igalo, I have to fight to keep my clinic now, for – as the major shareholder – the Government of Montenegro is to sell the Institute to the Brits for mere ten million.

Nothing is stable and lasting in the two lands of my native country. With each new authority, rules of life suffer changes. Which sometimes make me feel like a 'prodigal son' here. This might give me a reason why I should conclude my career of a doctor and a businessman in the United States.

[70] **Milo Djukanovic** (b. 1962) is said to be the most powerful person in Montenegro. He entered politics at an early age, becoming a member of the Yugoslav Communist League as high school student and standing out in youth activism. His ascent to power took place in the years preceding the collapse of Yugoslavia (1989-91), when he became Secretary of the Communist League of Montenegro. As the Communist League was succeeded by the Democratic Party of Socialists (DPS – *Demokratska partija socijalista*) in the newly-established multiparty system, Djukanovic was still one of the major leaders, loyal to Slobodan Milosevic in Serbia and his unitarian national policy until 1997, when he determinedly opposed him. When Milosevic was deposed in 2000, Djukanovic started to openly advocate secesstion from the Federal Republic of Yugoslavia. The country became a confederation under the name of the State Union of Serbia and Montenegro (2003-6), before Montenegro's 2006 independence referendum. Throughout the periods of change and until nowadays, Milo Djukanovic has ruled Montenegro in the posts of Prime Minister (1991-8; 2003-6; 2008-10; 2012-16) and President (1998-2002), with two formal resignations and retirements (2006-8; 2010-12) during which he pursued business. There is speculation about his possible running for presidency in 2017 again. – *Translator's note.*

[71] **Vlade Divac** (b. 1968) was a world-famous basketball player of Yugoslavia/Serbia who spent the major part of his career in the NBA; the first player born and trained outside of the U.S.A. to play in over 1,000 NBA matches. For two mandates (2009-2016) he was President of the Serbian Olympic Committee. – *Translator's note.*

[72] **Zoran Djindjic** – see the footnote in the chapter "Save Yugoslavia", Part Two of this book. –*Translator's note.*

[73] **Veselin Djuranovic** (1925-1997) was one of the highest ranking Montengrin politicians who rose to the top of Yugoslavia's federal administration as Prime Minister of the S.F.R.Y.(1077-82) and President of the Presidency of Yugoslavia (1984-5). – *Translator's note.*

A PROFITEER ON HIS SERBIAN IDENTITY

How far the false information about me, those produced by the Montenegrin media, reached can be seen from the fact that Miroslav Michael Djordjevich – in his book *Decade of Illusions 1990– 2000*, published in 2016 – wrote that I worked in the United States without the necessary licence. I cannot imagine the motives Mr. Djordjevich may have had to depict me the way he has in his book. This man, who portrays himself as the sole unifier of the Serbs in diaspora, probably did so in order to rise in the eyes of his readers, presenting himself as a faultless man of virtue. Had he wanted the truth, it would have sufficed to dial my phone number and ask if I had really practised surgery without the proper American licence.

I wrote to Michael Djordjevich and asked him what was the matter with the claim. Moreover, I sent an official disclaimer with regard to his untrue claims in the book *Decade of Illusions*. What Michael Djordjevich and I share in common – apart from the same surname – is that we both come from Serbia and work in the United States. He had taken light from our homeland, and I left in pursuit of further education. Michael was a young activist of the Republican Party, and I was a high-ranking Republican in charge of California. We both live in that state, the richest one in America. Miroslav Djordjevich was trying to unify the Serbs in diaspora with those in our homeland, and I was just a Serb serving his people. Yet it seems that, doing his patriotic business, Michael Djordjevich was first and foremost working for himself and his own pocket.

Miroslav Michael Djordjevich was born in Belgrade's Dorcol quarter where he graduated from the First Boys' High School. He emigrated to the United States as a volleyball player in 1956, enrolled in University of California, Berkeley to graduate therefrom in 1960. This young Republican politician became a businessman: he owned two companies in the field of finance – *USF&G Financial Security* and its successor *Capital Guaranty* Company. In the year 1990, he founded the Serbian Unity Congress at Cleveland, Ohio; this international organization was supposed to gather the Serb diaspora with the objective to maintain the Serbian identity and support the motherland in its reconstruction and progress. Over the next two decades, Michael was endeavoring to protect the Serb(ian) interests in the U.S.A. and (ex-)Yugoslavia. Toward the end of 1999, he organized a large-scale Szentendre Congress (Szentendre, Hungary) which gathered the Serbian diaspora from all over the world and the leaders of Serbia's Democratic Party. Next year, the united Serbian opposition parties won the elections (against Slobodan Milosevic) and transformed Serbia.

As an adroit bargainer with his Serbian identity, Miroslav Michael Djordjevich tried to reach a big deal with the Serbian authorities in the time of democratic changes which he claims to have enhanced with the political backup of the official Washington: His goal was to start a Serbian-American bank, based on a promise by PM Zoran Djindjic and Minister Miroljub Labus. He somehow managed to ensure a high scholarship for Mr. Labus' daughter Milica Labus. However, he never opened this private bank of his in Belgrade.

In an attempt to get payed for his patriotic work, Michael Djordjevich went to the Republic of Srpska where he – assisted by the politician Mladen Ivanic, as the media and the opposition claimed –opened the Southeastern-European Development Bank. It was a private bank founded partly with the capital of the Republic of Srpska. During the opening ceremony, Djordjevich expressed his special acknowledgment to PM Mladen Ivanic "for being a visionary and supporting the Bank".

– Our arrival is building a bridge between the Serb diaspora and the motherland, part of which is, as I see it, the Republic of Srpska. In addition to capital, we aspire to transfer hereto the Western knowledge, experience, working style. I would emphasize, besides our love which made us come here, that we have seen progress taking place in the Republic of Srpska. – Those were Djordjevich's words on the said occasion in 2002.

A couple of years later, Miroslav Michael Djordjevich and his partner Milan Mandaric, another American Serb, sold the bank. The transaction looked like a normal business deal, except for the fact that the Ministry of Finance, i.e. the Government of the R.S., did not follow the procedures prescribed by the law in preparing and selling the property/capital of the state.

– The state capital in the Development Bank was sold for KM 4.1 million (the currency of Bosnia-Herzegovina), whereby a statefounded commission expressed some doubts as to the choice of the bidder, for the best was not respected. It has been ascertained that Michael Djordjevich, who represented the Southeastern-European Development Bank (*Razvojna banka Jugoistocne Evrope*), was privileged in the process through some special conveniences that discriminated the other bidders. – This can be read in a Government paper of the Republic of Srpska.

Throughout his patriotic projects in his motherland, Miroslav Michael Djordjevich invariably sought privileges. He had the offices of the Serbian Unity Congress and his *Studenica* Foundation in the office building of the Ministry of Serbian Diaspora at No. 20 Vasina Street in downtown Belgrade, but the information of whether he payed any rent therefor has never been available to the public.

In his political memoirs, Djordjevich admits that the Serbian Unity Congress, i.e. the Serbian diaspora he coordinated, waged a heroic battle for the rescue of the fatherland and the Serbian nation.

– In this struggle, both the authorities and the opposition proved incompetent. We did not manage to unite our mother country and the diaspora because the relevant individuals in power in Belgrade were incapable and unprepared to do that, and some of them simply did not care. We did less than we wanted to, but more than the Serbian authorities deserved – claims Djordjevich nowadays.

The Chairperson of the said two organizations, Slavka Draskovic Jovanovic, worked at the office at No. 20 Vasina Street, while being the owner of a private firm of hers registered at the same address (*Poslovno vodjstvo*/'Business Leadership')

The 'business' handled by the firm and the Serbian Unity Congress was selling a program for the opening of Serbia's business world to the U.S.A. and cooperation with American businessmen/companies. This was carried out via some exhibitions of Serbian economy at American trade fairs (the fairs in Chicago and Las Vegas). Both of these trade read: Because all of these stories about him leave an impression of Miroslav Michael Djordjevich, who plays the role of a bridge-builder between the diaspora and the motherland, as a man who trades with his Serbian identity, a man who charges bridge toll and puts it in his pocket.

MY SON FOR AMERICAN PRESIDENT

MY LIFE HAS BEEN one of repeated ups and downs. I would climb up the ladder, both as a person and a professional/businessman, then fall down, yet stand up and rise again. People have often asked me: How did you survive the falls? Well, I account for that by a 'survival mechanism' I managed to build for myself. Hard work proved to be my salvation each time I needed it. Having gone through each of the crises – whether marital or business-related ones – I would resume hard work. I would 'shake off' all the hindrances and start building my private life or career anew.

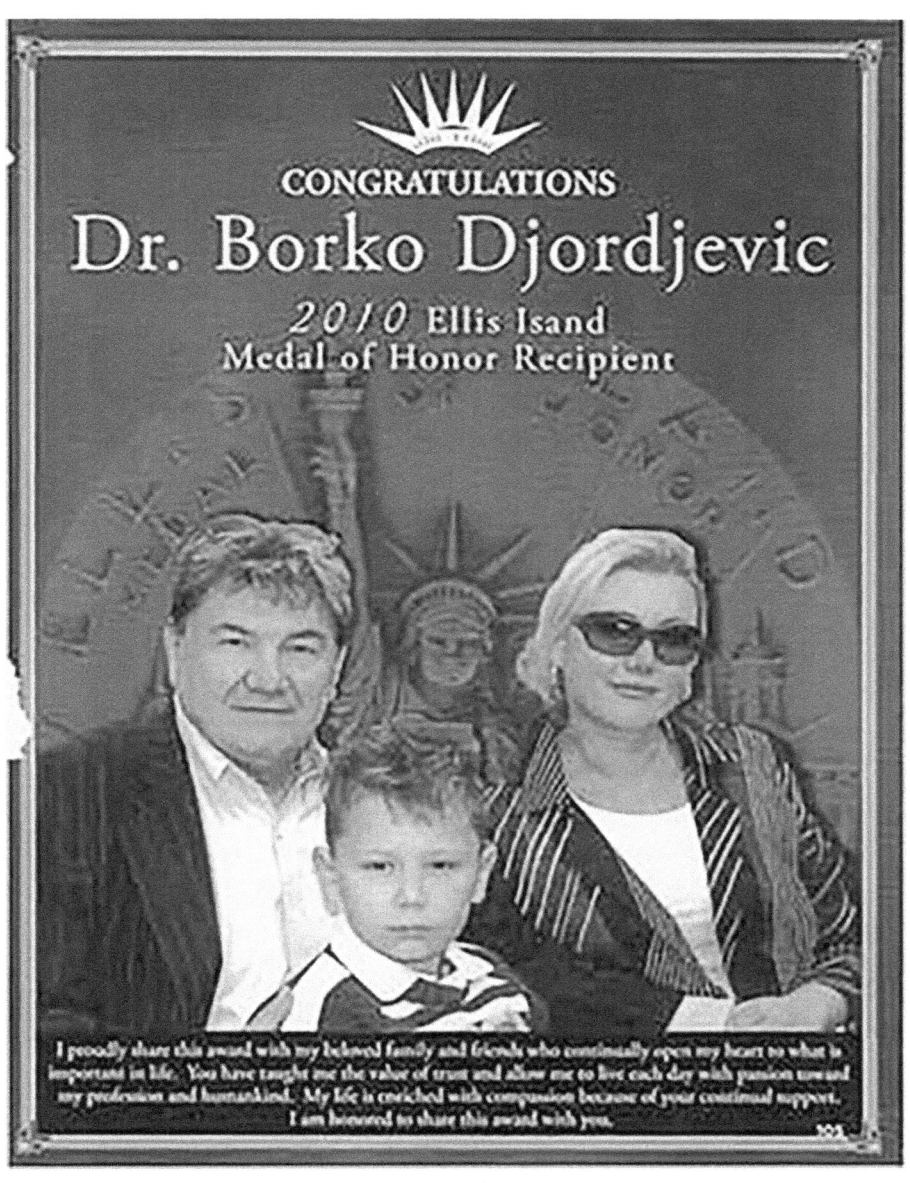

Invitation to Dr. Djordjevic's family for the Ellis Island Award ceremony

I am both a Serb and an American. Both good and evil have been my companions. I have felt it all, both good and evil, and endured. Privately, my family's happiness is the measure when I evaluate my life. Professionally, my last patient's happiness with my work, and testimony thereon, is the measure. Socially, my satisfaction comes from the help I provide to the people surrounding me. Those are the postulates of my life principles, and I still stick to them.

My life in America was quite normal until the year 2002. In that year, I was 'condemned' to divorce, for my second wife caught me in adultery. I left Palm Beach and our villa in Santa Barbara. My mother and sister went back to Belgrade, and I – together with Sandra Lucic –moved to Rancho Mirage. Thereafter, I regularly went to Belgrade to see my mother and my sisters. My mother, Marija Djordjevic, passed away in 2015, at the age of 94. In her last days, I was with her, in Belgrade.

It was only after my mother's death that I resumed my earlier working rhythm, which meant – as a Serbian saying goes – 'weaving on three looms at a time'. As to my family life, Sandra and I take care that our children Nikola and Nina grow up like all normal people, yet with the best conditions possible for their education. Our daughter Nina is a very nice young lady, dedicated to school, music and sports. Our son Nikola, clever and serene, takes after his grandfather Branko Djordjevic. Fond of studying, he has graduated from a special high school for talented mathematicians and wants to attend a college in Geneva. Considering his age, he is a strong, serious and ambitious young man who goes in for waterpolo and basketball.

As an American-born Serb, our son Nikola – educated in Serbia, Switzerland and the United States – is going to become the president of the United States of America one day. My efforts are invested into creating conditions (social, financial, political) which shall make it possible for Nikola – within three decades – to grow into the First Man of America.

*

While Americans tend to show off their success and the joy they draw therefrom, my fellow-Serbs tend to boast of working little and suffering much. When I left the former Yugoslavia, giving up politics and non-medical business to resume medical practice and surgery in California in 1997, my working hours – in my three clinics – lasted from 4 a.m. to midnight. Within a short while, I managed to restore my reputation in the States, for Americans hold industrious and successful people in high esteem.

Allene Arthur, California's reporter on the life of the jet set, published an article in The Desert Scene (March 2, 1997) titled "Borko's Hiatus":

Borko is back. [...] For most of the '80s [he] became a status symbol like a Rolls-Royce. [...] Abruptly, he left the world of gleaming Palm Springs society in 1988 to return to his native Yugoslavia. [...] Borko started a clinic in Igalo and taught plastic surgery in Belgrade. Getting caught in up in the Croatia-Serbia war, he repaired trauma patients and later worked on the children victims in Bosnia, the innocent amputees.[...] Djordjevic is back in his old Palm Springs office doing business as usual.

Next year, the screenwriter from London Stuart Urban wrote a script for a documentary film about me, one he entitled The Madiators. It was a story about a man of Serbian origin, a plastic surgeon who made an attempt at stopping the civil war in Bosnia/Yugoslavia. Unfortunately, the project never saw the light of the day.

In 2015, I came to Belgrade again, unhappy to see that nothing in the life of the Serbs had changed essentially. At that time, the U.S. Ambassador Michael Kirby said that "the Serbs are a bit schizophrenic, as their heart pulls toward the East, but the head directs them to the West".

And the CIA, the world's most powerful secret service, has emphasized this characteristic of the Serbs:

– The Serbs are greedy for small money!

My friend Marko Lopusina, a journalist and publicist, thinks that the Serbs are "a small, semiliterate nation, deluded by someone into thinking that they are a heavenly nation". Lopusina also says:

– When sitting at a table full of roast meat and beverage, we provide many solutions for any problem in the world, yet none for our own problems. – And he adds an aphorism of his own to describe the Serbian people in the 21st century:

– The Serbs know everything yet read nothing!

I share his opinion about "us, the Serbs" who "fail to learn from the errors of others, but learn from their own mistakes only". That is why our life experiences cost us dearly to a tragical degree. I would say that we, the Serbs, are masochists who do not aspire for happiness, remaining ever sad and woeful. Moreover, the Serbs are depressed people and, hence, unprepared for, and incapable of, accepting changes or triumphs; contrariwise, they are prepared for defeats and respond to these with an unhealthy dose of aggressiveness.

One of my American friends has the following experience of the Serbs:

– The Serbs make a lot of noise and work too little for a better life. They would rather say that they do not want something than admit they actually do! A Serb would rather say he doesn't want to eat, even when he's hungry. The Americans lack this ambiguity, so they can't understand this depressive and mercurial behavior of the Serbs. To a clear question, an American will expect or give a clear answer. When an American says 'No!', it means 'No!'. On the other hand, when a Serb says 'No!', it often means 'Yes!'. Along this line of thinking, the Serbs force their American in-laws to eat when the poor people are not hungry at all, so they, overeaten, throw up later.

This American guy is right. We are mercurial people. We used to adore Slobodan Milosevic, but we foreswore him rather quickly, arrested and sent him to prison. We were fond of Radovan Karadzic first, then delivered him to a foreign court as a war criminal. The political practice in Serbia and the Republic of Srpska has shown that, in elections, a Serb will vote for the worst candidate on the list; once the elected person becomes president or minister, the same voter will besmirch and ridicule him through joke-cracking.

This trait of the Serbian nature and satire is the national language of common sense. However, the fickleness has killed us in the eyes of the foreigners, for nobody can understand this kind of double play on our part: now we want it, now we don't; now we choose a 'vozhd', now we assassinate him.

The worst feature of the Serbian character is their tendency and skill in, to put it in a corresponding English/American phrasing, "sending someone on a wild goose chase". That is what I experienced from Slobodan Milosevic, Mira Markovic, Milan Panic, and later by Boris Tadic and Vojislav Kostunica. Therefore, whenever I am with the Serbs, I tend to 'function' like an American. I work hard and expect success. Considering my material/financial condition, it is obvious that I have accomplished full professional success as a physician.

*

My matrilineal grandaunt Erika Fey, a Jewish lady from Novi Sad, used to possess large property in the Autonomous Province of Vojvodina, which is now undergoing restitution processes. The Jewish Community in Novi Sad is now providing help to the inheritors of the once Jewish property, and we as a family hope to get back what rightfully belongs to us. I also have some property of the Djordjevic family in the vicinity of Nish, in the south of Serbia, but right now I prefer to wait for better circumstances in the society before I start a restitution process.

There are many people in Serbia who were deprived of their property in post-second-world-war years. The state (Communist Yugoslavia) acted like a criminal in these matters. Restitution has been under way for some time, but at an irritably slow pace, sometimes involving some political criteria. Less than one third has been restored, and the authorities talk about the process as a 'democratic gain'. But I cannot tolerate empty talk, 'ticking over' and endless dragging. After I had been through the wartime period of my life in which I was a doctor, a humanitarian, a missioner, and also a divorced man, I managed – by the year 2007 – to reach annual salary of $ 1.7 million, taxed in the United States. Next year, in 2008, I came back to Serbia and the neighboring Montenegro.

In my clinic *American Aesthetic Surgery Center Dr. Borko Djordjevic*, at Dr. Simo Milosevic Institute in Igalo, Montenegro, I have built and equipped four operation rooms. I promote new techniques in aesthetic medicine and plastic/cosmetic surgery, already applying the revolutionary and scalpel-free rejuvenation method using stem cells from adipose tissue (fat). Injection of these cells triggers formation of cells capable of generating new tissue and, in a revolutionary way, giving youthful look to the old tissue. And no scalpel is used thereby!

Stem cells were in an exploration stage for a long time. The toughest problem was the resistance showed by the Americans, for they generally opposed abortion: to them, the use of placenta was a matter of ethical and religious sacrilege, so the application of stem cells in practice was disapproved. It has only been over the last several years that the adult stem cells have been discovered in adipose tissue which play an amazingly important role in the generation of cells and rejuvenation of tissue. If inserted into the tissue of the muscles, brain or spinal cord, breast, pancreas or hypodermis, they are capable of regenerating the local tissue. Of vital importance for the process is 'snatching' of the fat in an adequate and precise way and to deliver it to the lab technician who is going to prepare them for further use/treatment.

This method, which involves stem cells, is truly novel and revolutionary, for it relies on a person's own stem cells; in other words, here we deal with autogenic transfer of one's own tissue which has the 'task' to substitute the old, broken and cracked collagen with newly-generated, young collagen. The method leads to the (re)creation of a new, fresh and young face. In aesthetic/cosmetic surgery, the method is part of anti-aging medicine. Actually, rearward leap in time has been accomplished, and the tissue is rejuvenated according to the anti-aging protocol.

With "Mother Serbia" sculpture at the former Ministry of Diaspora

My patients are often middle-aged Montenegrin businessmen who come for eyelid lift (blepharoplasty) and rejuvenation. Male patients are also the foreigners who live or intermittently reside in Montenegro, mostly Russians. Youthful look is in highest demand, and that includes face lift, ironing out of wrinkles, embellishment of breasts and liposuction. Some of my patients are ladies formerly 'worked' at other private clinics; they ask me to 'repair' the previous 'handcrafting' performed by my so-called 'colleagues'. Unwilling to comment upon the results of other aesthetic surgeons, I cannot help noticing that among these there is a number of unsuccessful doctors and adherents to beauty dictatorship.

In the United States I learned that your worthiness corresponds to your knowledge and skill. The Americans do not care about your geographical background and prayer mode. In the Balkans, contrary habits rule. The first questions a Montenegrin will ask you is "Who are your family?" and "Where d'you hail from?". There is a similar habit in Serbia, although the nature of the curiosity is somewhat different. As my emotions are still tied to Belgrade, the capital of Serbia is also a haven for my family.

As a successful Serb-born American, I made a gift to the Serbian Ministry of Diaspora: a statue of a woman holding a pogaca (round, cake-like bread) in her hands. The figure has been named "Mother Serbia", and it was a symbolical announcement of my homecoming and my wish to bring a gift for my fatherland in the form of my medical competences and life experiences. For several years, the figure and the symbol of "Mother Serbia" was awarded to the most noble of the Serbs in diaspora. Today, "Mother Serbia" is standing alone and forgotten in a Belgrade office at No. 20 Vasina Street, the former seat of the Ministry of (Serbian) Diaspora, for the Ministry, intended for cooperation with, and taking care of, the Serbs living worldwide – exists no longer[74].

I have started a plastic surgery clinic in Belgrade, too. I have a good and comfortable life, but I also want my people to have a better life, too. The quality of plastic surgery in Belgrade/Serbia/the Balkans is high indeed, and I aspire to further improve it. Balkan women dream of looking like Barbie dolls. They dream of being strikingly bosomy and having very small nose; these features are their ideal of beauty. Serbian men aim at getting rid of their fat. Unlike American women, who are inclined to try whatever plastic surgery can offer, Serbian women go to extremes regarding their breasts and mouths, in terms of size. Which means that big bosom is their greatest fetish and this is the only part of their body they exaggarate with. The inclination is taken advantage of by the so-called 'show-bizz surgeons' who 'produce' grotesque-looking breasts and lips for the women in Serbia, thus making them ugly.

My business is to make beautiful individuals. Aesthetic surgery is as old as mankind: Humans have aspired for better look since the beginning of their kind. Modern surgical techniques can make their dreams come true. This line of surgery is an art which need not be associated with perfect beauty. Each patient is a special individual whom I approach accordingly and suggest the best solutions available. To 'sell' an operation is the least important aspect of the job. What does matter is that your patient leaves the clinic greatly satisfied. For that reason, I intend to make my art of face and body beautification available to the ladies in Serbia.

---

[74] In July 2012, this ministry merged with the Ministry of Culture. – *Translator's note.*

BARACK OBAMA'S NEIGHBOR

My clinic in Palm Spring operates normally when I am in the States. In California, I have a long list of patients, but also a much longer list of friends with whom I permanently keep in touch or exchange home/family visits. Since long ago I have had the habit of – regardless of my whereabouts worldwide – contacting my friends and acquaintances. I did that using fax-machine in old times, meanwhile replaced with e-mail and/or text messaging by cell phone.

In mid-April 2015, Joe Biden, Vice President of the United States, contacted me and asked if I was willing to transfer to the Democratic Party. I said I would have to think about that, considering the fact that I had been a Republican for decades. It was not so easy to leave the circles of Ronald Reagan and join those of President Barack Obama.

Frankly, I feel closer to the Democratic Party than the Republicans, for I like Barack Obama as a man who confronted the corporate societies as the swayers of the world, and because he understood and supported my friend Vuk Jeremic. The son of my friend Misko Jeremic has an opportunity to become Secretary-General of the United Nations. Long time ago, when Vuk was a young boy, I bought him his first computer as a gift. Today, Vuk is a world-ranking diplomat, a former President of the U.N. General Assembly and a candidate for the head of this world organization.

In his intention to run for the U.N. Secretary-General, the young Jeremic enjoys the support of Russia and China, of the former Mayor of New York Rudy Giuliani and of his best man who is an associate of the right hand of the present Secretary-General Ban Ki-moon.[75]

In their political analyses, the Americans have labelled Vuk Jeremic a Serbian nationalist. His mark was 2+/D+, which only tells that he is a genuine Serb with healthy national feeling and moderate in his public appearances. My mission of supporting Vuk Jeremic during his race for the U.N. consisted of some efforts to get the U.S. President be informed about the man and meet the young Serb in person.

It was through Oprah Winfrey that I managed to reach Barack Obama, who said:

– I have no comment on his candidacy!

This implied that the American President did not object to Jeremic as a candidate. Moreover, it meant that the U.S.A. would not veto a positive outcome, although not voting pro. In politics, American silence implies approval. But I am worried by the fact that Serbia kept silent about Jeremic's candidacy too long. Here in Belgrade, this was not interpreted as approval. On the contrary. Meanwhile, there was rumor about Serbia's support to Miroslav Lajčák, Slovak candidate. Another rumor concerned the reported readiness of Boris Tadic to run for the same post in the United Nations. In the end, Serbia has given support to the candidacy of Vuk Jeremic and he is preparing for the U.N. elections.

In the current constellation of the relations on the Old Continent, Vuk Jeremic would make an ideal mediator between the Russians, the Germans and the Americans (plus Ukrainians) in the search for a solution to the problem in Ukraine. Provided Vuk Jeremic takes the office of the U.N. Secretary-General, Serbia would have a man of her own heading the world organization for the next twelve years.

Within my campaign in support of Vuk Jeremic, I am getting ever closer to President Barack Obama in order to exert some influence on the Americans possibly and formally backing up the son of my friend Misko Jeremic. My chances to influence the opinion of the U.S. President have been growing, especially now that I hear of Barack Obama's purchase of a house in my Palm Springs neighborhood. He has payed $ 4.5 million for it. Obama will not have any difficulty paying it off, for a former American president may receive up to $ 150,000 for a speech or presentation delivered. That is to say: Barack Obama intends to live here as my neighbor once he retires from presidency.

The White House advised me that Vuk Jeremic should get Serbia's formal approval of his candidacy for the post of the U.N. Secretary-General and go public with it while Barack Obama was still in power. The candidacy after the U.S. presidential elections would be hazardous because of the possibility that Hillary Clinton becomes the next President of America.

It is a well-know fact that Hillary Clinton conducts an anti-Serbian policy, for she belonged to the creators of Serbia's province of Kosovo as an 'American state' in the Balkans; therefore, she would be unwilling to see a Serb, be it Vuk Jeremic with his favorable background, holding the office of the U.N. Secretary-General and eventually becoming a presidential candidate in the United States. If that happens, a chance will occur for my son Nikola to start his career as a staffer of Vuk Jeremic as U.N. secretary-general and rise to the position of a future candidate for the U.S. president.

As the saying goes among the Serbian and other peoples:
Wait and see; or: Time will tell.

---

[25] The race ended in the fall of 2016, with Vuk Jeremic finishing with the second highest cumulative number of positive votes in the six rounds of straw polls carried out by the Security Council, right behind the eventual winner António Guterres. – *Translator's note.*

DOCUMENTS

AUTHORIZATION FOR DR. BORKO DJORDJEVIC BY RADOVAN KARADZIC

[With official letterhead of the Republic of Srpska, seal and personal signature.]

This is to certify that Mr. Borko Djordjevic, MD Ph.D. Passport No: 035192453, USA, a special representative of The Republic of Srpska (Bosnian Serbs) is fully authorized to negotiate the matters of peace agreement, and mediate in creation of the maps between us and others concerned parties, which will be subject to our final approval.

He is also authorized to represent The Republic of Srpska in mediation in variety other matters, such as economic and financial activities.

Dr Radovan Karadzic
President, The Republic of Srpska

Pale, 28. 12. 94.

JIMMY CARTER AMONG THE DANGEROUS SERBS

Excerpt from the book
Jimmy Carter: ***Beyond the White House: Waging Peace, Fighting Disease, Building Hope,***
Simon and Schuster, 2007.

Our first involvement with Bosnia-Herzegovina was in June 1994, when Chris Spiro, former speaker of the New Hampshire House of Representatives, brought Serbian Ambassador Milan Milutinovic to our home in Plains to deliver a personal message from President Slobodan Milosevic. In summary, it said that he was ready to conclude a comprehensive settlement in the Balkans but needed to be treated with respect by the U.S. government. I knew that the European-UN peace effort had reached a dead end, and there was no confidence that the Europeans would enforce an agreement even if one were reached.

The lack of progress was due to the fact that the United States had not played a strong role, imposing rather than proposing a comprehensive peace. The main message was that Milosevic wanted me to come to Belgrade, representing either the Carter Center or the U.S. government. I responded that there were multiple channels for peace and that I had no desire to become involved in the Balkans. I relayed his message to President Clinton.

The situation continued to deteriorate, and our Center began to monitor developments very carefully, primarily using the services of our interns. We subsequently became involved, to help prevent an all-out war and multiple human rights violations. Our work in this area was an intriguing experience that involved three men who have since been indicted for war crimes and genocide by the International Criminal Tribunal in The Hague. One of them (Milosevic) was arrested and died during his trial. The other two are now international fugitives, with $5 million bounties, offered by the U.S. government, on their heads.

Early in December 1994, I received a handwritten letter from the Bosnian Serb leader, Radovan Karadzic, requesting I meet with a delegation to explore ways for the Serbs to accept the latest recommendations of the International Contact Group (United States, United Kingdom, France, Germany, Italy and Russia). I was not very familiar with the political situation in the former area of

Yugoslavia, although I had welcomed Marshal Tito to the White House for a formal visit.

Rosalynn and I still remember the thirty-five-minute toast that he gave after the state banquet, which then had to be translated into English. At that time, multiple ethnic and political groups constituted Yugoslavia, and Tito was holding them together with his political shrewdness, the power of his personality, and his reputation as a hero who had resisted the Nazis during World War II and later defied Stalin and the Soviets.

After Tito's death, in May 1980, Rosalynn and I were the first visitors to Yugoslavia to meet with the ruling committee, which we found fragmented and confused. Ethnic tensions grew as the peoples of the republics of Slovenia, Croatia, Kosovo and Serbia made conflicting demands for power and autonomy.

Radovan Karadžić was a poet and a psychiatrist who was accused of holding some UN hostages and was growing increasingly independent from Slobodan Milošević, the elected ruler of the Serbs, who also sought dominion over the other provinces. In April 1992, Bosnia had come to be recognized as an independent state, and Karadžić became the first president of the Bosnian Serb administration, with its capital in the mountain town of Pale. As a Greek Orthodox Christian, he had reached out to fellow Orthodox countries and publicly stated, "The Bosnian Serbs have only two friends God, and the Greeks." This was a fairly accurate statement at the time we received his letter.

Earlier that same year, The Carter Center and I had been accused of being excessively intrusive and independent in going to North Korea and Haiti, and I was determined to be very careful not to become involved with the Serbs without approval from both the White House and the State Department. I immediately called President Bill Clinton, who encouraged my meeting with Karadžić's emissaries and asked that I give him a report immediately.

Within a few days, former ambassador Harry Barnes, director of our conflict resolution program, and Dr. Joyce Neu, assistant director, brought Slavko Obradović and Dr. Djordjević to our home in Plains, and they explained that the Contact Group was refusing to deal with the Bosnian Serbs and communicating only with Milošević in Belgrade. The U.S. State Department had the same policy. There were excellent telephone communications, and the men spoke often with Karadžić during our meeting. They said he would make the necessary peace concessions directly to me if I would come to Pale and Sarajevo to talk to him and to the Bosnian Muslims personally. His representatives got him on the phone, and Karadžić pledged to me that he would do the following:

a. Permit normal movement of all UN relief convoys throughout Bosnia;
b. Remove any existing restraints on the free movement of representatives of the United Nations;
c. Release all Muslim prisoners of war who were aged nineteen years or younger. He resisted total releases because he needed assurance that Bosnian Serb captives would be freed by the Bosnian Muslim authorities;
d. Honor a cease-fire around Sarajevo, which he did not control, and open the airport, which was controlled (or under attack) by his forces;
e. Guarantee human rights both now and in the future.

He assured me that all of these things would be announced within three hours and could be implemented within a day. I understood that these were major concessions demanded by the Contact Group, so I informed Karadžić that I would notify President Clinton. I did so while the Serb emissaries were still in Plains. Clinton was pleased but somewhat skeptical. I informed him that I would go to Sarajevo and Pale only if Karadžić first implemented his promises to me. We informed UN Secretary General Boutros Boutros-Ghali and carried out an agreement with Karadžić that I also inform CNN, so that he could repeat his commitments and reveal his planned actions to their reporter in Bosnia.

That evening, Judy Woodruff interviewed Karadžić live on CNN, and he repeated the promises he had made to me, stating that the Serbs just needed someone who was trustworthy to communicate with them. I called the State Department and informed them about my tentative plans and said that if promises were kept I would go to the region without political status, representing only The Carter Center.

National Security Adviser Sandy Berger and Assistant Secretary of State Peter Tarnoff called and asked me about two additional points I had discussed with Karadžić and mentioned to the President: a comprehensive cease-fire and acceptance of the Contact Group's plan as a basis for negotiations. I explained that this was not to be announced in advance but that Karadžić would con firm it when I arrived in Bosnia. I mentioned the need for transportation from some major airport in Europe through Zagreb to Sarajevo and outlined my tentative schedule. They approved this request, but it was clear to me that White House officials were being careful to distance themselves from my involvement and the United Nations was much more supportive.

Secretary of State Warren Christopher called and suggested that I meet with Bosnian government leaders first and reminded me that the critical issue would be a cease-fire. Bosnian Muslims did not want a permanent cease-fire, which would freeze the present territorial gains of the Serbs, and they had offered three to four months maximum. Christopher suggested that if I could get Karadžić to accept the Contact Group proposal as a basis for negotiation and implement a cease-fire, I should let State, not The Carter Center, do the subsequent negotiation. I had no objection to this.

Once our trip was publicized, we were inundated with advice. French Foreign Minister Alain Juppé said that Karadžić's commitments to me were an "unacceptable provocation". He insisted that I should refer only to the Muslims as representing the Bosnian people. Democratic Senator Patrick Leahy of Vermont asked me not to promise anyone immunity from war crimes trial. The Greek American Chris Spiro called from New Hampshire to say that nothing could be done in the Balkans without Milošević's approval; that Karadžić and Milošević were irreconcilable; and that Milošević controlled the borders, the military, space, and communications, and could have peace within two months while Karadžić would not survive six months. He said that Milošević wanted to meet with me, and I replied that I planned to meet with both Milošević and Karadžić and that the White House knew this.

The UN assistant secretary-general (later secretary-general) Kofi Annan called to welcome my trip, wish me well, and offer me full support. Lawrence Eagleburger, secretary of state under

George W.H. Bush, attacked the Bosnia effort, as he had my visits to North Korea and Haiti, and stated that I was a loundering former president looking for publicity who hardly knew where Yugoslavia was located.

Before leaving home, I assessed all the information and advice and prepared a draft agreement that I hoped to consummate after meeting with Milošević, Karadžić, leaders of the Muslim Bosnians (Bozniaks) and representatives of the Contact Group.

With support from the White House, the State Department, and the United Nations, we went first to Frankfurt and then to Zagreb, where we met with the prime minister of Bosnia and the president of Croatia. Then we travelled to Sarajevo for a meeting with Alija Izetbegović, officially the president of Bosnia-Herzegovina. He was skeptical about our mission and had some fairly harsh demands, but none that deviated substantially from the prepared text I had in my pocket.

After a brief tour of war-ravaged Sarajevo, we drove to Pale. Because the direct road was mined, our route was circuitous (a seventy- five minute drive to travel nine miles), through beautiful and undamaged farms, pastures, and mountain slopes reminiscent of the Alps. Realizing that Karadžić would have to obtain approval from the military leaders, I was glad that Ratko Mladić and other top generals and political leaders were present. Then Karadžić and his wife (also a psychiatrist) joined Rosalynn and me in a small room, with our peace fellow Harry Barnes coming in on occasion.

[PP. 68-69 not available to Translator; Recommendation: to be copied and inserted by the Author or the Publisher]

This agreement was signed December 20, 1994, by Alija Izetbegović, witnessed by me.

Then we went back to Pale, where I finally accepted two improvements:

1. The cease-fire will commence at noon on December 23, 1994, monitored by UN forces, with the intent to conclude the agreement by January 1, 1995.

2. Based on assurances that convoys and humanitarian services will pass freely, the Bosnian forces will withdraw from the demilitarized zones before commencement of the negotiations described in item 1.

This agreement was signed December 21 by Radovan karadzic, witnessed by me.

My work was almost over, and when I arrived at the airport I obtained approval of the two changes from President Izetbegovic before announcing the to the assembled news media and walking to our plane, guarded by a huge UN truck that shielded us from possible firing. Since the cease-fire had not commenced, we took off with our flak jackets on, knowing that the previous plane had taked four bullets through its left side. I took the hard drive out of my computer and put it and the signed documents inside my flak jacket.

It was snowing heavily in Zagreb, and we gave a brief report to UN Envoy Yasushi Akashi, then flew to Belgrade, where the weather was good. We were met with enthusiasm by Slobodan Milosevic, who was accompanied every minute by Chris Spiro. We were served a banquet in the president's private office, sitting around a little coffee table. As did all the other leaders from the region, Milosevic had to give me the history lesson first, but Rosalynn and I were thankful that he began with World War I instead of the twelfth century. I asked him repeatedly what it would take for him to restore relations with Karadzic, and he finally said that if his parliament voted for the "Carter Plan", this would be adequate.

I called Secretary of State Christopher to give him a report. He thanked me and promised that the U.S. government would be resolute in implementing all the agreements. Finally, on the way home from Frankfurt on a Delta Air Lines plane, we were annoyed when some last-minute duty-free Christmas presents were delivered to us in a Marlboro bag. I wrote Delta's CEO to complain about the airline's advertising cigarettes and urged him to ban all smoking on their flights.

I received an urgent message from Yasushi Akashi the next morning, reporting that the cease-fire had been negotiating, everything was quiet, and a provision called for any violations to be publicized, not concealed. It was signed by Izetbegovic, Karadzic, Bosnian General Delic, and Serbian General Ratko Mladic. The State Department called to say that the cease-fire was workin "better than we had hoped" and the implementation agreement would be signed on December 30.

Under pressure from the Russians and Europeans, the Contact Group still refused to meet with any Bosnian Serbs, having all their eggs in Milosevic's basket. We had provided only four months to negotiate a permanent peace agreement, and they were stalemated on this point. I sent Milosevic a letter urging him to advise the Contact Group to deal with Karadzic if and when the Serb parliament approved the peace deal.

The cease-fire held for five months instead of four, but the Contact Group frittered away the time, refusing to meet with the Bosnian Serbs, who offered to go to Geneva and negotiate on the basis of the Contact Group plan, as clarified by our agreement.

The situation deteriorated rapidly, and I finally decided in June 1995 to accept an invitation from Senator Sam Nunn to testify before a Senate committee about the stalemate. He said that General John Galvin, former supreme allied commander, Europe, and commander-in-chief of the U.S. European Command, agreed with me and would also testify. At the Senate, Nunn pointed out that I was the fifth president ever to testify, Truman having been the most recent. No Democrat or Republican disagreed with our basic premise: that peace talks between Bosnian Serbs and Muslim Croats should be exhausted before any military action was taken. I went by the White House to share our views with National Security Adviser Anthony Lake.

Sweden's former prime minister Carl Bildt called to tell me that he represented the European Union and agreed with our proposals involving the Bosnian Serbs but that the Contact Group would stick with Milosevic for a short time. Secretary-General Boutros-Ghali told me that he agreed completely with my testimony and would try to shift attention to peace talks including the Bosnian Serbs.

We at the Carter Center urged the Bosnian Serb leadership to comply with UN demands to prevent the use of weapons against Sarajevo. At the same time, we attempted to find a way to assure that the Serb areas would not be attacked by Muslim Croat forces if all heavy weapons were removed. My suggestion was that the United States or NATO guarantee that these Bosnian promises would be honored if the Serbs would remove "a significant number" of their heavy weapons and let the remaining ones be placed under observation by the UN forces.

In late August, Carl Bildt sent me a copy of their latest proposals, which was what we had been trying to get since December, including a nine-month lifting of sanctions against Yugoslavia to test Milosevic's good faith. However, that same morning Croatia launched what seemed to be a war against the Serbs in the south, a Serbian shell fell on a market in Sarajevo, and NATO forces began a tremendous bombing of Serbian sites. Assistant Secretary of State Richard Holbrooke was in Belgrade, seeking some end to the conflict and using the Carter Center as an avenue to the Bosnian Serbs, when he was informed that Karadzic had agreed to let Milosevic speak for all Serbs.

Finally, in November 1995, the parties agreed to meet in Dayton, Ohio, to negotiate a peace treaty under the supervision of the United States. The Croats and Serbs were left out of the negotiations, with their interests represented by Croatia's president Franjo Tudjman and Serbia's president, respectively. Alija Izetbegovic represented the Bosnian government. The conference was chaired by Richard Holbrooke, with European Union Special Representative Carl Bildt and First Deputy Foreign Minister of Russia Igor Ivanov as co-chairmen.

As this agreement brought a temporary end to the war in Bosnia, Milosevic was credited in the West with being one of the pillars of Balkan peace. The Dayton Agreement did not grant amnesty for the war crimes committed during the conflict.

A contingent of Albanians formed an armed force and contested control by Milosevic of portions of Yugoslavia. Although the Serbian response was at first fairly restrained, by mid 1999 hundreds had died in escalating rretaliations, and more than 100,000 Kosovo Albanian's were reported to have been forced from their homes. The conflict culminated in the Kosovo War, which began in March 1999, with seventy-eight days of bombing by the air forces of the United States and NATO's other member nations. They flew over 36,000 sorties, and the Serbs were hit by more than 400 cruise missiles and 23,000 bombs, including cluster bombs and highly toxic depleted uranium bombs. This bombardment caused terrible destruction and eventually forced Milosevic to back down.

Within three weeks, more than 800,000 Albanians had returned home, but about 250,000 Serbs, Bosniaks, and Gypsies fled to avoid revenge from the Albanians. To preserve the fragile peace, NATO now maintains a peacekeeping force of 45,000 troops in Kosovo.

It is interesting to conjecture about how many human rights atrocities, refugees, and deaths might have been avoided if our agreements and suggestions had been honored by the international community."

COMPREHENSIVE PEACE AGREEMENT

[Serb side]

We the undersigned agree that we and those under our authority will:

1. Commence negotiations on an agreement for a cessation of hostilities on December 27, 1994, with the intent to conclude the agreement by January 15, 1995. This agreement would be implemented immediately by instituting a v by interposition of U.N. forces along the line of confrontation, by cessation of all military activities and the exchange of prisoners, etc. This cessation of hostilities will last for four months or for a longer period if mutually agreed by both parties.

2. We agree that while the cessation of hostilities is in effect, we shall negotiate a comprehensive peace agreement, with the proposal of the Contact Group as the basis for negotiation of all points. This will be done at a mutually acceptable site, under the auspices of the Contact Group, using mediators proposed by the Contact Group and mutually agreed by the parties. All issues are to be resolved in full cooperation with the Contact Group. In all respects, both sides will be given equal treatment.

3. During this period there will be unrestricted movement of relief convoys, use of the airport at Sarajevo in accordance with existing agreements, and the delivery of humanitarian services by oficial institutions and non-governmental organizations. Each side may join with UNPROFOR inspectors to assure that no armaments or weapons of war are included in the cargoes to be delivered.

4. Each side will be responsible within its controlled areas for the total elimination and prevention of the firing of any guns or weapons of any kind that might be damaging to people or property.

5. Each side will be responsible within its controlled areas for the protection of human rights in accordance with international standards. All people, regardless of age, sex, or ethnic origin, shall have the right to live in a location of their choice. International observers, including the Special Rapporteur of the Commission on Human Rights, will be free to observe compliance with this agreement.

6. There will be an early exchange of all detainees, under the auspices of the International Red Cross and in accordance with the Geneva Conventions. The ICRC will have unimpeded access to all detainees to insure that the provisions of this agreement are fulfilled.

7. In a final agreement, all has to be agreed: otherwise, nothing is agreed.

It is realized that other difficult issues and unresolved questions will have to be resolved. This will be done peacefully, utilizing the services of the Contact Group or UNPROFOR as appropriate.

Signed 19 December 1994

Radovan Karadžić (signed)
Ratko Mladić (signed)
Jimmy Carter, Witness (signed)

Additional Agreement to that of 19 December

[Serb side]

20 December 1994

1) It is agreed that the negotiations to establish a total cessation of hostilities will commence on 23 December, 1994, with the intent to conclude the agreement by 1 January 1995.

2) A complete ceasefire, throughout Bosnia-Hercegovina, will be implemented at noon, 23 December 1994 monitored by U.N. forces along all lines of confrontation, by cessation of all military activities.

3) Based on Assurances that convoys [unreadable] humanitarian services will pass freely, the Bosnoan forces will withdraw from the Igman demilitarized zone in accordance with the existing agreement prior to the commencement of the negotiations described in item (1) above.

Radovan Karadzic [signed]

Witnessed: Jimmy Carter [signed]

COMPREHENSIVE PEACE AGREEMENT

[Bosniak side]

We the undersigned agree that we and those under our authority will:

1. Immediately implement a cease-fire, monitored by the U.N. forces along all lines of confrontation, by cessation of all military activities and the exchange of prisoners, etc., as described below.

2. Commence negotiations on an agreement for a total cessation of hostilities on December 27, 1994, with the intent to conclude the agreement by January 15, 1995.

This cessation of hostilities will last for four months or for a longer period if mutually agreed by both parties.

3. While the cessation of hostilities is in effect, negotiate a comprehensive peace agreement, on the basis of the acceptance of the peace plan of the Contact Group as a starting point. This will be done at a mutually acceptable site, under the auspices of the Contact Group, using mediators proposed by the Contact Group and mutually agreed by the parties. All issues are to be resolved in full cooperation with the Contact Group.

It is understood that there will be unrestricted movement of relief convoys, use of the airport at Sarajevo in accordance with existing agreements, and the delivery of humanitarian services by official institutions and non-governmental organizations. Each side may join with UNPROFOR inspectors to assure that no armaments or weapons of war are included in the cargoes to be delivered.

Each side will be responsible within its controlled areas for the total elimination and prevention of the firing of any guns or weapons of any kind that might be damaging to people or property.

Each side will be responsible within its controlled areas for the protection of human rights in accordance with international standards. All people, regardless of age, sex, or ethnic origin, shall have the right to live in a location of their choice. International observers, including the Special Rapporteur of the Commission on Human Rights, will be free to observe compliance with this agreement.

There will be an early exchange of all detainees, under the auspices of the International Red Cross. In accordance with the Geneva Conventions, the ICRC will have unimpeded access to all detainees to insure that the provisions of this agreement are fulfilled. In a final agreement, all has to be agreed: otherwise, nothing is agreed.

It is realized that other difficult issues and unresolved questions will have to be resolved. This will be done peacefully, utilizing the services of the Contact Group or UNPROFOR as appropriate.

Signed 20 December 1994:

Alija Izetbegovic, President [signed]
Rasim Delic, Supreme Commander [signed]
Jimmy Carter, Witness [signed]

LETTER BY PRESIDENT KARADZIC TO PRESIDENT CARTER
of December 26, 1994

[Original unavailable to Translator]

LETTER BY YASUSHI AKASHI,
Special U.N. Envoy, to Radovan Karadzic
(December 22, 1994)

[Original unavailable to Translator]

STATEMENT BY THE CONTACT GROUP,
issued in London and Bonn on December 22, 1994 at 11 a.m.

[Original unavailable to Translator]

ANNEX II
AGREEMENT ON COMPLETE CESSATION OF HOSTILITIES

1. Following the Cease-fire Agreement, signed on 23 December 1994, the parties agree to a complete cessation of hostilities with effect from 1200 hours on 1 January 1995 along all lines of confrontation. This agreement will be in effect for an initial period of four months, subject to renewal under these same conditions by agreement of the parties.

2. The cessation of hostilities will be supervised and monitored by the United nations Protection Force (UNPROFOR) through the establishment of joint commissions. A Central Joint Commission shall be established under the chairmanship of UNPROFOR, with initial meetings at the sarajevo Airport, and regional joint commissions shall also be established in permanent session as needed and as determined by the Central Joint Commission.

3. Liaison officers will be exchanged between UNPROFOR and the parties by 15 january 1995 and afterwards where deemed appropriate.

4. Cessation of hostilities will include the following measures:
   a) Separation of forces in conflict to mutually agreed positions and the positioning of UNPROFOR forces for observation and monitoring, to include interpositioning;
   b) The parties agree to refrain from the use of all explosive munitions, and the use of weapons used to fire explosive munitions. In addition, talks will begin immediately on the modalities for the withdrawal and monitoring by UNPROFOR of heavy weapons of 12.7 mm calibre and above.

5. Full freedom of movement with appropriate procedures shall exist for UNPROFOR and other of icial international agencies, in particular the Of ice of the United Nations High Commissioner for Refugees (UNHCR), in order to implement this agreement, to monitor human rights and to deliver humanitarian aid, including medical supplies and evacuations. The parties commit themselves to full respect for the safety and security of UNPROFOR and related personnel. UNPROFOR shall continue to prevent any abuse of freedom of movement by its personnel or convoys which might be of military benefit to either party.

6. The parties agree to comply immediately and fully with all existing agreements, including the 5 June 1992 Sarajevo Airport Agreement, the 24 April 1993 Srebrenica Agreement, the 8 May 1993 Srebrenica and Zepa Agreement, the 14 August 1993 Mount Igman Demilitarized Zone Agreement, the 9 February 1994 Sarajevo Airport Agreement, the 17 March 1994 Agreement regarding the use of civilian traffic across Sarajevo Airport, the 23 April 1994 Gorazde Agreement and the 14 August 1994 Anti-Sniping Agreement.

7. The parties agree to assist fully in the total restoration of utilities and the establishment of joint economic activities aimed at the normalization of life in all territories, and in particular in and around the Safe Areas. These activities shall be undertaken on a reciprocal basis.

8. The parties agree to work continuously and simultaneously on processes for the early release of persons detained in relation with the conflict, as well as for the provision and cross-checking of all available information on persons unaccounted for. This work will be undertaken under the auspices of the International Committee of the Red Cross (ICRC), in accordance with their standard procedures. The parties commit themselves to commencing the processes by 15 January 1995.

9. The parties agree to cooperate with UNPROFOR in the monitoring and observation of the withdrawal of all foreign troops. UNPROFOR will perform this specific task on the basis of this agreement with the parties to the conflict and in accordance with its obligations under the relevant Security Council resolutions and statements.

10. This agreement is to be without prejudice to the final political or territorial solution.

31 December 1994

(Signed) Alija IZETBEGOVIC (Signed) Rasim DELIC
(Signed) Radovan KARADZIC (Signed) Ratko MLADIC
(Signed) Kresimir ZUBAK
(Signed) Vladimir SOLJIC

Witnessed by: (Signed) Yasushi AKASHI
(Signed) Sir Michael Rose

(There was also a version in the Serbian Cyrillic alphabet.)

HOW HOLBROOKE DODGED MEETING WITH KARADZIC

Having completed his political and intelligence mission in the Balkans, Ambassador Richard Holbrooke became U.S. representative in the United Nations Organization. He wrote memoirs about the 'Road to Dayton', first in the form of an article entitled "The Road to Sarajevo", first published in two parts by New Yorker on October 21 and 26, then in his book To End a War [Random House, 1998]. He admitted that Slobodan Milosevic could be persuaded much easier than Radovan Karadzic, and for that reason he avoided meeting with Dr. Karadzic whenever it was possible. This practice of his has been described in the above said memoirs:

[Translator's recommendation: Find the New Yorker article or the book To End a War by Richard Holbrooke, Random House, 1998 and insert the relevant citation!]

The green-marked lines indicate the part of the book/article relevant for citing.

[...]

Standing with Slobodan Milosevic 13 years ago on the veranda of a government hunting lodge outside Belgrade, I saw two men in the distance. They left their twin Mercedes and, in fading light, started toward us. I felt a jolt go through my body; they were unmistakable. Ratko Mladic, in combat fatigues, stocky, walking as though through a muddy field; and Radovan Karadzic, taller, wearing a suit, with his wild, but carefully coiffed, shock of white hair.

[...]

I did not shake hands, although both Karadzic and Mladic tried to. Some of our team did; others did not. It was their choice. We sat down at a long table on the patio facing each other and began to talk.

[...]

– We are ready for peace, – he said in English. – Why did you bomb us?

[...]

DR. BORKO DJORDJEVIC'S PARTNERSHIP WITH DR. SIMO MILOSEVIC INSTITUTE AT IGALO, MONTENEGRO

- Two letters to the Author's lawyers Radojica Lazic and Zeljko Aprcovic -

Letter One

Dear Radojica and Zeljko,

When I came back from America, in December 2007, while inspecting the surgery ward, I found two rear operation rooms completely flooded by water and all the equipment destroyed, including the fixtures, which required a thorough restoration of both operation rooms anew. For the restoration works I took a credit from Hypo Alpe Bank, the amount was € 300,000, which was an additional investment into the damaged operation rooms – both building works and installment of the fixtures (wiring, distribution system for gases –oxygen and nitric oxygen), while the container with new equipment, currently estimated at € 136,000, had to be imported from America (2008) so as to substitute the previously damaged equipment.

I shall not dwell here on how much there is to repair and clean on daily basis, due to the constant damage caused by the cracking of the pipes on the floor above ours.

Although we are partners who should share both the expenditures and the pro it, as I have said, the Institute has 'kidnapped' the entire regular business and directed it into the private hands of some individuals employed therein.

Find enclosed the Assessment Report.

Regards,

Borko Djordjevic

Letter Two

Dear Radojica and Zeljko,
Happy Holiday!

In the preparation of the letter to be written to the Institute, it would be recommendable for me to have the reasons cited by Director Bosnjak and others why they would not cooperate with me, so I can provide you with my feedback.

Chronologically and historically, my relations with the Institute, after the fall of Director Bato Djurovic, have never been stable or good, or financially profitable either. Before the disintegration of Yugoslavia, when I used to work with the Institute under a service agreement, it was highly profitable and satisfactory to both parties.

Since the very beginning, the doctors' lobby never approved of private practice within the Institute. When Director Djurovic left, and it was with him that I had signed the original contract on joint venture, Brano Radojcic, neurosurgeon from Risan took the post of director.

From the day of signing the original agreement, in 1992, until the lifting of the sanctions, very little work was done with patients, for some building works prevailed, i.r. building of the surgery ward (4 operation rooms). In 1997, I left for America and rarely worked at the Institute. The reasons were as follows:

1. I had a serious conflict with the Minister of Healthcare Miomir Mugosa, who closed my clinic twice (in 1995 and '96) on banale grounds. He required that my firm payed 10,000 Mark to the Ministry of Healthcare, which I was not willing to do.

2. The previously made agreement with the Norwegians and the Dutch about sending their patients straight into the Surgery Ward was blocked by Radojcic, the new Director, from 2001 until now, for he was a protégé of Mugosa, so Mugosa still, indirectly, controlled the ongoings in the healthcare system.

In the meanwhile, the local physicians such as Dr. Marina Delic and others, began to develop a parallel private practice and use uninvasive cosmetic surgery (Botox, Restylane and the like); as their position entitled them for triage of new patients, all of the patients from abroad ended in their private offices.

Nothing was allocated to our joint firm, so there was no joint revenue. Brano Radojcic, Member of the Board representing the Institute, quit the Board in 1910 because, as he claimed, my company *Atalanta*, registered in Switzerland, and a signatory of the agreement, no longer existed. It is true that I had closed the Swiss company *Atalanta SA*, and that I transferred all of its properties to my name, for I had been the sole owner; accordingly, I transferred my part, 60%, of ownership in the Mediterranean Surgery Center to my personal name, so that currently I claim the titular right to the 60% of the capital invested into the Mediterranean Surgery Center and the sole proprietor registered at the Commercial Court of Montenegro. The original agreement allowed for all of these moves.

The whole period of Brano Radojcic's directorship, with practically the same persons in the Management Board, gradually and systematically led to the deterioration of the Institute's infrastructure. Even today, the Institute has still not been given the utility permit for electricity supply, and the water pipes have completely decayed due to the use of harmful industrial mineral water from the local sources, which caused the fissures in the pipes and damages in the walls and structures of the Institute itself. Some patients emerged with legionnaires disease (as a consequence of the low-temperature water in the pipes) – three people from Norway, which has never been admitted in public.

My advertisement panel, which should have stood at the reception of the Institute's main entrance, was removed and thrown away into the boiler room. In spite of all that, I did not want to terminate the agreement, for financially it was not in my interest – after the capital had been invested into the infrastructure of the surgery ward.

Although the whole coast, that is, the hospitals in Kotor, Risan and Meljine together had 4 operation rooms, and I alone had the same number of these, there was no good will or interest to establish a general hospital on the local level, despite the minimum investment required.

It seems to me that the local authorities and administration tend to kidnap the Institute for their personal needs, and for that purpose – since the day I signed the agreement, the Institute – as the cadaster register shows – has been burdened with more than 6 million Euro loan for the sake of covering the expenditures of that non-profitable organization. Despite the well-known fact that the Institute used to be extremely profitable in the past, and the fact that plastic surgery was coceived as a complementary branch of medicine to the spa center, the local managers, headed by Radojcic and Marina Delic, were redirecting the possible joint pro it outside the Institute and for their personal interests.

Long time ago I separated private practice from the state-run one, and the applied model of joint venture was supposed to help transition of the public capital to the private one. That was not possible owing to the local management. Although the state was the owner, the social self-management led to the collapse and non-pro it-making work of the Institute, which in turn led to the drop (4 times) in its value to €350-450 per square meter. The Institute has turned doomed like all the other social enterprises which failed to find their way in the process of property transition.

Today, the so-called Spa Center is oversized and incapable of pro it making, so no foreign investor can see his interest in such a place where the costs of maintenance and salaries with all the taxes/contributions surpass the profitability potential. If the State hired a foreign management company to run the Institute and payed it 30% of the gross pro it, whereby both the revenue and the loss would clearly be discerned, that would prove better than having the local managers practically steal from the potential joint earnings for their personal interest; thus, all the local managers so far, since the 1990's to this day, have improved their personal financial status, evidence of which does exist.

Although my motivation was never grounded on the prospects of earning big money but on enjoying my professional work, it certainly did not imply my investing money to lose it later, or to work for operating loss.

That is why I am extremely interested in what the management and Bosnjak have to say about why they obstruct our work, and specify their reasons.

My invested capital has been assessed and registered with the Commercial Court by an independent appraiser. The current price of one square meter of this range [in the building] has been assessed in the last tender to € 350. My investment surpasses the value for the space of 1,400 sq m. Provided the agreement is terminated, I claim a return of the invested amount in compliance with the agreement which says that in such a case the investment, with percentage calculation applied, amounts to more than 2.5 million Euro (we have not made an accountance entry for the additional value of the newly imported equipment). Or, the whole space of 1,400 sq m should be registered as my property and entered so in the cadaster register. We can thus avoid the arbitration process and the costs of such a process. Moreover, it would be of no avail that the issue becomes one of public debate, unless necessary.

Finally, everybody minds his own interest and, despite my good will, I have no intention to turn my investment into a gift to anyone.

This has been an abridged chronology of the events for which there is evidence, and the principal witnesses will be the representatives of the Netherland's *Fontana* tourist company, as well as the representatives of the Norwegian Administration who used to partner with the Institute's management.

Anyway, I find the status quo unacceptable, and so does – I guess – the Institute. Whoever appears as a future partner cannot be expected to make large investments, for it takes huge amounts to renovate the space so as to meet international standards, be profitable and attract foreigners and foreign capital, whereas my line of work within the MedSpa is in high demand nowadays.

Today, social property hardly exists anywhere, and it should not exist here either, for it obviously hinders growth and normal functioning.

I categorically refuse any belittling of my past professional success, convinced that it comes out of jealousy and personal interests of the interested subjects, and I shall categorically defend my pursuit of efficient professional work.! The time has come when one has to work hard for one's living.

This should never have happened: that this Institute has been managed for 15 years by a drunken doctor such as Brano Radojcic, and an incompetent marketing manager such as the psychiatrist Paunovic. That was a recipe for collapse, which has eventually proved true.

Borko Djordjevic

BORKO DJORDJEVIC, MD: CAREER OVERVIEW

As a prominent physician in his field(s) for many years, Borko Djordjevic, MD, has always been among the leaders in the cutting-edge cosmetic and reconstructive surgery. A holder of the Certificate issued by the American Board of Plastic and Reconstructive Surgery, and a Member of the American Academy of Cosmetic Surgery (AACS), Dr. Borko Djordjevic is a specialist in General Plastic Surgery and Aesthetic & Reconstructive Surgery which includes facelifting (rhytidectomy), rhinoplasty, blepharoplasty, chemical peeling, augmentation/reduction of breasts, hands, feet; reduction and sculpture of hips and abdomen, liposuction, genital repair and reconstruction.

QUALIFICATIONS
Dr. Borko Djordjevic was head of the group of physicians specializing in plastic and reconstructive surgery, surgery of hands and genitalia, and cosmetic surgery – at the Riverside Methodist Hospital in Columbus, Ohio. His education continued at prestigious institutions such as Stanford and Northwestern Universities. Committed to mastering novel techniques, he participated in numerous international symposia with some of the world's most renowned surgeons. Dr. Borko Djordjevic has published his scientific output in many books and medical journals.

The university-related career of Dr. Borko Djordjevic includes his assistant-professorship for the subject Plastic and Reconstructive Surgery at the School of Medicine, University of Belgrade, as well as correspondent editorship for the university-published *Journal of Medical Research* and Head of Cosmetic Surgery Fellowship Training Program.

In the year 1994, Dr. Borko Djordjevic was specially appointed by the former U.S. President Jimmy Carter as an assisting associate missioner at the Carter Center, Atlanta, Ga., in the Center's efforts to accomplish peace in Bosnia and former Yugoslavia; in that capacity, he is personally credited with the realization of President Carter's trip to Bosnia.

COMMITMENT TO WORK

Dr. Borko Djordjevic is first and foremost dedicated to good communication with his patients in order to properly understand their aims and aspirations related to the operation they wish to undergo. For, he believes that the psychological condition of the patient is equally important as the physical one. "Prior to a surgery, one has to consider the patient's basic motivation," – he claims. "For instance, if the person in question has suffered a loss in the family, like a wife having lost her husband, she seeks a way to feel better. However, no matter how successful the operation proves to be, it will not alleviate the real source of the problem. On the other hand, when such a patient reconciles herself with the loss, the surgery may have a very positive effect."

The techniques practised by Dr. Borko Djordjevic have reached perfection. After he had recently spent some time in his native Yugoslavia, helping war casualties and operating under most primitive conditions, his hand has advanced in sensitiveness and precision. Work in critical circumstances and with great hazards has taken his skill and resourcefulness to the utmost. The result has been that he manages to do more within less time, also learning how to reduce the duration of his patients' recovery period.

EDUCATION, CERTIFICATIONS AND TRAINING PROFILE
Specializations

Speciality: General Surgery at Mountainside Hospital, Montclair, New Jersey, USA

Speciality: General Surgery at The Graduate Hospital University of Pennsylvania Philadelphia, Pennsylvania, USA

Speciality: Plastic and Reconstructive Surgery, hand and genitalia surgery, cosmetic surgery at Riverside Methodist Hospital - Affiliate of Ohio State University Columbus, Ohio, USA

American Board of Plastic and Reconstructive Surgery: Board Certificate

CONTINUING MEDICAL EDUCATION

Medical Review Course St. Barnabas Medical Center Livingstone, New Jersey, USA 1970 – 1971
Annual Meeting: Ohio Valley of Plastic and Reconstructive Surgery Society Maceno Island, Michigan, USA 1976
ASPRS/PSEF/ASMS Annual Scientific Meeting, Boston, Massachusetts, USA, 1976
Backer's Cosmetic Surgery Meeting, Mount Sinai, Miami Beach, Florida, USA, 1977
Chief Surgical Resident in Plastic and Reconstructive Surgery Conference, Chicago, Illinois, USA (Presented paper: Theratoma Of The Neck), 1977
American Society of Aesthetic Surgery, Annual Meeting, USA, February 1977
American Cleft Palate Education Foundation, Annual Meeting, USA, March 1977
ASPRS Educational Foundation, Chief Residents' Annual Meeting, March 1977
Ohio Valley Society of Plastic and Reconstructive Surgeons, Ohio Valley Meeting, USA, June 1977
Eastern Virginia Medical Society Conference on Reconstructive Surgery, USA, June 1977
Northwestern University, Plastic Surgery Department Postgraduate Course in Plastic Surgery, September 1977
Indio Community Hospital (John F. Kennedy Memorial Hospital) Grand Rounds September, 1977 – June, 1978
Eisenhower Medical Center, Rancho Mirage, California, USA Weekly Conferences, April 1978
Impotence: Perspectives for Evaluation and Management, April 1978
Desert Hospital, Palm Springs, California, Cardiovascular Exam (CPR) May, 1978
Plastic Surgery Research Foundation, Breast Reconstructions Following Mastectomy, December, 1978
Review Course Plastic and Reconstructive Surgery, Stanford University, Palo Alto, California, USA 1978
American Society of Aesthetic Surgery, Problems in Aesthetic Surgery, January 1979
American Society of Plastic and Reconstructive Surgeons, Annual Meeting, New Orleans, Louisiana, USA September, 1980
Review Course American Board of Plastic and Reconstructive Surgery, Northwest University, Chicago, Illinois, USA (Written exam) 1983
ASPRS/PSEF/ASMS Annual Scientific Meeting, New Orleans, Louisiana, USA 1986
Review Course American Board of Plastic and Reconstructive Surgery Stanford University, Palo Alto, California, USA (Oral exam) 1987
Review Course American Board of Plastic and Reconstructive Surgery, Stanford University, Palo Alto, California, USA 1988
ASPRS/PSEF/ASMS Annual Scientific Meeting Washington Convention Center, Washington, D.C., USA 1992
International Symposium on Plastic Surgery, Firenze, Italy 1994
Doctoral thesis Secondary Rhinoplasty, University of Belgrade, School of Medicine, Belgrade, Yugoslavia Degree: Doctor of Medical Sciences 1994
APRS/PSEF/ASMS Annual Scientific Meeting, Dallas, Texas, USA 1996
Advances in Aesthetic Plastic Surgery, The Cutting Edge Symposium Manhattan Eye, Ear and Throat Hospital, New York 1996
Laser Workshop: Treatment of Cutaneous Lesions, Skin Laser Center, New Jersey, USA 1997
American Academy of Cosmetic Surgeons Annual Meeting, Century City, California, USA 1999
16th Annual Plastic Surgery Day-Annual Meeting Cedars-Sinai Medical Center Los Angeles, California, USA 1999
California Academy of Cosmetic Surgery Annual Meeting and Education Program, Annenberg Center-Eisenhower Medical Center, Rancho Mirage, California, USA 1999
American Academy of Plastic Surgeons Annual Scientific Meeting Los Angeles, California, USA 2000
17th Annual Plastic Surgery Day – Annual Meeting Cedars-Sinai Medical Center Los Angels, California, USA 2000
California Academy of Cosmetic Surgery: Annual Meeting and Education Program Annenberg Center-Eisenhower Medical Center, Rancho Mirage, California, USA 2000
ASPS/PSEF/ASMS Annual Scientific Meeting Los Angeles, California, USA 2000

PSEF– In-Service Exam 2001
CME – Medical Ethics – 4th Edition 2001ASPS/ACCME In-Service Exam 2001
ASPS/PSEF/ASMS Courses 2001
19th Plastic Surgery Day Cedars-Sinai Medical Center Los Angeles, California, USA 2002
ASPS/PSEF/ASMS Scientific Meeting 2002
University of Belgrade, Serbia: Taught at the School of Medicine 2002
American Society of Plastic Surgeons PSEF In-Service Exam 2003
International College of Surgeons CA Division Surgical Update 2003
Medical Educational Resources Advances in Cosmetic Surgery 2003
18th Annual Symposium on the Latest Advances in Facial Plastic Surgery Newport Beach, California, USA 2004
19th Annual Symposium on the Latest Advances in Facial Plastic Surgery Newport Beach, California, USA 2005
Cosmetic Surgery Board Annual Board Meeting San Diego, California, USA 2005
The Foundation for Facial Plastic Surgery The 20th Annual Symposium on the Latest Advances in Facial Plastic Surgery Newport Beach, California, USA 2006

PRESENT MEDICAL AND SURGICAL APPOINTMENTS

Director and Chairman, Department of Plastic and Reconstructive Surgery Mediterranean Surgery Center, Igalo, Yugoslavia/Montenegro
Director, Cosmetic Surgery Fellowship Training Program, University of Belgrade, Yugoslavia/Serbia
Contributing Editor, Journal of Medical Research, University of Belgrade, Yugoslavia/Serbia
Associate Professor, Plastic and Reconstructive Surgery, University of Belgrade, School of Medicine, Belgrade, Yugoslavia/Serbia
Member Investigator, Western Institutional Review Board (WIRB) Study: "Adjunct Study of Mentor H/S Silicone Gel-filled Mammary Prosthesis"

FORMER APPOINTMENTS

Medical Exam Commissioner of the State of California Board of Medical Quality Assurance, USA
Special Appointment by former President Jimmy Carter, to assist the Carter Center of Atlanta, Georgia, in their efforts to further peace in the Bosnian-Yugoslavian countries. Solely responsible for bringing President Carter personally to Bosnia in December 1994 to further the peace efforts.
Chairman of the Board and Chief Executive Officer Oil Securities, Inc. (NASDAQ): Acquisition and management of numerous domestic oil and gas properties in North America with special emphasis on alternative energy sources.

PUBLISHED WORKS

1. Djordjevic, B., M.D., Ph.D., *Surgery of the Hand*, Medicinska Kniga, Belgrade, Yugoslavia, 1994
2. Djordjevic, B., M.D., Ph. D., *Plastic and Reconstructive Surgery*: Principles of Anatomy and Technique, Vol. I, Atalanta International, Ltd, Belgrade, Yugoslavia, 1995
3. Djordjevic, B., M.D., Ph. D., *Plastic and Reconstructive Surgery:* Head and Neck, Vol. II, Atalanta International, Ltd, Belgrade, Yugoslavia, 1996
4. "Tumors of the Skin and Subcutaneous Tissue Facial Lesions Laser and Microsurgery", Djordjevic, B., M.D., Ph.D., *Plastic and Reconstructive Surgery*, Vol. III, Atalanta International, Ltd., Belgrade, Yugoslavia, 1997 "Burns Reconstruction of the Face, Scalp, Eyes, Nose and Ears"
5. Djordjevic, B., M.D., Ph. D., *Plastic and Reconstructive Surgery,* Vol. IV, Atalanta International Ltd., Belgrade, Yugoslavia, 1998 "Cleft Palate Cleft Lip Craniofacial Anomalies Facial Fractures"

CERTIFICATIONS

EFCMG
FLEx
American Board of Plastic and Reconstructive Surgery (written)
American Board of Cosmetic Surgery
Doctor of Medical Sciences – Ph. D., University of Belgrade
Associate Professor, University of Belgrade, School of Medicine
BCLS/CPR „C" – Health Care Provider, Life Saver Systems

ACADEMIC APPOINTMENTS
Instructor of Physiology, University of Belgrade, Yugoslavia/Serbia
Deputy Governor, American Biographical Institute Research Association North Carolina, USA
Professor of Surgery, University of Belgrade, Yugoslavia/Serbia

AWARDS AND CITATIONS
Distinguished Citizen of State of New Jersey, USA
Who is Who – California, USA
Man of the Year – American Biological Institute
California Medical Association – Certificate of Excellence
American Medical Association – Physician Recognition Award
20th Century Award of Achievement
Distinguished Leadership Award, International Directory
Humanitarian Award – Golden Palm Star – Palm Springs, California
Man of the Year Award – Greater Palm Springs Celebrity Golf Classic
Republican Senatorial Medal of Freedom

MEMBERSHIP AND FELLOWSHIPS IN PROFESSIONAL SOCIETIES
1. American Medical Association
2. The New York Academy of Medicine
3. Palm Springs Academy of Medicine
4. American Academy of Cosmetic Surgery
5. American Society of Lipo-Suction Surgery
6. American Society of Hair Restoration Surgery
7. International College of Surgeons
8. American Board of Plastic Surgery, Board Qualified

PHYSICIAN PROFILE
Robert P. Sengelmann, M.D.

CERTIFICATION
American Board of Plastic Surgery – 1974

EDUCATION
Undergraduate, Stanford University, 1961
Medical School, University of California at Los Angeles, 1965, with Honors
Postgraduate, Stanford University Medical Center, General Surgery and Plastic and Reconstructive Surgery, 1973
Teaching Appointment: Stanford University Medical Center, Clinical Professor of Plastic Surgery
Teaching Appointment: American Society of Aesthetic Plastic Surgery, Visiting Professor 1999-2001
American Association for the Accreditation of Ambulatory Surgical Facilities, President
American Board of Plastic Surgeons, Director
American Society for Aesthetic Plastic Surgery, former Editor of *Aesthetic Society News*
American Society of Plastic Surgeons, former President
American Society of Plastic Surgeons, former Editor of *Plastic Surgery News*
California Society of Plastic Surgeons, former President

SOCIETY MEMBERSHIPS:
American Society of Plastic Surgeons
The Aesthetic Surgery EducaAmerican Society of Plastic Surgeons
The Aesthetic Surgery Education & Research Foundation, Charter Member
Alameda-Contra Costa Medical Association
American Association for Accreditation of Ambulatory Surgery Facilities
American Association of Plastic Surgeons
American Board of Plastic Surgery
American Medical Association
American Society for Aesthetic Plastic Surgery
International Confederation of Plastic, Reconstructive and Aesthetic Surgery (IPRAS) Plastic Surgery Education Foundation

PHOTOS & PRESS CLIPPINGS

Dr. Borko Djordjevic (right), Prof Dr. Senigzazov and Mrs. Irina Yakovleva, wife of the Governor of Saint-Petersburg, after a surgery in Switzerland (1996)

Dr. Djordjevic with his mother Mara and a friend of hers during his birthday party (1978)

Dr. Borko Djordjevic and the actress Eva Gabor

Jolie Gabor and her daughters

Jolie Gabor, mother of the famed Gabor sisters

Borko Djordjevic at a party in Zsa Zsa Gabor's Bel Air home (1983)

Magda and Eva Gabor during dinner in Borko Djordjevic's Palm Springs villa

Borko Djordjevic with the actress Bonnie Swearingen and her husband John

Front page of the newspaper Globe after his operation on the famed American televangelist Jim Bakker

Accompanied by the Hollywood media mogul Merv Griffin

Borko Djordjevic with a Hollywood friend

Dr. Djordjevic's patient — Rebel Randall, the first Coca-Cola Girl in advertisements

Borko Djordjevic in the Kentucky Derby Club with Shirley Rosen, owner of the stallion which won the 1984 Breeders' Cup

With the famous heart surgeon Denton A. Cooley whose wife was Borko's patient in Belgrade in 1995, and Slavko Simeunovic, Deputy Dean of Belgrade's Faculty of Medicine

Dr. Borko Djordjevic and his favorite Mercedes car — the plate reads BODY MD

With Larry King, iconic TV and radio host

With music superstar Elton John and actress Fran Drescher at the 1998 Oscar Award Ceremony

With actress Elke Sommer at a cocktail party

With Zoran Kojic, Director of the Intercontinental Hotel, and his wife

With singer and actress Barbara McNair

Borko Djordjevic celebrating 30-years' school reunion at Kalemegdan (1991)

[square meters to be 'transcribed' into square yards or feet]

Dr. Djordjevic's 7,000-sq m home at Palm Springs in 1981: his neighbors were Steve McQuinn and William Holden, and his five surgeries a day yielded $ 50,000 each

With Casey Kasem, host and co-creator of the American Top 40 Show, and his wife at Oscar Award Ceremony (LA, 1998)

Exhausted, Dr. Borko Djordjevic fell asleep while in a restaurant

Dr. Borko Djordjevic and Misko Jeremic (father of Vuk Jeremic, President of U.N. Assembly 2012–13) in London, negotiating Texaco's privatization of Serbian Jugopetrol (1992)

With Iraqi military a ache Mahmoud H. Al-Modafar, Saddam Hussein's staffer and creator of the 'Long-Range Cannon' project

With Mahmoud H. Al-Modafar in Baghdad, during the 1996 visit to President Saddam Hussein

With Nebojsa Dimitrijevic, Yugoslav diplomat in Geneva, who was promised the post of foreign minister in Z. Djindjic's Government, yet unfairly remained unappointed

Dr. Borko Djordjevic receiving a Certificate of Appreciation from Minister of Serbian Diaspora V. Vukcevic during Minister's 2004 visit to California

Jimmy Carter in his home at Plains, Ga. with Bill Clinton on the line, in the presence of Borko Djordjevic, Slavko Lazarevic, Tom Hanley and Harry Barnes

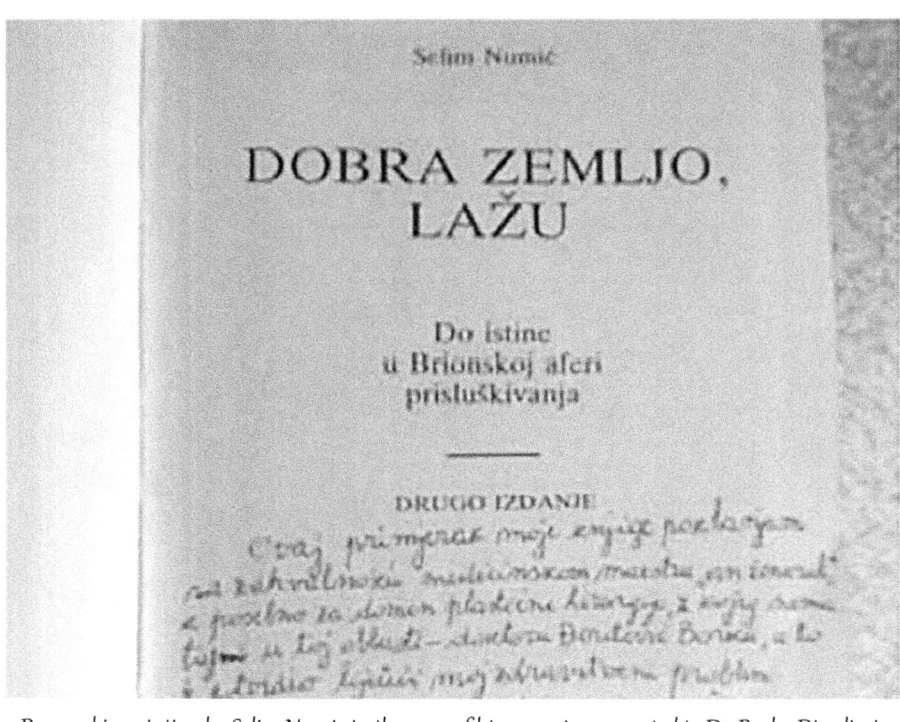

Personal inscription by Selim Numic in the copy of his memoirs presented to Dr. Borko Djordjevic

Inaugural ceremony for Dr. Borko Djordjevic as Fellow of the International College of Surgeons, Vancouver, 1996

With Mrs. George Deukmejian, Governor of California's spouse, at Palm springs (1981)

In a Georgia co on field on return from the visit to Jimmy Carter at Plains

Borko Djordjevic and Svetozar Marovic, President of the former State Union of Serbia and Montenegro

The once rulers of Serbia: Slobodan Milosevic and his wife Mirjana Markovic

Charter of Membership in the Republican Presidential Task Force awarded to Borko Djordjevic

Delegation led by banker Guido Schmidt-Chiari received by M. Unkovic, Mayor of Belgrade

New York's businessmen visiting M. Unkovic, Mayor of Belgrade, in 1990: They proposed Motorola's investment of 200 million dollars in Serbia's wireless telephony

Dr. Borko Djordjevic and Radovan Karadzic analyzing the effects of Jimmy Carter's visit to Pale (1994)

With Radovan and Ljiljana Karadzic, and Gen. Ratko Mladic

Dr. Borko Djordjevic, Radovan Karadzic and Borko's lawyer Tom Hanley sketching the maps of Bosnia-Herzegovina and the Republic of Srpska

Drawing the map of Bosnia-Herzegovina with 51 percent Serb-held territory

Dr. Borko Djordjevic talking to the former U.S. President Jimmy Carter

Jimmy Carter and Radovan Karadzic during a friendly chat

Dr. Borko Djordjevic with H.E.S. Sadoun, Iraqi Ambassador to Belgrade (1996)

Dr. Borko Djordjevic with former U.S. President Gerald Ford in Palm Springs

DESERT SCENE

ALLENE ARTHUR

Doctors vary prescriptions for lifestyle

Borko's hiatus

Borko is back. You remember plastic surgeon Dr. Borko Djordjevic. He flashed into town in the late 1970s and for most of the '80s became a status symbol, like a Rolls-Royce.

He face-lifted many of the social queens, including three out of four Gabors. The handsome doc met his prospective patients at swell parties, and hosted them himself at his Southridge home, the former hilltop showplace of esteemed designer Arthur Elrod. Borko almost married Eva Gabor, did marry a socialite patient and later married the Jonny Cat heiress.

Abruptly, he left the world of gleaming Palm Springs society in 1988 to return to his native Yugoslavia. "I wanted to cleanse the soul, to give something back to the country that educated me and to my own people," he said.

Borko started a clinic in his hometown of Igalo and taught plastic surgery at a medical school in Belgrade. Getting caught up in the Croatia-Serbia war, he repaired trauma patients and later worked on the children victims in Bosnia, the innocent amputees.

His soul apparently cleansed, Djordjevic is back in his old Palm Springs office doing business as usual. He's donating a $15,000 facelift to be auctioned at the Debutante Ball at The Ritz-Carlton on March 15 to benefit Northwood University's scholarship program.

We don't expect a facelift to be a hot item among the tender young debs, but it may be among the more well-seasoned post-debs who attend charity balls.

Californian newspaper writing about Dr. Djordjevic's return from Serbia to the United states (1997)

Borko B. Djordjevic, M.D., Ph.D., F.I.C.S.
PLASTIC AND RECONSTRUCTIVE SURGERY

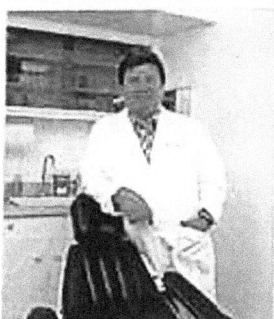

Facsimile of the article about Dr. Djordjevic published in Palm Springs Life

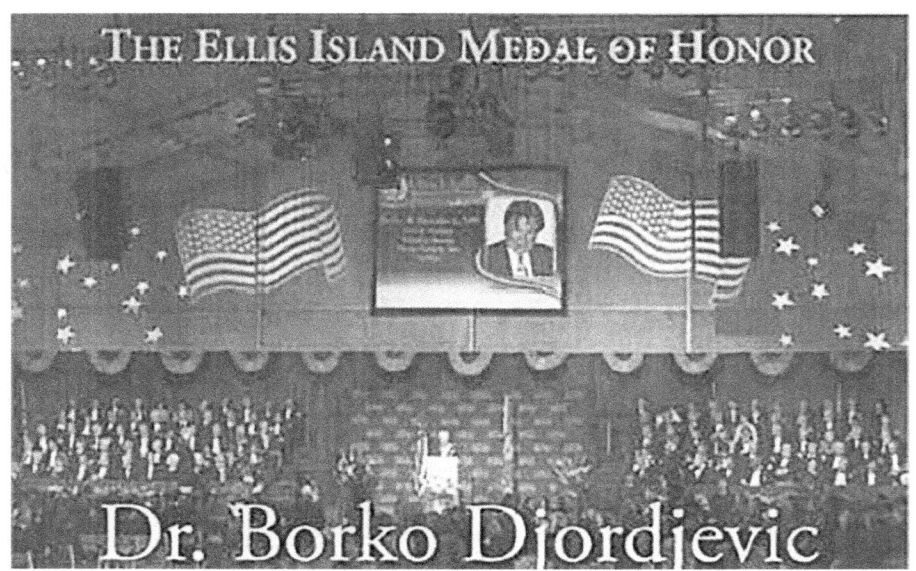
Dr. Borko Djordjevic as a recipient of the Ellis Island Medal of Honor

Invitation brochure and medal

JIMMY CARTER

January 11, 2018

To Dr. Borko Djordjevic

Rosalynn joins me in thanking you for sending us copies of your book. It is a welcome addition to our collection, and we appreciate your remembering us in such a thoughtful way. You have our best wishes for continued success.

Sincerely,

Jimmy Carter